CHINA

EMPIRE AND CIVILIZATION

CHINA

EMPIRE AND CIVILIZATION

General Editor:
Edward L. Shaughnessy

OXFORD

UNIVERSITY PRESS

Oxford University Press

Oxford   New York
Athens   Auckland   Bangkok   Bogotá   Buenos Aires
Calcutta   Cape Town   Chennai   Dar es Salaam   Delhi
Florence   Hong Kong   Istanbul   Karachi   Kuala Lumpur
Madrid   Melbourne   Mexico City   Mumbai   Nairobi   Paris
São Paolo   Singapore   Taipei   Tokyo   Toronto   Warsaw

and associated companies in
Berlin   Ibadan

First published in the United States of America in 2000 by
Oxford University Press, Inc.
198 Madison Avenue, New York, N.Y. 10016–4314
Oxford is a registered trademark of Oxford University Press

Conceived, created, and designed by
Duncan Baird Publishers, London, England

Library of Congress Cataloging-in-Publication Data is available

Senior Editor: Peter Bently
Editor: Joanne Levêque
Designers: Paul Reid and Lloyd Tilbury at Cobalt id
Picture Researcher: Cee Weston-Baker
Commissioned Maps: Michael Hill
Decorative Borders: Sally Taylor
Indexer: Mary Kirkness

Typeset in Sabon 10/15pt
Color reproduction by Colourscan, Singapore
Printed and bound in China by Imago

NOTES
The abbreviations CE and BCE are used throughout this book:
CE   Common Era (the equivalent of AD)
BCE   Before the Common Era (the equivalent of BC)

10 9 8 7 6 5 4 3 2 1

CONTENTS

INTRODUCTION **6**
Edward L. Shaughnessy

Captions to pages 1–3:
PAGE 1 *The Forbidden City, Beijing.*
Ming-dynasty painting on silk.
PAGE 2 *Qing-dynasty imperial pavilion.*
Beihai park and lake, Beijing.
PAGE 3 *A mythical beast with a smaller*
creature on its back. Inlaid bronze,
Eastern Zhou period, ca. 500BCE.

INTRODUCTION

In China, a keen awareness of the past has in most periods gone hand in hand with an openness to innovation. The form of this large 18th-century cloisonné *enamel vase, almost 29 inches (73 cm) tall, is consciously derived from ancient bronze ritual vessels, and the symbolism of the decoration is also traditionally Chinese (for example, the deer and cranes represent longevity). However, the technique of enameling was of foreign origin, being adopted from the Middle East in the 14th century.*

The opening section of the *Yi Jing* (the *Classic of Changes*), foremost among China's classic literary works, takes as its organizing image the heavenly dragon: first hidden in watery depths beneath the horizon, the dragon then appears in the fields before suddenly jumping up to fly through the summer sky. However, even the dragon cannot fly forever. When it gets too high—and too arrogant—it is cut off at the neck to descend once more into the watery depths.

The motion of the heavenly dragon has meant many different things to different interpreters: some modern scholars view it as a simple reference to the Dragon constellation of the Chinese star system, whereas traditional readers had tended to see it as a symbol of the emperor or ruler, or perhaps a virtuous person. The image has been adapted to philosophical, religious, literary, artistic, and certainly also political expression. A saying attributed to Confucius in the recently discovered Mawangdui manuscript of the *Yi Jing* catches one aspect of its timelessness: "As for the sage's establishment of government, it is like climbing a tree: the higher one gets, the more one fears what is below."

The notion that what is below will eventually rise is so fundamental to Chinese thought that even time is visualized as moving up before one's eyes, with past time already above the horizon and future time below it. But like the movement of the dragon, in China time is considered to be cyclical: when what is below moves up, what is above moves down, ready to rise again. This marks a stark contrast with Western notions of time moving in a straight line. It is perhaps easy for us to see that future time eventually becomes past time. Less clear, however, is the notion in Chinese thought and culture that past time also becomes future time, yet this is what lies behind the famous saying of Sima Qian (ca. 145–86 BCE), China's first great historian: "Those who do not forget the past are the masters of the future."

China focuses on the past, which has quite literally risen back into view. In the last several decades, China's archaeologists have unearthed tens of thousands of cultural artifacts, many of a sublime beauty. As well as filling hundreds of new museums in every Chinese city and county seat and prompting numerous exhibitions in Europe and America, these discoveries have provided dramatic new evidence with which to answer the question "Who were the Chinese people?" For instance, it is now known that the Shang dynasty, the earliest state in China of which there are written records, coexisted with other remarkable, and

equally distinctive, Chinese cultures. Even in ancient times, therefore, the civilization of China was far from homogeneous. With this in mind, we can venture a long way toward answering the question "Who *are* the Chinese people?"

China explores these questions. On each page, full-color photographs illustrate many of the most recent discoveries made by Chinese archaeologists. But the book has a wider focus than a museum catalog or a volume on art or archaeology, and does not neglect the many other cultural artifacts or types of cultural expression that have long been above ground—and which have therefore had an even greater influence on Chinese culture.

The organization of the book, with essays written by leading experts on Chinese civilization, allows for all of these artifacts to be situated within their place and time. While focussing on the imperial period

A celestial dragon, part of the ceramic "Nine Dragon Screen" in the imperial palace (the Forbidden City), Beijing. The dragon is an ancient symbol of transformation and adaptability, characteristics that are the key to the resilience of Chinese civilization over at least forty centuries.

The temple that stands at the top of Taishan (Mount Tai, or "Great Mountain"), one of the five most sacred peaks of traditional Chinese religion, has drawn pilgrims and visitors for many centuries.

that began in the third century BCE and ended in 1912, its scope stretches from the very beginning of China's traditional history and into the twentieth century, and covers the breadth of China's vast landscape. *China* is divided into three main parts:

1. The Chinese World

This section surveys the geography, political history, and traditional society of China, discussing such aspects as the diversity of Chinese landscapes, the role of the emperor, the workings of the imperial bureaucracy, and the ethnic and linguistic variety to be found within China's frontiers.

2. Belief and Ritual

The second section looks at the philosophies, religions, and sacred practices of traditional China. Encompassing the three formal systems of Confucianism, Daoism, and Buddhism, as well as the supernatural world of ghosts and popular deities, this section also explores other ancient cosmological and metaphysical ideas that are both fundamental to, and profoundly expressive of, the traditional Chinese worldview.

3. Creation and Discovery
This third section looks at the extraordinary physical adornments of Chinese civilization, ranging from magnificent art produced in a range of two- and three-dimensional media to the equally distinctive products of China's technological, medical, and architectural expertise.

A concluding essay, **The Legacy of 4,000 Years**, looks at how radical change and enduring tradition have interacted—and continue to interact—in post-imperial China. The book ends with a reference section that includes a brief guide to the Chinese language and a table of the dynasties that ruled in China from the second millennium BCE to 1912.

The reader who chooses to read traditionally from front to back will find a clearly traced narrative. Others, perhaps inspired by the *Yi Jing*, which encourages readers to change sequence with each new reading, will find it possible to trace their own path by following the extensive cross-references, leading them perhaps from the planning of the Forbidden City in Beijing to the notion of *feng shui*, or geomancy, and thence to the belief in heavenly portents, cults of immortality, and perhaps eventually to alchemy or Chinese medicine.

For anyone who seeks to understand the China of yesterday, of today, or even of the future, this book provides new ways of seeing one of the world's most astonishing and resilient civilizations.

This painted scroll of the Tang dynasty depicts the emperor Xuanzong (ruled 712–756CE) (right) watching his favorite consort, Yang Guifei, as she mounts a horse. Xuanzong was one of the most noted imperial patrons of the arts.

Part 1

THE CHINESE WORLD

Dreaming of Immortality in a Thatched Cottage *by Tang Yin (1470–1524) (detail). China's sharply etched landscape of deep valleys and steep mountains has long been one of the chief sources of artistic inspiration.*

OPPOSITE: *Rice terraces in Guangxi Autonomous Region in southern China. Once thickly forested, China's hillsides were largely cleared for firewood and agriculture. Terracing is one method of preventing the serious soil erosion caused by widespread deforestation.*

● CHAPTER 1 *Richard von Glahn*

"ALL UNDER HEAVEN"

BORDERS OF LAND AND SEA

Since the time of Confucius (551–479BCE), the Chinese have considered the North China Plain—which they refer to as the "Central Plain"—as the heartland of their country. The first Chinese state, the Shang dynasty (ca. 1500–1045BCE), arose on the North China Plain, and throughout his career as a wandering statesman Confucius never ventured beyond this region. For Confucius and his contemporaries, the "Central States" (Zhongguo) that occupied the North China Plain defined the limits of Chinese civilization. Later, after the unification of China under a single emperor, the term "Zhongguo" came to be understood as a singular noun denoting the empire, the "Middle Kingdom." Today it serves as the usual name for China.

Down through the centuries the Chinese continued to regard the North China Plain as the ancestral heart of Chinese civilization, even as the Chinese world steadily expanded southward. By the time of the founding of the Qin empire in 221BCE (see pp.28–9), its realm stretched from Sichuan in the southwest to the shores of the South China Sea, and northward to the grasslands of central Asia. Among its accomplishments, the Qin unified a series of existing walls that had defended the territories of individual states against incursions by horse-riding nomad warriors of the steppe into a single "Great Wall" (or "Long Wall" in Chinese) across its northern border (see pp.214–15).

Although the Great Wall proved only sporadically effective as a bulwark against foreign invasion, in the Chinese mind it loomed as a great barrier dividing the civilized realm of settled farmers and city-based government from the rootless and masterless peoples of the steppe. The idea of the Great Wall marking a fundamental rift between two different worlds expressed the perpetual antagonism between the Chinese of the Central States and the peoples of central and northern Asia, who periodically threatened China with invasion and conquest.

However, the empires forged by foreign conquerors of China such as the Mongols (Yuan dynasty) and Manchus (Qing dynasty) erased this conceptual boundary, and radically reshaped the territorial compass of "China." The present borders of the People's Republic of China were

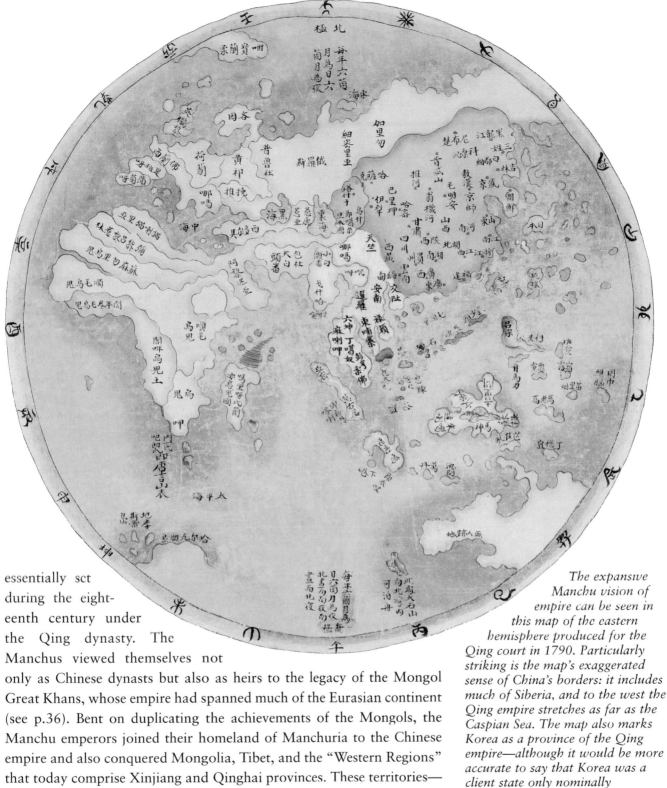

essentially sct during the eighteenth century under the Qing dynasty. The Manchus viewed themselves not only as Chinese dynasts but also as heirs to the legacy of the Mongol Great Khans, whose empire had spanned much of the Eurasian continent (see p.36). Bent on duplicating the achievements of the Mongols, the Manchu emperors joined their homeland of Manchuria to the Chinese empire and also conquered Mongolia, Tibet, and the "Western Regions" that today comprise Xinjiang and Qinghai provinces. These territories—and also Taiwan, likewise first incorporated into the Chinese empire by the Manchus—are now claimed as integral parts of the Chinese nation. Today, therefore, the concept of the "Central Plain" has broadened to encompass the boreal alpine forests of Manchuria, the lush tropics of monsoon Asia, the vast Gobi and Taklamakan deserts, and the equally alien mountain fastnesses of Tibet and the Himalayas.

The expansive Manchu vision of empire can be seen in this map of the eastern hemisphere produced for the Qing court in 1790. Particularly striking is the map's exaggerated sense of China's borders: it includes much of Siberia, and to the west the Qing empire stretches as far as the Caspian Sea. The map also marks Korea as a province of the Qing empire—although it would be more accurate to say that Korea was a client state only nominally subordinate to Qing suzerainty. The hemispherical perspective betrays the influence of Jesuit cartographers from Europe employed at the Manchu court.

MOUNTAINS AND WATER

China's landscape exhibits a checkerboard pattern formed by two contrary forces: the uplift of mountain ranges oriented along both north–south and east–west axes; and the erosive power of three great rivers (the Yellow, the Yangzi, and the Pearl) flowing from west to east. These rivers cut through the mountain ranges and link together a series of basins to form three tiers of human settlement, each with its own distinctive ecology and habitat.

The remarkable contrasts between the Yellow river valley in the north and the Yangzi river valley farther south can largely be attributed to differences in rainfall. The Himalayas and the high Tibetan plateau prevent the monsoon rains of the Indian Ocean from reaching north China. Consequently, northern and western China are arid regions. To the north and west of the Ordos plateau lie steppe grasslands that recede toward barren deserts. The grasslands once contained many lakes but as the climate has become cooler and drier over the past three millennia, these have vanished into billowing deserts.

The Yangzi river winds its way through southern China. The section shown here is near the Yangzi Gorges region (see map, opposite).

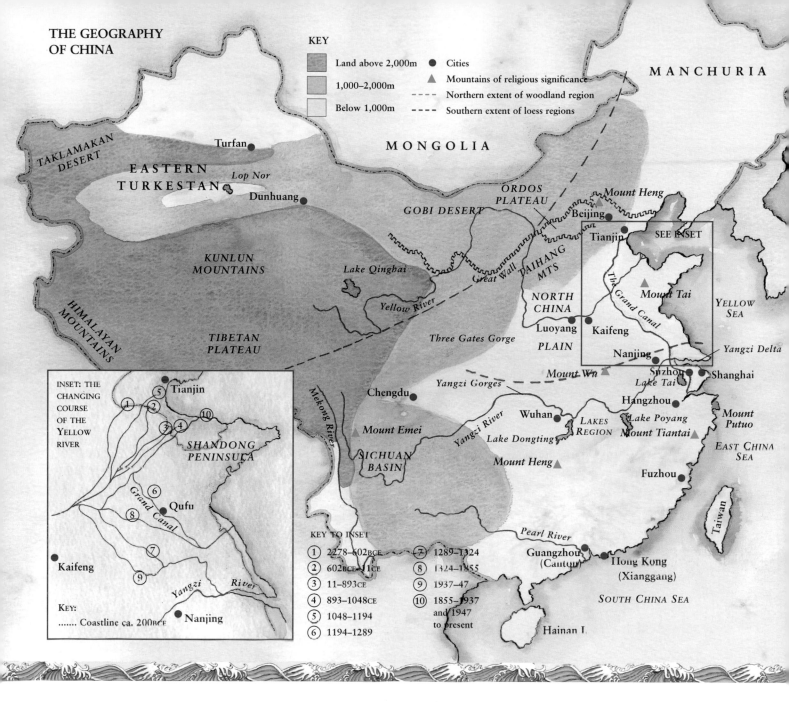

THE GEOGRAPHY OF CHINA

KEY

	Land above 2,000m	● Cities
	1,000–2,000m	▲ Mountains of religious significance
	Below 1,000m	– – – Northern extent of woodland region
		– – – Southern extent of loess regions

MANCHURIA

TAKLAMAKAN DESERT

EASTERN TURKESTAN

Lop Nor

Turfan

Dunhuang

MONGOLIA

GOBI DESERT

ORDOS PLATEAU

Mount Heng

Beijing

Tianjin

SEE INSET

KUNLUN MOUNTAINS

Lake Qinghai

Great Wall

TAIHANG MTS

NORTH CHINA

Mount Tai

YELLOW SEA

HIMALAYAN MOUNTAINS

TIBETAN PLATEAU

Yellow River

Three Gates Gorge

Luoyang

PLAIN

Kaifeng

The Grand Canal

Nanjing

Yangzi Delta

Mount Wu

Suzhou

Shanghai

Lake Tai

INSET: THE CHANGING COURSE OF THE YELLOW RIVER

Tianjin

⑤

①

②

⑩

③ ④

SHANDONG PENINSULA

Grand Canal

⑥

Qufu

⑧

⑦

Kaifeng

⑨

Yangzi River

Nanjing

KEY:
...... Coastline ca. 200BCE

Mekong River

Chengdu

Yangzi Gorges

Mount Emei

SICHUAN BASIN

Yangzi River

Wuhan

Lake Dongting

LAKES REGION

Lake Poyang

Mount Tiantai

Mount Putuo

EAST CHINA SEA

Mount Heng

Fuzhou

Taiwan

KEY TO INSET
① 2278–602BCE	⑦ 1289–1324
② 602BCE–11CE	⑧ 1324–1855
③ 11–893CE	⑨ 1937–47
④ 893–1048CE	⑩ 1855–1937
⑤ 1048–1194	and 1947
⑥ 1194–1289	to present

Pearl River

Guangzhou (Canton)

Hong Kong (Xianggang)

SOUTH CHINA SEA

Hainan I.

The upper course of the Yellow river snakes through rugged mountain ranges thrown up by tectonic lifting and folding. The seismic faults running along the edges of the Taihang mountains, west of Beijing, are among the most unstable in the world, and north China has suffered many devastating earthquakes. The Yellow river bursts through these mountains at Three Gates gorge onto the North China Plain, a large alluvial fan built up by repeated flooding and silt deposition. The inhabitants of the plain have been constantly menaced by the floodwaters of the river, which has changed course several times (see map, above, and sidebar, p.17).

The verdant landscape of south China offers a stark contrast to the dun and ocher hues of the north. The monsoon rains reach as far as the Yangzi river valley, which is very wet and humid. The Yangzi winds

LANDSCAPES IN CHINESE PAINTING

Many people who see Chinese landscape paintings for the first time instinctively assume that the precipitous mountains with their soaring peaks and contorted shapes display extravagant artistic license. Yet the interaction between climate and geology in southern China has created just such a sharply etched landscape of deep valleys and steep mountains. Monsoon rains and high humidity have eroded the surface soils, leaving bare, steep-flanked mountains of volcanic rock. Human settlers have cleared most of the original forest cover in south China and thus contributed to the process of erosion (see caption, p.19).

The mountainous regions of Hunan, southern Anhui (see pp.106–7), and Zhejiang provinces are full of such dramatic scenery, and over the centuries became a favorite subject of Chinese painters. In representing these startlingly beautiful landscapes, devoid of apparent signs of human meddling, *literati* painters (see pp.196–7) and poets eloquently expressed their sense of detachment from political and social turmoil.

ABOVE Taking a Zither to a Friend, *attributed to the Ming artist Jiang Song (active ca. 1500), a painter of the Zhe school, named from Zhejiang province in southeast China. The tiny figures of a gentleman and his servant (who carries a* qin, *the seven-stringed zither beloved of the Chinese* literati) *are dominated by the misty mountain landscape.*

LEFT *Mount Tian Zi in Hunan province, another region where natural erosion and a volcanic geology have created an extraordinary landscape of dramatic peaks and valleys.*

through three basins: Sichuan in the west, an ancient inland sea; the Lakes region of central China; and the massive delta where the river meets the sea. The landscape of the Yangzi valley alternates between these broad, flat basins and rugged mountain ranges (see box, opposite).

In the far south, the Pearl river drains a much smaller area than the Yellow and the Yangzi. This region is fully tropical, much of it originally rain forest, and dense vegetation and tropical diseases inhibited human settlement here until late imperial times. The year-round growing season enables farmers to harvest as many as three crops of rice a year.

Soil and water have been the key forces shaping human settlement in China. North China, although arid, is blessed with rich soils, thanks to the steady removal of loess, a type of yellow soil that is such a distinctive feature of the north Chinese landscape that "Yellow Earth" has become a common metaphor for "China." Loess is borne by wind from the uplands of the west to the alluvial plains of the east, where deposits can be nearly 250 feet (80m) deep. In the subtropical south, in contrast, heavy rainfall leaches nutrients from the soil, resulting in relatively poor fertility. However, by using advanced techniques of cultivation and applying fertilizers, farmers can produce bountiful harvests of rice on the same fields year after year without having to allow the fields to lie fallow and recover their fertility.

Intensive human settlement and exploitation of natural resources have also transformed the natural environment. The lowland lake basins of central China and the Yangzi delta were once huge swamps crisscrossed with meanders and shallow lakes. The ecological demands of irrigated rice farming, which requires level fields and an abundant supply of water, forced Chinese farmers to intensify cultivation of these basins and valley bottoms. Farmers steadily encroached upon the swamps, reclaiming land for agriculture while building dikes to protect their fields from flood. Deprived of natural outlets for its floodwaters, the Yangzi river began to flow more rapidly and deposited greater amounts of silt on the river bottom, increasing the pressure on its confining dikes. Thus, the more human beings tried to control the river, the greater the potential for catastrophic flooding.

However, drought was an even greater menace than flood, even in the monsoon belt of south China. Droughts in the north might last for years, turning whole provinces into dust bowls. For rice farmers in the south, ten days without rain at a critical time could spell disaster. In most years farmers could count on the timely arrival of the "plum rains" (so-called because they coincide with the ripening of plums) in late May and early June, when the young rice plants are most vulnerable. For insurance, though, prudent farmers also dug water storage ponds, sacrificing valuable cropland to ensure an ample supply of water throughout the year.

THE CHANGING COURSE OF THE YELLOW RIVER

The earliest recorded change in the course of the Yellow river dates back to 602BCE. Presumably, the shift in the river's course at that time resulted from environmental rather than human causes. During the past millennium, however, human intervention has had a significant impact on the river's behavior. Maintenance of the flood dikes along the river was always a chief priority of the imperial government and necessitated mobilizing hundreds of thousands of laborers. In 1855, the dikes, weakened by years of neglect, collapsed. The river broke loose from the southerly channel in which it had been contained for five centuries and found a new outlet to the coast—some 250 miles (400km) farther north. More recently, in 1937 and again in 1947, government leaders deliberately destroyed the dikes along the Yellow river in order to alter its course and stem the advance of the Japanese and then the Communist Chinese armies. In each case, millions of people suffered from the devastation and famine that ensued (see map, p.15).

RESOURCES AND ECOLOGY

The human impact on the Chinese landscape has been profound. Once, warm-temperature species such as elephants, rhinoceros, tapirs, and tigers roamed many parts of north China. The cooler climate that has prevailed since ca. 2000BCE reduced the range of these large mammals, but their virtual extinction, even in subtropical southern China, has resulted from the progress of human settlement.

More than any other human activity, farming has taken a heavy toll on China's natural resources. The primeval forests that covered nearly all of eastern and southern China have vanished except in the southwest; the rows of willows, poplars, and elms that line roads and waterways in the North China Plain and the Yangzi delta signify a human rather than natural landscape. Deforestation, already acute in northern China by the Tang dynasty, rendered timber and fuel scarce. The Chinese therefore built dwellings of sun-dried brick or pounded earth, reserving wood for roof-beams and coffins. Dire fuel shortages encouraged a rapid expansion of

Rice paddies in Guizhou province, southwest China. As rice farmers expanded into deforested upland areas, they built elaborate terraces to contain the water needed for irrigation, thereby creating—perhaps unwittingly—an effective means of soil erosion control.

coal mining. The half million residents of Kaifeng, the Northern Song dynasty capital, relied almost exclusively on coal for cooking and heating—Marco Polo observed that everyone in Cathay (north China) bathed at least three times a week in water heated by coal.

Aware of the ecological costs of their way of life, Chinese people have traditionally made painstaking efforts to use their environment in the most efficient manner. Houses are tightly clustered in compact villages to maximize the amount of land available for cultivation. Fish and ducks are raised in irrigation ponds, while hillsides are planted with bamboo, tea, and other useful plants. In the plains of the Yangzi delta the traditional checkerboard panorama of rice paddies is interrupted only by an occasional small hill crowned with a dense thicket of gravestones.

The burden of feeding China's huge population places immense strain on the environment. At the margins of the long-settled parts of China the advance of agriculture is quickening. Even in the arid northwest, mountain slopes have been carved into terraced fields. In recent years, the mammoth and controversial Yangzi Gorges dam project has been inspired by the growing need to divert the plentiful water of the Yangzi river to the parched farmlands of northern China.

Deer in a Forest (detail), by an anonymous artist. The mixed deciduous woodland depicted in this Song dynasty painting has largely disappeared. Southern China was once thick with tall forests of oaks, broad-leaved evergreens, and Chinese fir. But from early historical times farmers burned down the trees and converted the land into rice paddies. Mountain forests were cut down for fuel, papermaking, construction, and shipbuilding, to be replaced by tea, sweet potatoes, and other crops. Deforestation led to erosion, which compounded the problem of flooding in the valleys and basins, because soil was washed into rivers, raising their beds.

PROVINCES AND PEOPLES

This mosque in Turfan in western China was built in 1778.

MUSLIMS IN CHINA
Islamic communities can be found in many parts of China. Muslims initially came to China as merchants, journeying by caravan across the Silk Road, or by ship from the Indian Ocean to southern China. The Mongol rulers of China relied heavily on Muslims as administrators, and encouraged the founding of Muslim congregations and mosques. These communities have retained their distinct identity within the surrounding Chinese community in many major cities of present-day China. The Manchu conquests in central Asia brought large Muslim populations of many different ethnic backgrounds under the Chinese rulers' political control. The People's Republic categorizes central Asian Muslim peoples, such as the Uighurs, as nationalities who share a common culture, language, and homeland, while Muslims living in the metropolitan areas of China are recognized as a separate nationality (Hui) chiefly on the basis of their religion.

The People's Republic of China (PRC), which occupies essentially the same territory as the late Qing empire, recognizes 56 official "nationalities." More than 90 percent of China's population is comprised of the "Han" people, Chinese-speaking inhabitants of territories long ago incorporated into the Chinese empire. Some of the minority nationalities, such as the Tibetans and Uighurs, can be readily defined by virtue of their distinct homeland, culture, and language. Other groups, such as Chinese Muslims (Hui) and Manchus, have been largely assimilated and cannot be easily typified by ethnic labels. The nationalities of modern China should be recognized as products of modern ideology and political practice. Nationality labels tell us little about the historical consciousness and social identity of the Chinese people.

In Confucius' day a sharp line was drawn between civilized and barbarian peoples. Yet the distinction was expressed in cultural rather than ethnic or racial terms. For Confucius, to be Chinese meant to share in the cultural heritage of the Zhou dynasty and respect its values. He believed that the moral charisma of the Chinese sovereign could convert barbarian peoples to civilized ways. The idea of a "Han" people reflects this belief in the transformative power of the virtuous ruler. "Han" originated as a term of political allegiance (to the Han dynasty), and throughout much of China's history its rulers were disposed toward policies of assimilation rather than exclusion. Nonetheless, the sheer size of the empire promoted strong regional and provincial identities. For example, the Cantonese of Guangdong province call themselves "Tang" people rather than "Han," since Chinese first settled in Guangdong in large numbers during the Tang dynasty.

The Ming conquests in the southwest and the expansion of the empire under the Manchus brought many non-Han peoples under the suzerainty of the Chinese empire. The Manchus conceived of their empire as a federation of five peoples—Manchus, Chinese, Mongols, Tibetans, and Muslims—joined by an emperor who transcended any single cultural identity. This definition of China as a multinational state persists today. In many outlying areas, "national minorities" remain the majority of the local population and are allowed a limited degree of self-government.

Although most of the provinces of modern China have long existed as distinct cultural regions, it was not until the Ming dynasty that the provinces became formal units of the imperial government. The two metropolitan regions (centered on the two Ming capitals of Beijing and Nanjing) and thirteen provinces of the Ming (see p.33) have survived down to the present in largely unchanged form, except that two of those provinces have been split in two, producing seventeen provinces altogether. The Qing dynasty's incorporation of Manchuria, Tibet, other central Asian territories, and Taiwan ultimately added eleven new provinces. Today, China is divided into 30 units with provincial status: three metropolitan regions (Beijing, Shanghai, and Tianjin), 22 provinces, and five autonomous regions with non-Han majorities (Tibet, Xinjiang, Ningxia, Inner Mongolia, and Guangxi).

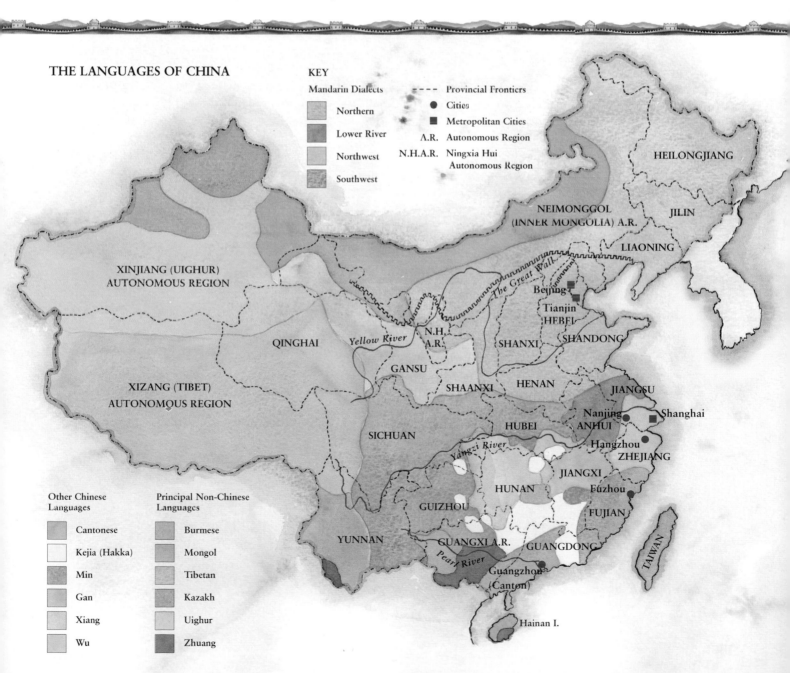

THE LANGUAGES OF CHINA

KEY

Mandarin Dialects

Northern

Lower River

Northwest

Southwest

- - - -   Provincial Frontiers
●   Cities
■   Metropolitan Cities
A.R.   Autonomous Region
N.H.A.R.   Ningxia Hui Autonomous Region

Other Chinese Languages

Cantonese

Kejia (Hakka)

Min

Gan

Xiang

Wu

Principal Non-Chinese Languages

Burmese

Mongol

Tibetan

Kazakh

Uighur

Zhuang

HEILONGJIANG

NEIMONGGOL (INNER MONGOLIA) A.R.

JILIN

LIAONING

XINJIANG (UIGHUR) AUTONOMOUS REGION

The Great Wall

Beijing

Tianjin

HEBEI

QINGHAI

Yellow River

N.H. A.R.

SHANXI

SHANDONG

GANSU

XIZANG (TIBET) AUTONOMOUS REGION

SHAANXI

HENAN

JIANGSU

Nanjing

Shanghai

SICHUAN

HUBEI

ANHUI

Hangzhou

ZHEJIANG

Yangzi River

JIANGXI

HUNAN

Fuzhou

GUIZHOU

FUJIAN

TAIWAN

YUNNAN

GUANGXI A.R.

GUANGDONG

Pearl River

Guangzhou (Canton)

Hainan I.

COMMUNICATION ROUTES

North China has always been plagued by poor transportation, especially before the onset of railroad building at the end of the nineteenth century. The Yellow river was navigable only over short stretches, and the alluvial North China Plain lacked the stone needed to surface roads. Most roads were little more than ox-cart ruts that became quagmires after heavy rain. The Qin and Han dynasties created highway networks, mainly for military use. Governments maintained a rapid courier system, but merchants often had to carry passports and pay customs duties at key junctions. Although travelers on official highways might cover 25 miles (40km) a day, movement on ordinary roads was much slower (see also p.174).

South China, in contrast, has ample navigable waterways. The Yangzi is navigable for 1,630 miles (2,700km), although porterage was

THE GRAND CANAL

Except for the ocean, there is no natural transport route between north and south China. China's capitals have usually been located in the north, but by the sixth century CE the government had come to depend on the transport of grain from the south to feed the population of the capital and armies stationed along the northern frontier. Provisioning the capital at Chang'an (modern Xi'an) was especially difficult because of its location far inland.

Already in the Han dynasty the imperial government constructed a series of canals to link Chang'an to the North China Plain. Emperor Yangdi (ruled 604–617CE) of the Sui dynasty rebuilt the old canals and extended the canal system southward across the low-lying eastern plains to Yangzhou, on the northern bank of the Yangzi river. He also added a new segment across the Yangzi delta to Hangzhou. Contemporaries roundly denounced Yangdi for the great burden of labor service he imposed on his subjects to complete this "Grand Canal." But the canal certainly strengthened both the economic and military might of the imperial state, by providing rulers in the north with an efficient means of tapping the agricultural riches of the south (see also p.174).

An 18th-century painting on silk depicting the emperor Yangdi inspecting the new extension of the Grand Canal at Hangzhou.

once necessary to traverse the rapids in the Yangzi Gorges region of western China. The Yangzi also has numerous navigable tributaries that enable ships to reach most parts of its huge basin. The building of the Grand Canal in the seventh century CE (see box, opposite) made easy passage between north and south China possible for the first time.

Under the early empires, China's main artery of international commerce was the Silk Road, which followed a chain of oasis towns across the central Asian steppes to Chang'an. The Han and Tang dynasties built forts and customs stations along this route well beyond the Great Wall. However, after the eighth century CE, Chinese rulers lost control of these territories and trade along the Silk Road dwindled.

Typhoons and seasonal winds hindered sea voyages beyond the sight of land. The monsoons—which brought strong southwesterlies in summer and strong northeasterlies in winter—meant that ships could make the round trip between China and India at most only once a year. However, the invention of the nautical compass in the Song period and improvements in marine technology (see pp.175) spurred a rapid growth in overseas trade with Korea, Japan, southeast Asia, and the Indian Ocean.

Traffic on the Grand Canal in Suzhou. Under the Song, the inhabitants of the Yangzi delta began to take advantage of the flat terrain to dredge innumerable canals that facilitated irrigation, flood control, and commercial traffic. A web of waterways connected virtually every village in the delta to local market towns and the great metropolises of Suzhou and Hangzhou. River and canal boats carried heavy cargoes on average 45 miles (75km) per day, twice as fast as ox-drawn carts and much more cheaply.

This elaborately decorated ivory beaker with turquoise inlay comes from the tomb of Fu Hao, the wife of the Shang dynasty king Wu Ding (ruled ca. 1215–1190BCE).

● CHAPTER 2   *Mark Edward Lewis*

CONTINUITY AND CHANGE

THE ARCHAIC STATES

The earliest Chinese state, the Shang, emerged ca. 1500BCE out of a Neolithic world of ancestor-worshipping villagers who dwelt on hilltops above their fields in the river valleys. The creation of this state entailed the introduction of writing, the building of walled settlements, the appearance of an élite who extracted obedience and goods from the common people, and the use of large-scale military forces. These inter-linked changes formed the first Chinese civilization.

The earliest surviving script in China forms a complete writing system that was used by the Shang kings and their close allies to communicate with ancestors or gods through "oracle bone" divination (see pp.132–3). Almost every aspect of royal activity was preceded by divination, accompanied by specified sacrifices, offered chiefly to the Shang royal ancestors. These were potent divinities in their own right and the sole intercessors with the high god Di, or Shang Di, a remote deity who lay beyond human offerings. The Shang kings were thus essentially the high priests of a theocratic tribal coalition, whose progressive extension had entailed the incorporation of many local cults into a shared pantheon and genealogy.

The gradual transformation of priests into nobility was marked by the creation of a new type of urban settlement amid the villages, distinguished by larger walls and by the presence of functional divisions. The main divisions were those of the nobles' palaces or temples, and the workshop area, where artisans produced bronze weapons and ritual vessels, finely carved jades, and other material attributes of the nobility. The nobles of the Shang walled towns organized themselves in military units. The Shang army consisted

Shang civilization coexisted with a number of remarkable ancient Chinese cultures, as this extraordinary 6-foot (2m) tall bronze statue illustrates. It was discovered at Sanxingdui in Sichuan (see p.185) and its purpose is unknown.

WOMEN IN THE SHANG STATE
Inscriptions and archaeological finds, such as the richly furnished tomb of the royal consort Fu Hao (see p.140, and illustration, opposite), show that women wielded considerable power in the Shang state—some of them even commanded armies. They may also have influenced the succession. In general, the throne passed from brother to brother, but at certain points it shifted to the next generation, at times that may have been determined by the status of the candidates' mothers. This may have occurred when the king's wife was deemed of higher status than the next brother (the heir), in which case the succession would pass to her son by the king. The succeeding Zhou state used primogeniture and denied such importance to women—Zhou propaganda denounced the Shang kings for being female-dominated.

of infantry, and inscriptions mention forces as large as 13,000 men. These imposed order on the Shang's subject population, guarded against hostile peoples, and secured prisoners to be sacrificed in royal burials.

The Shang state was a linked network of these towns and their immediate hinterlands, and dispersed among the Shang settlements were villages of peoples with whom the Shang were frequently at war. Thus the Shang rulers presided over a league of settlements, and not a "state" in the modern sense of a contiguous territory defined by boundaries. This league of settlements had no bureaucracy and was essentially an extension of the royal household. The Shang king rarely delegated powers, and then only to immediate relatives or followers. He traveled constantly to impose his authority, and relied on brothers, sons, and sons of sons as the base of his power. The capital was thus inhabited by a large royal clan that secured the monarchy and regulated the succession. Even the Shang queens performed political tasks. The only significant non-kinspeople who were active in the Shang government were advisers and diviners, who came to the Shang capital from allied tribes.

THE TERRITORIAL STATES

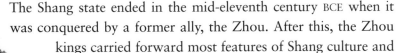

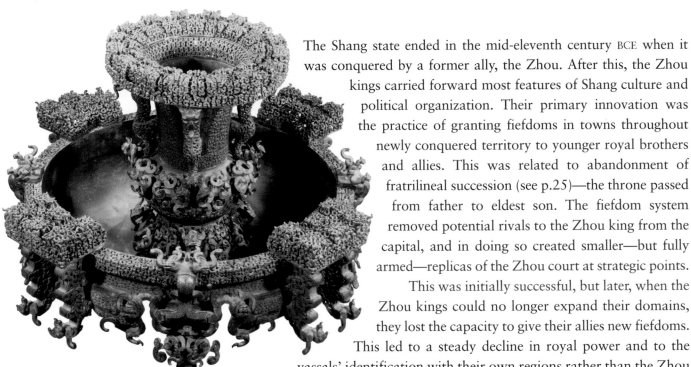

An Eastern Zhou bronze ritual vessel from the tomb of Lord Yi of Zeng, who died ca. 433BCE (see also p.125).

A NEW VISION OF WARFARE
Sun Wu, or Sunzi ("Master Sun"), is the shadowy author of the earliest and greatest work of Chinese military thought, the *Sunzi Bingfa* (*Sunzi's Art of War*). The source of military theory throughout east Asia, it has become increasingly influential in the West, and not just among soldiers, since a French version appeared in the eighteenth century. The text clearly reflects the rise of mass armies in the Eastern Zhou period. It rejects the earlier heroic vision of war, downgrading combat in favor of the arts of the commander, who is advised to use illusion and deception to manipulate his opponent's mind. If combat proves necessary, he obtains victory through stealth, speed, and striking at weak points.

The Shang state ended in the mid-eleventh century BCE when it was conquered by a former ally, the Zhou. After this, the Zhou kings carried forward most features of Shang culture and political organization. Their primary innovation was the practice of granting fiefdoms in towns throughout newly conquered territory to younger royal brothers and allies. This was related to abandonment of fratrilineal succession (see p.25)—the throne passed from father to eldest son. The fiefdom system removed potential rivals to the Zhou king from the capital, and in doing so created smaller—but fully armed—replicas of the Zhou court at strategic points.

This was initially successful, but later, when the Zhou kings could no longer expand their domains, they lost the capacity to give their allies new fiefdoms. This led to a steady decline in royal power and to the vassals' identification with their own regions rather than the Zhou house. In 770BCE an alliance of Rong barbarians and rebel nobles forced the king to resettle near modern Luoyang in the east of the kingdom.

The centuries following the eastward shift of the royal court are known as the Eastern Zhou period (ca. 770–221BCE). In the early Eastern Zhou, the former Zhou fiefdoms preserved an uneasy alliance against non-Zhou peoples while struggling for military dominance among themselves. In the seventh century BCE the states began to expand their infantry forces through the mobilization of peasants, who in return received absolute title to their land.

Technical innovations, such as the crossbow, made infantry more effective, and large-scale workshop production made such forces cheap to equip. In the mid-seventh century BCE some states adopted the use of cavalry from northern nomads. These changes dramatically increased the size of armies—some contained as many as 100,000 men—and states that had made more thorough military reforms conquered those that had not.

This extension of military service also entailed an administrative revolution. The peasants and their land had to be accurately registered. For legal and security purposes the state grouped households into units, and rewarded success in battle with ranks in a state-imposed hierarchy. Order was preserved through the imposition of state law.

The cumulative effect of these changes was the political and social transformation of the Chinese world. In place of hundreds of semi-inde-

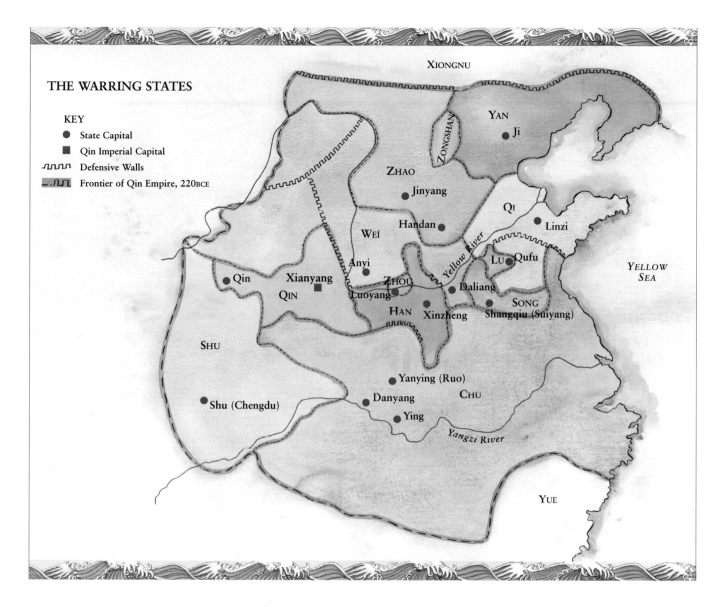

THE WARRING STATES

KEY
● State Capital
■ Qin Imperial Capital
⌁⌁⌁ Defensive Walls
⌁⌁ Frontier of Qin Empire, 220BCE

XIONGNU

YAN
Ji

ZONGSHAN

ZHAO
Jinyang

Qi

WEI
Handan
Linzi

Anyi
LU
Qufu

Qin
Xianyang
ZHOU
Daliang

QIN
Luoyang
SONG

HAN
Xinzheng
Shangqiu (Suiyang)

SHU

Yanying (Ruo)

Danyang
CHU

Shu (Chengdu)
Ying

Yangzi River

YELLOW
SEA

Yellow River

YUE

pendent city-states inhabited by warrior nobles fighting on chariots, the former Zhou vassals created new states that were continuous, territorial entities marked by fixed boundaries and separated by walls. With the subsequent conquest of weaker states by more powerful ones, the Chinese world came to be divided among seven powers collectively known as the "Warring States." These great territorial states had full-blown bureaucracies administering peasant households who provided military service in infantry armies. The individual household became the standard form of family organization, outside which the state alone provided cohesion and rank.

The great states of the later Eastern Zhou period, being designed solely for military expansion, were inherently unstable. Ever more destructive and bloody warfare could end only if one state swallowed the rest, or if a wholly new type of state emerged.

THE FIRST EMPIRES

QIN DYNASTY

Qin Shihuangdi	221–210BCE
Er Shi	210–207BCE

WESTERN HAN DYNASTY

Gaodi	206–195BCE
Huidi	195–188BCE
(Lu Hou, Regent 188–180BCE)	
Wendi	180–157BCE
Jingdi	157–141BCE
Wudi	141–87BCE
Zhaodi	87–74BCE
Xuandi	74–49BCE
Yuandi	49–33BCE
Chengdi	33–7BCE
Aidi	7–1BCE
Pingdi	1BCE–6CE
Ruzi	7–9CE
Reign of Wang Mang	
("Xin dynasty")	9–23CE

EASTERN HAN DYNASTY

Guang Wudi	25–57CE
Mingdi	57–75CE
Zhangdi	75–88CE
Hedi	88–106CE
Shangdi	106CE
Andi	106–125CE
Shundi	125–144CE
Chongdi	144–145CE
Zhidi	145–146CE
Huandi	146–168CE
Lingdi	168–189CE
Xiandi	189–220CE

The Warring States period ended in the triumph of the state of Qin, which conquered its last rival in 221BCE. The Qin unification of China was without precedent. It was marked by the king of Qin's adoption of a new title—he called himself Shihuangdi, "First August Emperor"—and by a succession of notable measures including an attempt to confiscate all weapons, the tearing down of walls between states, the imposition of a uniform administration, the unification of the Chinese script, and the standardization of weights and measures. Nevertheless, Qin failed to adjust to the cessation of warfare, employing its armies in pointless southern expeditions and massive public works such as the building of the first "long wall" (see p.51). These projects aroused great resentment and a civil war erupted shortly after the First Emperor's death in 210BCE. His successor, Er Shi, ruled for only three troubled years before the Qin empire crumbled.

Emerging from the civil strife that followed Qin's collapse, the Han dynasty inherited its predecessor's institutions. Over four centuries the dynasty introduced innovations that provided the basis for a lasting empire. To begin with, the Han elaborated the office and role of the emperor. While Qin had established the title "emperor," the institution itself developed gradually. The Han inherited the idea that the emperor was the source of law, highest judge, and chief administrator, constrained only by obedience to his ancestors and ancestral precedent. He was also distinguished by a panoply of privileges: garments, insignia, chariots, and even roads were reserved for his sole use. Religious reforms culminated in the revival of the Zhou cult of the divinity Heaven (Tian) and in the concept of the Mandate of Heaven, under which the emperor derived his power from on high (see pp.45–6). The Han emperors became progressively detached from their original Guanzhong base to become the embodiment of a monarchy that transcended local loyalties. The second important change was the abolition in 32CE of the annual mobilization and training of peasants. Now limited to the frontiers, warfare required a permanent army, paid for by a tax that replaced universal military service.

No longer organized for warfare, the state justified itself as the protector of social order. This included police action, ritual performances to secure nature's beneficence, and the propagation of morality. To this end, Emperor Wudi (ruled 141–87BCE) established an Imperial Academy with a curriculum defined by the Confucian canon (see pp.82–3). By the end of the first century BCE an education based on the Confucian classic texts became the principal route to public office and élite status.

The final major development of the Han era was the creation of a

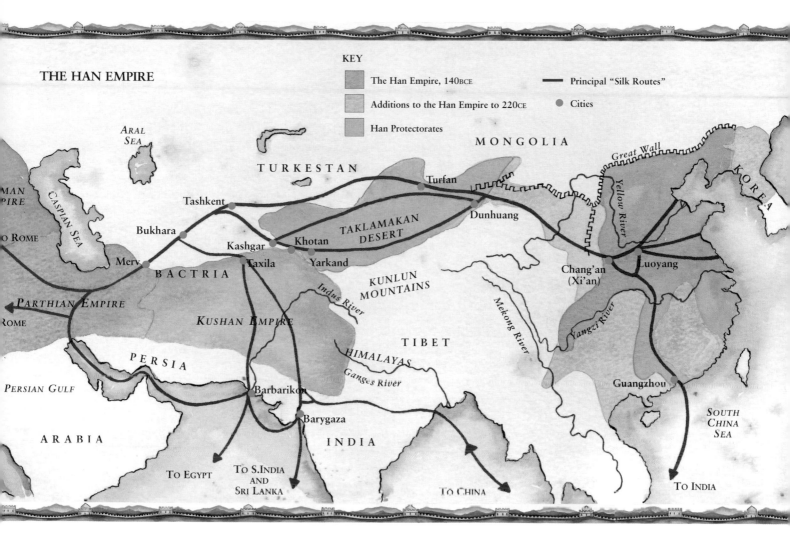

THE HAN EMPIRE

KEY

The Han Empire, 140 BCE

Additions to the Han Empire to 220 CE

Han Protectorates

Principal "Silk Routes"

● Cities

new élite. Land was the primary source of wealth, but the system of shared inheritance (see p.71) meant that estates had to be constantly rebuilt through the purchase of new land with income derived from some alternative source. The most profitable source was public office, and so landowner families educated their sons to gain office, while officials purchased land to acquire more lasting wealth. Taxes against merchants pushed them, too, to invest in land and to secure land through studying for office. By the first century CE a single group of great families combined landowning, officeholding, and trade to secure their social dominance.

In the long term these changes provided a firm basis for imperial China, but they combined to destroy the Han. Power became concentrated in the hands of those closest to the emperor, namely his relatives by marriage and eunuchs. This progressively alienated the great families, who strengthened their local bases and social networks. When a millenarian rebellion in 184 CE led to armed struggle in the capital, military forces were controlled entirely by barbarian chiefs, frontier generals, and great families. Thus the Han collapse initiated the first age of warlords.

Under the Han, exotic animals and artifacts were especially prized. Central Asian horses, such as the one depicted in this bronze, were particularly sought after for their speed and large size.

A TIME OF DISUNION

TALES OF THE STRANGE

The Period of Disunion witnessed the emergence in China of prose fiction. Such tales appeared in anthologies of "uncanny" phenomena outside normal experience that could highlight its principles and limits. The early collections claimed to be true and patterned themselves on histories. However, in many stories of ghosts and fox spirits, the sheer interest in the narrative eclipses any supposed truth. Elaborate fictions in the literary language developed even further in the Tang dynasty, and the earliest stories dealing with human romance grew directly from the themes and structures of these tales of uncanny encounters. Notable examples are *The Tale of Ying Ying* by Yuan Zhen (779–831CE) and *The Tale of Li Wa* by Bo Xingjian (776–826CE).

The Han dynasty's final collapse in 220CE led to the break up of the empire into three rival kingdoms and ushered a long era of political division. Two features define the three centuries known as the Period of Disunion (265–618CE)—great families forming a proto-nobility (see box, below), and the rise of military dynasticism. When non-Chinese chieftains seized the two former Han capitals in 311CE and 316CE, the ruling Jin house shifted to the lower Yangzi, near modern Nanjing, in a regime controlled by a coalition of great families. The north, meanwhile, was divided among a succession of short-lived barbarian states called the "Sixteen Kingdoms." This marked the low point of imperial power and the zenith of the aristocracy.

The revival of the unified empire relied on hereditary military households formed from refugees allocated abandoned land by the government. These were eliminated by the Jin in the late third century. However, the powerful families who fled south with the Jin court in 316CE used poor refugees to provide hereditary labor and military service.

In the fourth century an ambitious clan in the mid-Yangzi region

NOBLE ARTS

The proto-nobility of the Period of Disunion distinguished themselves from rivals through their cultivation of the arts. The earliest of these included "pure conversation"—bon mots and apt allusions used to encapsulate people's characters—lyric poetry, calligraphy, and playing the lute. All these activities were performed at banquets and excursions, often accompanied by alcohol, as an adjunct of refined fellowship. The "Seven Sages of the Bamboo Grove" emerged as the idealized embodiments of this life (see pp.90–91).

When the court and leading clans moved south, the new physical environment altered the character of such noble arts and added new ones. Poetry increasingly dealt with the theme of rural life, a rustic vision of the nobles' estates, and the celebration of mountain landscapes. The painting of such landscapes and their artificial recreation as gardens also became elements of noble self-refinement. Under the reunited empire these arts spread across China as hallmarks of the élite.

A mural of mounted warriors from the tomb of Prince Zhanghuai, Xi'an. The Period of Disunion was an age when nobles cultivated the arts as much as the warlike pursuits reflected in the rise of military dynasties.

created a "Western Command Army" of hereditary refugee soldiers. Those in the Jin capital region established a rival "Northern Command Army," which thwarted an invasion by the western forces and suppressed a religious rebellion. Then, a commoner who had risen through the ranks took control of the army and seized the Jin capital. In 420CE he established the Liu Song dynasty, the first military regime. These military dynasts broke the proto-nobles' dominance of the court and reasserted imperial power.

A similar process took place in the barbarian-occupied north. Among the "Sixteen Kingdoms" one tribal coalition, the Murong, had established a state that combined the use of nomadic troops with a Chinese-style bureaucracy administering the peasantry. This pattern was adopted by Toba people, who from their base near modern Datong reunited all of north China. Following a civil war in the 520s, a successor state was founded in the Guanzhong region and this developed a new style of hereditary army, the "Divisional Troops," that allowed it to reunite the north. After a coup d'état established the Sui dynasty, this army finally reunified the whole empire by conquering the south in 589CE.

THE THREE KINGDOMS	
WEI	220–264
WU	222–280
SHU HAN	221–223

THE PERIOD OF DISUNION	
Western Jin dyn.	265–316
Eastern Jin dyn.	317–419
Liu Song dynasty	420–479
Qi dynasty	479–501
Liang dynasty	502–556
Chen dynasty	557–589
Sui dynasty	581–618

Buddhist guardian figures at Longmen caves, Henan (ca. 500CE). Buddhism became firmly established in China during the Period of Disunion (see p.110).

MEDIEVAL EMPIRES

Representations of mountain landscapes were very popular among the Tang nobility (see box, p.30). Entitled Journey of Minhuang to Shu, *this northern landscape painting on silk is a later copy of an eighth-century original. The picture reads from left to right and depicts three separate episodes.*

TANG DYNASTY

Gaozu	618–626
Taizong	626–649
Gaozong	649–683
Zhongzong	684, 705–710
Ruizong	684–690, 710–712
Wu Zetian	690–705
Xuanzong	712–756
Suzong	756–762
Daizong	762–779
Dezong	779–805
Shunzong	805
Xianzong	805–820
Muzong	820–824
Jingzong	824–827
Wenzong	827–840
Wuzong	840–846
Xuanzong	846–859
Yizong	859–873
Xizong	873–888
Zhaozong	888–904
Aidi (Zhaoxuan)	904–907

The Sui empire, like the Qin, was short-lived, and it was the Tang that truly restored imperial unity. Many of its institutions dated from the Han, but the intervening centuries had wrought great changes, including limited legal recognition of the nobility, a system of state-owned land, forms of hereditary soldiery, and state sponsorship of Buddhism and Daoism. The Tang incorporated these to fashion a new, medieval empire.

The Tang state sponsored several genealogies listing and ranking the powerful clans in a hierarchy based on offices held by clan members under the Tang. Sons of high officials had an automatic right to a post. Under the Tang legal code, high rank entailed immunity from torture and other privileges. The code also ranked the entire population as officials, commoners, "base people," or slaves. Consequently, a reduced form of nobility survived, one that depended upon obtaining high office.

The state ownership of land derived from the practice of military dynasts, who had issued abandoned lands to refugees in exchange for service. Under the Tang, all families (at least in the north) received a small amount of land in perpetuity plus additional lands that they held for as long as they gave service and taxes.

Hereditary military households took several forms. However, the need for long-term garrisons led to their decline and an increasing reliance on professional troops, to which the Tang's Turkic allies also contributed.

The state sponsored both Daoism and Buddhism, and, although the numbers of temples, monks, and priests were limited, religious institutions were exempt from taxation. Buddhist temples built up large estates.

The final great change under the Tang was the formation of smaller replica states that took on many aspects of Tang culture, including the legal code and writing system. Many of them, such as Korea and Japan, also adopted Buddhism via China. Foreigners from central Asia and further afield were also drawn to the Tang, whether on pilgrimages, for trade, or to offer tribute, and played a key role in the Tang urban economy.

However, the An Lushan rebellion of 755CE changed everything (see sidebar, right). In its aftermath, Tibetans or military governors ruled much of the north, and the state-owned land system vanished. The government began to base taxes on actual wealth, and it relied increasingly on salt and iron monopolies. New men with fiscal expertise rose to power under the military governors and monopolies. This confined the great families' influence to the court, and even there they were supplanted by eunuchs. There were massacres of foreigners in some cities. When the dynasty finally fell in 907CE, its institutions and social foundations had long vanished.

THE AN LUSHAN REBELLION

The rebellion of An Lushan divided not only the Tang dynasty but the whole history of imperial China. An Lushan was the Sogdian-born commander of three army groups based around modern Beijing. When his patron at court died, An Lushan feared for his position and marched on the capital in the winter of 755CE. Tang resistance collapsed, and he entered the capital unopposed.

An Lushan died in 757CE, but the rebellion was suppressed only in 763CE, largely with the aid of Uighur and Tibetan troops. The dynasty was restored but its institutional base had been destroyed, and its social foundations were soon to follow. This rebellion not only led to the disappearance of such major features as semi-hereditary nobility and service classes, but it also marked the permanent shift southward of the center of Chinese civilization to the Yangzi valley.

THE SOUTHWARD SHIFT

THE RISE OF LITERACY

Government policy and economic developments in the Song led to a massive extension of literacy and access to written materials. Whereas the Tang government had only one academy in the capital for examination preparation, the Song established such schools, endowed with land and provided with texts, in every prefectural town, and decreed the establishment of elementary schools in every county town. Schools were also set up by clans and private educators. The spread of printing dramatically reduced the price of books between the ninth and eleventh centuries (see p.182). Those engaged in the booming urban economy trained their children in basic literacy and numeracy, and even rural villages had elementary schools.

In the century of disorder that lasted from the final decades of the Tang to the founding of the Song dynasty in 960CE, power devolved into the hands first of local warlords and then of their palace armies. The commander of one such army, Zhao Kuangyin (later the emperor Taizu), restored unity and ended more than two centuries of semi-independent regional armies. The Song dynasty that Taizu established secured the dominance of scholar-officials, a move aided by the shift of the center of Chinese civilization from the north, with its martial heritage, to the Yangzi valley.

The new dynasty faced a serious challenge from two powerful states to the north founded by non-Chinese nomads, the Khitan state of Liao and the Tangut state of Xia. Like the earlier Toba Wei, these states combined nomadic military forces with a Chinese-style bureaucracy to administer peasant populations (see pp.36–7). The Song signed a series of treaties recognizing Liao and Xia as *de facto* equals and agreeing to give them large annual payments. But periodic warfare continued, and the Song were forced to spend an ever larger portion of their budget on defense.

THE NEO-CONFUCIAN RITUAL REVIVAL

Often treated as a philosophical movement, the revival of Confucianism in the Song was also a religious revival propagated by scholar-official "missionaries." At its core was an attempt to reduce the influence of Buddhism, especially on burials. The Buddhist establishment had come to play an increasingly large role in funerary rites, and for poor peasants and even *literati*, cremation or the abandonment of the bodies of deceased relatives to monasteries had become cheap and convenient alternatives to traditional burials.

To reverse this development, some Confucian *literati* endowed charitable cemeteries where poor peasants could have their parents buried without charge. More important, leading scholar-officials such as Zhu Xi composed manuals to standardize traditional Confucian rituals. These were then printed in editions of varying quality to make widely known the basic elements of key rites, and to encourage their practice. Over the centuries, simplified versions of these texts were disseminated even to remote villages (see also pp.84–5).

This Song-dynasty painting depicts a scene exemplifying the Confucian virtue of filial piety.

A view of the Yangzi valley, the center of Chinese civilization under the Song dynasty. Here a commercial revolution and the introduction of new varieties of rice led to tremendous population growth and the development of many great cities (see p.71).

These wars led to many technological innovations, including the introduction of gunpowder weapons (see pp.176–7) and the development by the Song of a large war fleet constructed with new shipbuilding methods.

Despite its military problems, the Song government was dominated by a civil élite recruited through examinations, which in the Song became the standard route to significant office. This produced the new ideal of the *literati*, the scholar-officials skilled in the arts and diverse intellectual fields. They came from the powerful landlord and merchant families that flourished in the booming Song economy.

The Song was in many ways a golden age of scholar-officials, when even emperors were open to their suggestions and criticism. However, without an institutional mechanism to resolve disputes, debates over policy led to protracted and fierce struggles between rival cliques, most notably over the reforms advocated by Wang Anshi (see p.67). Also, bureaucratization entailed the production of countless written regulations covering every aspect of government activity.

In 1126 the Manchurian state of Jurchen Jin overran all of north China and carried off the Song emperor and much of his family from the capital, Kaifeng. But one prince, Zhao Gou (later the emperor Gaozong), escaped south to Hangzhou, where he revived the dynasty, hereafter known as the Southern Song. Many Chinese scholars blamed the disaster of 1126 on the dynasty's excessive interest in such arts as poetry and painting. Others sought to purify China by reviving Confucianism (see box, opposite).

The reduced empire of the Southern Song flourished and its naval technology held off further foreign invasions for more than a century.

THE FIVE DYNASTIES

Later Liang	907–923
Later Tang	923–935
Later Jin	936–947
Later Han	947–951
Later Zhou	951–960

NORTHERN SONG DYNASTY

Taizu	960–976
Taizong	976–997
Zhenzong	998–1022
Renzong	1022–1063
Yingzong	1064–1067
Shenzong	1068–1085
Zhezong	1086–1101
Huizong	1101–1125
Qinzong	1126

SOUTHERN SONG DYNASTY

Gaozong	1127–1162
Xiazong	1163–1190
Guangzong	1190–1194
Ningzong	1195–1224
Lizong	1225–1264
Duzong	1265–1274
Gongzong	1275
Duanzong	1276–1278
Bing Di	1279

THE CONQUEST DYNASTIES

The non-Chinese states that ultimately conquered the Song were a new phenomenon in Chinese history. Chinese states had long been in contact with nomadic warrior tribes which, in times of political breakdown, had occupied part or all of north China. From the tenth century the Tangut, Khitan, Jurchen, and Mongol peoples founded something like states on the Chinese model, using Chinese administrative methods. In military terms, these "conquest dynasties" matched the Song at its peak and came to occupy ever increasing amounts of its territory.

The first important state was the Liao, established by the Khitan people in southern Manchuria. As Tang power collapsed a Khitan chieftain named Abaoji united several tribes and established himself as emperor of a dynasty. The Liao dynasty created a dual state, with the Khitan settled in the north under their own institutions and the Chinese, nominally under a civil bureaucracy, in the south of the state.

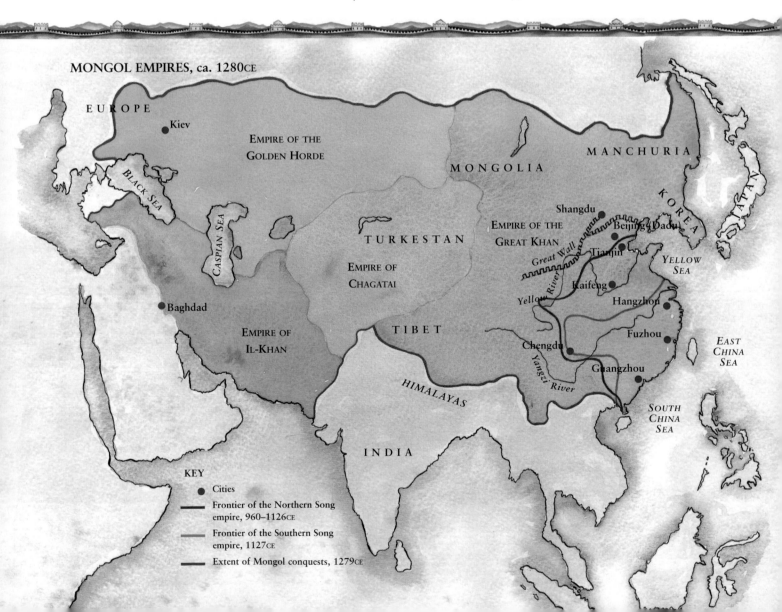

MONGOL EMPIRES, ca. 1280CE

EUROPE

Kiev

EMPIRE OF THE
GOLDEN HORDE

MANCHURIA

MONGOLIA

BLACK SEA

CASPIAN SEA

TURKESTAN

EMPIRE OF THE
GREAT KHAN

Shangdu

Beijing Dadu

KOREA

JAPAN

EMPIRE OF
CHAGATAI

Great Wall

Tianjin

YELLOW
SEA

Yellow River

Kaifeng

Baghdad

Yellow River

Hangzhou

EMPIRE OF
IL-KHAN

TIBET

Chengdu

Fuzhou

EAST
CHINA
SEA

Yangzi River

Guangzhou

HIMALAYAS

SOUTH
CHINA
SEA

INDIA

KEY

● Cities

── Frontier of the Northern Song empire, 960–1126CE

── Frontier of the Southern Song empire, 1127CE

── Extent of Mongol conquests, 1279CE

The Liao state was destroyed in 1125 by the Jurchen, a people from eastern Manchuria who were ancestors of the Manchus. Their Jin dynasty allied with the Song, but after destroying the Liao they turned on their former allies and in 1127 conquered north China with the aid of Chinese experts who introduced the use of siege engines and gunpowder against walled Chinese cities. To control their newly extended empire, the Jin resettled Jurchen people throughout north China. They had become largely indistinguishable from the Chinese by 1212, when the Mongols invaded. The Mongol armies completed their conquest of Jin in 1234.

For decades the Southern Song emperors successfully resisted the Mongols, aided by their control of the rivers, canals, and lakes of the south. Like the Jin, the Mongols ultimately succeeded by recruiting Chinese experts, who helped them build a fleet which in 1273 captured the important city of Xiangyang. The rapid conquest of the rest of the south—accompanied by the systematic massacres of entire cities—was completed in 1279.

Ruling China as the Yuan dynasty, the Mongols divided the population into ethnic groups (see pp.20–1). Each group was subject to different rules for taxation, law, and administration, all based on ethnic traditions. When the Confucian examinations were restored in 1315, quotas guaranteed that Mongols and other non-Chinese obtained half the degrees awarded. However, graduates filled only two percent of all government posts, and many key positions were occupied by non-Chinese.

Particularly severe restrictions were placed on the Chinese, who were forbidden to own weapons, congregate in public, intermarry with Mongols, or take Mongol names. Taxation was ruinous, and much land was confiscated. There were few opportunities for government service, and those Chinese who took them were often treated as traitors.

The population was further divided into hereditary castes—including farmers, doctors, soldiers, artisans, entertainers, and miners—and social mobility was prohibited.

These conquests were in many ways a disaster for China. The great iron industry of north China was destroyed, never to recover. The registered population fell by half, in part due to massacres and plagues, and some regions did not recover for centuries. There were even more lasting political changes. China acquired a new capital in the north, even though its economic and cultural heart remained in the south. Beijing, a minor frontier town, was the southern provinical capital of the Liao and a temporary capital of the Jin. It became a true capital in the Chinese style when the first Mongol emperor, Khubilai Khan, built the imperial city of Dadu there. The Jin also introduced the practice of flogging court officials, and this increasing imperial autocracy and reliance on force were to continue in later dynasties.

Mounted archers were the mainstay of the Mongol armies that swept across Asia and into Europe. This painting of a Mongol bowman dates from the Ming dynasty.

YUAN (MONGOL) DYNASTY

Khubilai Khan	1279–1294
Temur Oljeitu	1294–1307
Khaishan	1308–1311
Ayurbarwada	1311–1320
Shidebala	1321–1323
Yesun Temur	1323–1328
Tugh Temur	1328–1329; 1329–1332
Khoshila	1329
Toghon Temur	1333–1368

THE RISE OF AUTOCRACY

MING DYNASTY

Hongwu	1368–1398
Jianwen	1399–1402
Yongle	1403–1424
Hongxi	1425
Xuande	1426–1435
Zhengtong/Tianshun	
	1436–1449; 1457–1464
Jingtai	1450–1457
Chenghua	1465–1487
Hongzhi	1488–1505
Zhengde	1506–1521
Jiajing	1522–1567
Longqing	1567–1572
Wanli	1573–1620
Taichang	1620
Tianqi	1621–1627
Chongzhen	1628–1644

Drought, floods, and monetary collapse provoked a wave of millenarian rebellions that brought the Yuan (Mongol) dynasty to an end in 1368 with the establishment of the Ming dynasty under a former peasant and Buddhist monk, Zhu Yuanzhang. In an attempt to reduce peasant suffering, Zhu (the emperor Hongwu) intensified imperial autocracy and the extraction of services from people in fixed hereditary occupations.

Hongwu divided the population into hereditary peasants, soldiers, and craftsmen. He relied on the peasants themselves to allocate and collect taxes. Soldiers received land to provision themselves, reducing the tax burden. Craftsmen were either attached to imperial workshops or obliged to provide periods of service. This system excluded only the mercantile and scholarly élites in the south of the country, whom Hongwu distrusted and taxed heavily. He suspended the examinations, and later punished examiners if southern scholars were too successful. In theory, fixing all people in occupations to provide both for themselves and the state reduced expenditures. But Hongwu's vision was unworkable in a mobile, increasingly commercialized society.

The rise of imperial autocracy, inherited from the conquest dynasties, proved more enduring. Hongwu continued the policy of flogging officials who displeased him, while personally overseeing all matters of state. The burden proved too great, so his successors turned to eunuchs, who ultimately took charge of every aspect of administration (see p.46). These developments provoked a series of protests in which scholar-officials who challenged emperors and eunuchs were severely punished. The struggle ended only when the eunuch Wei Zhongxian, *de facto* ruler of China, was assassinated in 1628 on the accession of the last Ming emperor.

The conquest dynasties had drawn China into a world of international trade and diplomatic relations between equals. The Ming, however, attempted to restore the China-centered world of the Tang. To this end, the first two emperors launched a series of campaigns against the Mongols. Between 1405 and 1433 the Ming also dispatched fleets under the eunuch Zheng He in search of new tributary states.

Two officials of the Ming dynasty. The dynasty was marked by disputes between emperors and their scholar-officials. Notable among these was the Great Rites Controversy. When the Zhengde emperor was succeeded by a cousin, Jiajing, in 1522, officials expected the new ruler to worship Zhengde as his father so as to maintain continuity in the imperial ancestral cult. But Jiajing insisted on venerating his real father and punished those who opposed him. The dispute lasted over two decades before Jiajing prevailed.

THE MING EMPIRE

KEY
- National Capital
- Provincial Capital
- Other City
- Ming Empire, ca.1550
- Ming Empire, ca.1400

MONGOLIA
MANCHURIA
LIAOYANG
Yellow River
Great Wall
Beijing
BEIZHILI (JINGSHI)
SHANXI
Ji'nan
SHANDONG
YELLOW SEA
KOREA
SHAANXI
Kaifeng
HENAN
Xi'an
Nanjing
NANZHILI (NANJING)
KUNLUN MOUNTAINS
Chengdu
Yangzi River
SICHUAN
Hanyang
Hangzhou
Jingdezhen
ZHEJIANG
HUGUANG
Nanchang
JIANGXI
Jianning
EAST CHINA SEA
TIBET
Guiyang
GUIZHOU
FUJIAN
Yunnan
YUNNAN
Guilan
GUANGXI
GUANGDONG
Guangzhou (Canton)
Pearl River
SOUTH CHINA SEA

In 1449 the Ming emperor Zhengtong was captured by the Mongols. This led to decades of administrative paralysis, after which the Ming attempted a passive separation of China and the Mongols by rebuilding the Great Wall (see p.215). The dynasty sought to restrict foreign trade to a few ports; but this resulted in smuggling and an increase in coastal piracy.

In the last half century of Ming rule, eunuch corruption, a huge imperial clan, and disastrous campaigns in Korea drained the imperial coffers. Declining temperatures led to bad harvests, and the armies could not cope with growing bandit forces. In 1639 Japan and the Spanish in Manila cut off silver shipments to China, causing deflation, hoarding of goods, and famine. Within five years the Ming had collapsed.

ZENITH AND DECLINE

QING (MANCHU) DYNASTY	
Shunzhi	1644–1661
Kangxi	1661–1722
Yongzheng	1723–1735
Qianlong	1736–1795
Jiajing	1796–1820
Daoguang	1821–1850
Xianfeng	1851–1861
Tongzhi	1862–1874
Guangxu	1875–1908
Xuantong (Puyi)	1908–1912

A red lacquer throne made for the Qianlong emperor, whose reign marked the peak of Qing China's fortunes. Out of respect for his grandfather, Kangxi, who had reigned for 61 years, Qianlong abdicated after 59 years of rule. He died in 1799, aged 88.

The Manchus, a sedentary people living beyond the Great Wall in Manchuria, first established a state under Nurhaci (1559–1626). When peasant rebels took Beijing in 1644 and the last Ming emperor killed himself, Chinese generals supported a Manchu invasion in order to restore order. The invaders declared a new dynasty, the Qing, and confiscated large amounts of land to distribute to the Manchu "Banner Armies" (see p.55). With the final defeat of Chinese resistance in 1673, the Qing established a cosmopolitan state on the model of previous foreign dynasties.

The great achievement of the Qing was its unparalleled geographic expansion. It occupied Manchuria, Mongolia, Xinjiang, and Taiwan, and made Tibet a protectorate. Even European Jesuits played a role in this great multi-ethnic empire, mapping Xinjiang and helping to establish borders with Russia in treaties of 1689 and 1728. The fixing of the frontiers restricted nomad mobility and culminated in the final conquest of Xinjiang by the Qianlong emperor, under whom China was probably the wealthiest and most powerful country on earth.

Qing rule was intensely focused on the emperor, who developed government mechanisms that allowed him to gather information and make policy without reference to the bureaucracy. Thus while the Qing emperors avoided the open hostilities with officials that had marked the Ming, they were in practice even more autocratic.

China's zenith under Qianlong was followed by a century of decline. Between 1650 and 1850 the population trebled. Food needs were met by cultivating more land—primarily through the introduction of potatoes and maize from the Americas—but the use of marginal lands increased erosion and flooding (see pp.18–19). Declining rural conditions provoked a series of uprisings, culminating in the Taiping Rebellion (see box, opposite), while Xinjiang drained military and financial resources. The Western powers also had an impact, beginning with the Opium War of 1839–1842, in which Britain forced China to cede Hong Kong and accept opium imports from India. This set the pattern for a wave of "Unequal Treaties" imposed on China by foreign powers, who established zones of influence based on the "Treaty Ports."

By 1860 China was on the verge of collapse, with much of the Yangzi valley in the hands of the Taiping rebels, the Russians expanding into Chinese central

THE TAIPING REBELLION

The bloodiest uprising in the history of China began in 1850 and provided an epitome of the empire's weaknesses in the nineteenth century. The rebellion's leader, Hong Xiuquan, was a failed examination candidate, a type grown common because of population growth. After suffering a nervous breakdown owing to his repeated failure to pass the imperial civil service examination, Hong experienced visions of an egalitarian society which he explained through a garbled form of Christianity that he had learned from European missionaries at one of the Treaty Ports. Hong found a following for his vision among poor peasants of the Guangxi region who eked out a living on marginal land.

In 1850 Hong led an open revolt against the government. The Qing armies proved ineffectual and he swept north to occupy Nanjing. Although the movement subsequently disintegrated owing to rivalry among its generals, the imperial armies could not defeat it. Finally a scholar-official, Zeng Guofan, raised a new army based on his home province, but it took him a decade and 120,000 men to defeat the Taiping rebels.

A contemporary print of the Taiping rebels laying siege to the Treaty Port of Shanghai.

Asia, and Franco-British forces in Beijing to enforce a recent treaty. Attempts at modernization met with little success (see p.86) and further humiliations followed. Japan—which had pursued a rapid and highly successful modernization program—provoked a war over Korea in 1894 and destroyed the new Chinese fleet. A reform movement of 1898 (see p.85) ended abruptly when the dowager empress Cixi imprisoned the emperor. The Boxer Rising, a brutal anti-foreign revolt, culminated in 1900 with the siege of the legations in Beijing (see p.105). Cixi's disastrous support for the rising meant that when it was defeated the victorious foreign powers imposed an indemnity on China of twice the government's annual revenue.

In the first decade of the twentieth century the Qing government belatedly instituted major reforms, abolishing the ancient Confucian examinations, creating a modern police force, and establishing military academies. But the end of the imperial system was already under way (see sidebar, right).

THE END OF EMPIRE

Imperial rule collapsed in 1911, when a group of army officers seized Wuchang and declared independence from the Qing government. Within weeks fifteen provinces had followed suit. The head of the imperial armies, Yuan Shikai, negotiated a settlement for the establishment of a republic with himself as president. In February 1912 the seven-year-old emperor Xuantong—better known in the West by his birth name of Puyi—abdicated, bringing an end to imperial China. However, he was permitted to continue living in the Forbidden City until 1924. He ended his life as a gardener in Beijing, where he died in 1967.

THE ROLE OF
THE STATE

THE "SON OF HEAVEN"

FROM 221BCE TO THE END OF THE
EMPIRE IN 1912, THE CHINESE STATE
WAS CENTERED ON THE EMPEROR,
FROM WHOM ALL POWER WAS
DERIVED AND IN WHOSE NAME
EVERY GOVERNMENT ACTION WAS
PERFORMED. AS THE "SON OF HEAVEN"
HE ENJOYED THE SPECIAL FAVOR OF
THE GODS—WHO MIGHT, HOWEVER,
WITHDRAW THEIR APPROVAL. TO ASSIST
IN THE RUNNING OF A VAST STATE, THE
EMPERORS RELIED ON A HUGE
BUREAUCRACY, WHILE GREAT ARMIES
WERE REQUIRED TO GUARD THE
IMPERIAL FRONTIERS.

*The able and learned emperor
Kangxi, whose reign (1661–1722)
was the longest in Chinese history.
He is here portrayed in his library
as the ideal Confucian scholar.*

Until 1912 the supreme ruler of China was entitled "Son of Heaven."
Under the Zhou dynasty, Heaven (Tian) was the greatest deity, and the
conferment of this title upon the king not only acknowledged his position as the overlord of all the people of his kingdom but also gave him
the cachet of divine authority which no other man could share. This
unique relationship with Heaven remained the bedrock of imperial
authority through all successive dynasties.

The power and prestige of the emperor were formidable. He was
the high priest of all humanity who performed important sacrifices to
Heaven and Earth. He was the protector of the sources of human sustenance who offered sacrifices to the gods of agriculture, and a paragon
of filial piety who honored his ancestors by punctiliously following cus-
tomary ancestral rites (see pp.88–9). His word was law and he literally
exercised the power of life and death over his subjects. All legislative and
executive authority was ultimately his. He was treated with enormous
reverence and could be approached only by his closest advisors. The
minutest details of his daily life, even the clothes he wore, were considered of sufficient significance to be meticulously recorded for posterity.
However, he was never able to come into contact with his subjects and
was for the most part confined within the palace walls, only venturing
out to participate in important ceremonies or to make the occasional
inspection of part of his empire.

The imperial succession was hereditary. There was a convention
that the first son of the empress should normally be the heir, but ultimately it was the emperor who chose his successor. Sometimes his selec-
tion led to conflict, as when Gaozu (ruled 618–626CE), the first emperor
of the Tang dynasty, appointed as heir his eldest son, Li Jiancheng. This
was in accordance with convention, but Gaozu's second son, Li Shimin,
was more able and energetic and had already fought several victorious
campaigns on his father's behalf. Jealousy between Li Shimin and Li
Jiancheng, who was backed by another brother, led to open hostility.
After escaping several assassination attempts, Li Shimin ambushed Li

Jiancheng and put him to death. He then forced Gaozu to abdicate in his favor. As the emperor Taizong (ruled 626–649CE), Li Shimin proved a highly talented ruler, so the dynasty ultimately benefited from the outcome of this fratricidal strife.

Outstanding emperors emerged in all the major dynasties. However, most monarchies face the inherent problem of producing a long succession of able rulers and China was no exception. In an attempt to ensure the quality of the emperor's successor, the scholars at court took great pains over the education of the heir apparent. Yet some dynasties still suffered from a succession of weak rulers. Sometimes unscrupulous officials or eunuchs (see p.47) plotted to ensure that children would succeed to the throne, or that a new emperor would favor their particular court faction. Yet in spite of these instances there was usually sufficient strength in the Chinese bureaucratic monarchy to survive such periods. As long as there was an emperor in place and the structure of society and its cultural values were not threatened, the population was unlikely to rebel.

THE MANDATE OF HEAVEN

Well before the reign of the First Emperor, Qin Shihuangdi (221–210BCE; see p.28), Confucian scholars had elaborated a theory that curtailed the monarch's absolute right to rule. This was the concept of the "Mandate of Heaven," which asserted that just as Heaven had granted the ruler the authority to govern, this divine mandate might be withdrawn if the emperor departed too far from the path of benevolence. If this happened, the emperor might legitimately be overthrown and the mandate conferred upon another. Most Chinese dynasties were established after the internal decay of its predecessor had led to civil war, at the end of which the victorious rebel leader claimed the heavenly mandate.

According to Confucian thinking, Heaven's displeasure with an emperor might be demonstrated by omens, such as abnormal weather, floods, famines, plagues, or earthquakes. The disadvantage of the emperor's situation was that he was often regarded as being personally responsible for such events. There were several instances when an emperor confessed that his unworthiness had angered Heaven, thus bringing suffering to his people.

PALACE AND COURT

The gardens of the imperial palace (the Forbidden City) in Beijing.

The emperor lived in a magnificent complex of palace buildings which reflected his elevated status and his relationship to cosmic forces and to his family, advisors, and subjects. To those privileged enough to visit it, the palace provided an impressive display of imperial power and wealth. At the same time, its high walls excluded both the common people and, especially, potential enemies.

Being of timber construction, the palaces of early dynasties have all disappeared, most of them burnt by the rebels who overthrew their occupants. But in Beijing are preserved magnificent palace buildings of the last two imperial dynasties. Built by the third Ming emperor, Yongle (ruled 1403–1424), and inherited by the Qing dynasty in 1644, the Forbidden City palace complex measures 1,100 by 820 yards (1,000m by 750m). It is surrounded by a 33-foot (10m) high wall with watchtowers at the four corners and ceremonial gates at the four cardinal points.

Within the walls, arranged along a north–south axis, are a series of large ceremonial halls and throne rooms. The palace is divided into an "inner court" in the north and an "outer court" in the south. The inner court housed the emperor, the empress and his other consorts, his closest advisors, and the imperial guard. The outer court contained the offices of the executive arm of government, including the six boards, or ministries (see p.50). Large-scale ceremonies and parades were held in the courtyards of the outer palace (see illustration, p.48). The emperor also received foreign guests in one of the ceremonial halls. Among the other inhabitants of the palace was a substantial body of eunuchs (see box, below).

In addition to his wife, the empress, the emperor also had a small number of high-ranking consorts (*fei*), usually four. The criteria by which these consorts were selected varied; one Han emperor was advised to consider a woman's family background, virtue, age, and appearance. The emperor also had concubines. In antiquity there seem to have been relatively few but by the time of the Tang emperor Xuanzong (ruled 712–756CE), there were said to be thousands. At the other extreme, the Ming emperor Hongzhi (ruled 1488–1505) is reputed to have been the only monogamous ruler in Chinese history, apparently having relations with no other woman apart from his empress, Zhang. Sometimes a strong empress would insist on vetting the emperor's choice of concubine.

SEX AND PROTOCOL

Protocol surrounded all aspects of court routine and the emperor's sex life was no exception. If he wished to entertain a concubine, the emperor would choose her name from a tray of inscribed jade tablets. A eunuch would see she was stripped, bathed, depilated, and carried to the emperor wrapped only in a cloak so she could not conceal a weapon. The eunuch would wait outside the bedchamber for a suitable length of time then shout: "Time is up!" After three cries, he would enter the chamber and carry the woman back. Details of the visit would be recorded, since a concubine's status depended on how often the emperor had favored her. Some concubines waited for months, or even years, for such a visit.

THE IMPERIAL EUNUCHS

When the practice started is unclear, but eunuchs (castrated males) were certainly present as slaves of the Zhou kings. In the imperial period, they became a regular feature at court after the Han emperor Guang Wudi (ruled 25–57CE) insisted on castrating all male servants who attended court ladies. Emperors soon employed them as special confidants and advisors. Eunuch influence was rife under the Tang and Ming: toward the end of the Ming—when they may have numbered over ten thousand—eunuchs could dismiss officials, draft decrees, and control the imperial coffers. But many eunuchs served their rulers loyally and promoted constructive policies. Under the Qing their number fell and only just over one thousand eunuchs remained at the fall of the dynasty.

The imperial castrating shed stood just outside the palace walls. Some eunuchs volunteered to be castrated for the sake of a secure living at court; others were sold by their parents or child-traffickers. After recuperation, new eunuchs received a certificate and went to work in the palace. The majority had menial jobs in the kitchens or as sweepers. Others worked as musicians, actors, and puppeteers. The most senior had charge of the imperial seal of office. Eunuchs handled everything supplied to the royal family, from the emperor's concubines (see sidebar, above) to clothing, food, and toilet paper.

The imperial eunuch Li Lianying, 1890. Castration was a serious breach of the code of filial piety, since the body was considered a gift of one's parents. It was important that a person die and be buried complete, so eunuchs kept their mummified genitalia in a sealed bag or casket called a "treasure box."

GOVERNING THE STATE

In order for China to be ruled successfully it required a large, efficient, and loyal bureaucracy operating both at the center and in the provinces. The Qin dynasty laid the foundations for the creation of a nationwide bureaucracy by abolishing the feudal states and appointing all state officers directly from the center, and the succeeding Han dynasty established the theoretical basis of the Chinese system of government. In 137BCE the Han emperor Wudi declared Confucianism to be the official state ideology and the Confucian classics (see pp.82–3) became required reading for all politically ambitious scholars. Confucianism suited the aims of successive dynasties by upholding the emperor, the state, and the family in

SITTING EXAMINATIONS

In the Sui and Tang dynasties there were several types of open civil service examination. Most popular were the Classical Examination, which involved tests in the Confucian classics, and the Literary Examination (*jinshi*), which demanded a less extensive knowledge of the classics but required candidates to write various forms of verse. In both tests candidates had to write essays on moral principles and practical administrative problems, and to show a good knowledge of Chinese history.

In the Song dynasty the Classical Examination was gradually phased out so that by ca. 1100CE only the *jinshi* remained. Top graduates were selected for the Hanlin Academy, a body of influential scholars established by the first emperor of the Ming dynasty (see main text).

The Ming introduced a three-tier examination system. Those who passed the first test, the District Examination, held in the candidate's local town, were called Superior Talents (*xiucai*). Only a handful would go on to pass the Provincial Examination and become Promoted Scholars (*juren*), but those who did were set up for life, even if they did not proceed to the *jinshi*. Success in the *jinshi*, which was held in the capital, almost certainly led to a government post in Beijing or the provinces. The *jinshi* continued to be the highest degree up to the abolition of the imperial examinations in 1905.

The state examinations were administered by a special agency of the Board of Rites.

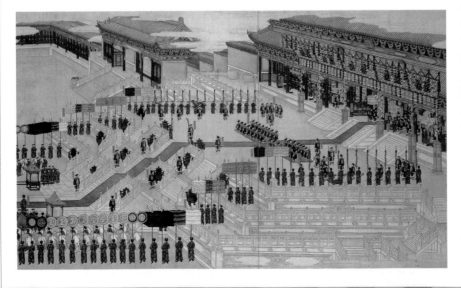

Imperial civil servants, all jinshi *graduates, parade before Emperor Guangxu (ruled 1875–1908) on the occasion of his wedding.*

A 17th-century map of a prefecture in Jiangxi province. The large town is the prefectural capital, Jiujiang.

one all-embracing ethical system. This Confucian-based bureaucratic monarchy was to last for two thousand years.

From the earliest times the success of a reign depended as much, if not more, on the quality of its officials as on the quality of the monarch. The sheer size of China made communications slow and hazardous, so it was doubly important to appoint officials of loyalty and integrity. Appointments were made at the center, but the capital and its immediate surroundings could not supply the number and quality of officials required to govern the whole empire. During the Han dynasty, therefore, governors of commanderies (see sidebar, right) were ordered to put forward local men of talent and virtue to serve the emperor. For such recommended scholars there was a form of examination, as advocated by the Confucian scholar-official Dong Zhongshu. Open civil service exams were introduced in the Sui and Tang dynasties (see box, opposite).

The Han established a two-tier structure of central government that was inherited, with occasional modifications, by all succeeding dynasties. The upper tier consisted of those officials closest to the emperor and

LOCAL GOVERNMENT

In the Han dynasty, the largest unit of local government was the commandery (*jun*). There were 83 *jun*, each ruled by a governor with a staff of civil and military officers. The commanderies were subdivided into *xian* (counties), each presided over by a "district magistrate" (see p.50). Subsequently, the larger *zhou* or *sheng* (province) replaced the *jun*. However, a greatly increased population led the Qing dynasty to interpose a new tier of local government, the prefecture (*fu*), between the province and the county.

An imperial civil servant's badge of rank. There were nine grades, grade one being the most senior; the peacock denotes grade three.

THE DISTRICT MAGISTRATES

The county (*xian*) was the basic unit of imperial rule throughout most of Chinese history. It was governed by an official usually known in English as a district magistrate who, as well as being a judge, was responsible for local security, tax collection, and conscription for labor and military service (see p.53). Like his superior, the provincial governor, he attended all important local religious ceremonies.

The district magistrate's office, the *yamen*, was always in a walled county town and was itself surrounded by walls and guarded by soldiers. The magistrate was aided by clerks and servants called "*yamen* runners" and had to be on good terms with the local scholar-gentry (see pp.66–7). Special handbooks reminded him of his moral duties—to protect the people and be sympathetic to them—and gave practical hints on the law and other matters. To diminish the danger of nepotism or corruption, a magistrate was never posted to his or his wife's native district.

might be described as a kind of legislature. For example, in the Tang dynasty, a body called the Grand Secretariat was responsible for formulating policies on important matters, which were reviewed by a second department, the Chancellery. Policies approved by the Chancellery were passed to the emperor for his approval.

A third department, the Department of State Affairs, was the main link between this upper (legislative) tier and the lower (executive) tier of government. Policies that had received imperial assent were handed down by the department to the relevant ministry for implementation. There were six ministries, or boards: the Board of Personnel (Li Bu), which dealt with matters concerning the bureaucracy, such as the grading and placement of officials; the Board of Revenue, or Finance (Hu Bu, literally "Board of Households"), which was in charge of taxation; the Board of Rites (Li Bu), which oversaw state ceremonies, examinations, and protocol; the Army Board (Bing Bu, literally "Board of Soldiers"), which administered military affairs; the Board of Punishments (Xing Bu), which oversaw all judicial matters (see pp.52–3); and the Board of Works (Gong Bu), which was concerned with public construction projects. More specialized central agencies dealt with agriculture, justice, imperial banquets, imperial sacrifices, diplomatic receptions, the imperial stables, waterways, education, and the imperial workshops.

Also included in the top level of government were the Censorate and the Hanlin Academy. The Censorate was created to oversee the bureaucracy and to make recommendations in case of maladministration or corruption either at central or provincial level. In theory, censors were obliged to speak their minds without fear or favor. Many did so, but there were cases of courageous censors who were severely punished for challenging imperial decisions. The Hanlin Academy was a body of academic high-fliers. Its main responsibility was advisory, although for a period in the Ming dynasty the academy took over many of the responsibilities of other organs in the upper echelon.

In addition to the advice of his ministers, the emperor might receive proposals submitted by officials of provincial level or below. These submissions, which were termed "memorials," were handed up the chain of command from official to official to the Grand Secretariat, which would forward them to the emperor if they were considered of sufficient importance. If the emperor approved a memorial it would be returned to the Grand Secretariat bearing his assent and might then be reformulated as an imperial edict.

THE BUILDING OF THE GREAT WALL

The imperial state was capable of astonishing feats of organization in order to accomplish major public works. The most famous example was the construction of the Great Wall. In the Eastern Zhou period, many states built defensive walls against the "barbarians" who menaced their northern borders. When the First Emperor, Qin Shihuangdi (ruled 221–210BCE), conquered these states, one of the first unification measures he undertook was to order his general, Meng Tian, to reconstruct, link, and augment the northern frontier walls to form a continuous barrier running from the northwest to the northeast for an estimated 4,000 miles (6,400km).

Meng Tian deployed a labor force of three hundred thousand soldiers, augmented by criminals, inefficient civil servants, and conscripts from all over the empire. His wall was mostly constructed of beaten earth, reinforced by courses of brushwood. Forts and watchtowers were constructed on high points and military barracks in the valleys.

The hardships endured by the laborers on the Qin Great Wall are still remembered in folktales. One tale relates how the husband of Lady Meng Jiang was conscripted to work on the wall. On the approach of winter, she traveled hundreds of miles bearing warm clothes for him, only to find that he had already perished. She could not find his body so lay down by the wall and wept for days on end. The wall was so touched by her grief that a section of it collapsed to reveal her husband's remains, which she took back to his ancestral burial ground.

The Great Wall snakes over the hills north of Beijing. The best preserved sections of the wall were built of stone under the Ming dynasty (see pp.214–15).

JUSTICE AND THE LAW

From early times China had a well-developed legal system based on an impressive and detailed legal code. This changed over the dynasties, but many of its provisions remained constant. The Qing dynasty code of 1740 was based on the Ming code of 1397, which in turn had much in common with the Tang code of 737CE. The reason there were so few major changes over such a great span of time was that those who drafted the codes were guided by the same idea: that law should be based on moral principles, which Confucius and other sages derived from practical experience of life. Chinese law reflected social practice, rather than claiming to be divinely inspired.

Confucian values are clearly reflected in the differing penalties imposed on people of different social or family status. The Tang code set out clear distinctions between franchized citizens and various categories of

CRIME FICTION

In the Song dynasty, the growth of commerce and urban society created a demand for many new forms of popular entertainment. "Stories about criminal cases" were among the new types of vernacular fiction that developed from the Song to the Ming periods. Written in colloquial rather than literary Chinese, they nearly always featured district magistrates or judges in the higher courts. The plots usually begin with a description of the crime (often including much realistic detail of contemporary life) and culminate in the exposure of the deed and the punishment of the guilty. Sometimes two solutions to a mystery are posited, but the correct solution is reached through the perspicacity of a brilliant judge.

The most celebrated hero of such tales was Judge Bao Cheng, or "Dragon Plan Bao," who was originally based on a historical person. Featuring in hundreds of stories,

Bao became the archetype of the incorruptible official in a society in which miscarriages of justice in favor of the rich and powerful were all too common. Not all crime stories have happy endings, and some were evidently written with the aim of exposing the brutal methods of corrupt judges who—often after accepting bribes—extracted false confessions by torture and condemned innocent people to death.

In some tales, the crimes are exposed with the aid of supernatural forces, but others display features common in Western crime fiction. For example, in one tale the dimwitted investigator is upstaged by the patient and methodical investigation of his junior.

This ceramic box lid from the reign of the Ming emperor Wanli (1573–1620) depicts a case being tried before a district magistrate, who is seated at his desk.

bondsmen. It also distinguished between officials, who enjoyed certain privileges, and those who held no official post. As far as family law was concerned, if a son struck his father this was a serious case of unfilial behavior that in extreme cases could lead to decapitation. But if a father beat his disobedient son to death he might, if judged to have been intolerably provoked, be let off. A woman who hit her husband would be punished with a beating, but a man who struck his wife would not be punished at all unless she were badly injured. Adultery by a woman was also viewed as much more serious than by a man.

In China the supreme legal authority was the emperor and the law was seen primarily as an aid to government rather than as an independent arm of the state. There was no judiciary separate from the imperial administration and, therefore, no distinct legal profession. People who sought to gain a living by advising litigants were regarded with suspicion.

The highest government body dealing with the law was the aptly named Board of Punishments, but the operation of justice was mostly the responsibility of the district magistrates, who in addition to their administrative duties as heads of counties (see p.50) had important police and judicial functions. As well as trying criminal cases and passing judgment on the guilty, the district magistrate headed investigations, collected evidence, apprehended criminals, and summoned witnesses.

Sentencing depended partly on a confession. This was simply a procedural matter of regarding the case closed only when the guilty party had confessed, and there was no obligation to treat anyone who did so less harshly. Torture might be used if a confession was not forthcoming. Any witness suspected of perjury might also be tortured or beaten.

All cases were reported to superior courts, and it was possible for defendants to appeal. The district magistrate was not empowered to pass sentence on the most serious cases; this was the responsibility of the higher courts at prefecture or province level.

There were no government officers at village level and local civil disputes were usually settled by arbitration. Any party who remained dissatisfied could still take their case to the district magistrate. Recent studies of cases coming before magistrates in the Qing dynasty show that they often dealt with civil disputes over land, debts, marriage, and inheritance. But to many ordinary citizens the district magistrate was an awesome figure, and most people were reluctant to go to law for fear of having to pay hidden expenses, such as bribes. They also feared being punished themselves should the case go against them.

A late Qing dynasty print of ca. 1900 showing two officers of the yamen *(district magistrate's office) extracting a confession by torture.*

CRIMINAL PENALTIES

There were five grades of punishment for serious crimes: beating with light bamboo, beating with heavy bamboo, penal servitude, exile, and death. In the case of beating, the number of blows to be administered was specified.

Capital cases were referred to the emperor, who alone could impose a death sentence. There were three main methods of execution, depending on the circumstances of the crime: strangulation, decapitation, and "death by slow slicing," a gruesome punishment for serious crimes (such as treason) in which successive cuts were inflicted on the offender. It was known in the West as "death by a thousand cuts," although the number of cuts ranged from eight to 120. The first cut was to the eyes, so that the victim could not see those that followed.

Lighter punishments included the yoke, stocks, cages, and imprisonment.

THE MILITARY

An archer from the famous army of 7,000 terracotta soldiers buried in 210BCE close to the tomb of the First Emperor, Qin Shihuangdi (ruled 221–210BCE), at Lintong, near present-day Xi'an, and discovered in 1974. His armor was designed to allow great flexibility of movement and he wears his hair in a topknot—only officers wore headgear (see also p.187).

The status of the army was not high in the traditional Chinese hierarchy—as an old saying put it, "good iron is not used for nails and good men do not become soldiers"—but in practice the military was of great importance to every Chinese dynasty, and a large part of government expenditure was on military matters. On the northern borders, the constant presence of warlike nomads meant that systems of frontier guards were a permanent necessity, and armies were needed to suppress rebellion and keep trade routes open through central Asia. But most dynasties sought to avoid the creation of large professional standing armies, which might provide a focus of power to rival the imperial court. Chinese armies were manned largely by citizens who were called up to do their labor duty in the army, and by criminals sentenced to military service.

One solution to the empire's frontier defense problems was the *fubing* system of the Sui and Tang dynasties. Peasants were resettled in border regions to form militia colonies, producing food when they were not fighting or training. The state was nervous of creating permanent bonds between officers and men and in war the militias would serve under officers sent from elsewhere who were withdrawn once peace was restored. The morale and effectiveness of the militias suffered as a result.

The *fubing* system was abandoned in the early eighth century CE when the military situation made permanent frontier garrisons of regular troops necessary. Owing to inadequate government supervision some of the garrison commanders became very powerful, and in 755CE the mightiest of them, An Lushan, launched one of the most serious rebellions in imperial history (see p.33).

The nomads and seminomads on China's northern borders were the main threat to the Song dynasty, eventually driving it south and finally overrunning it (see pp.34–5). The Ming dynasty, by contrast, was founded on military power and initially was quite capable of dealing with the northern menace. The Ming established military colonies headed by officers from hereditary military families, with 70 percent of the soldiers engaged in agriculture. These colonies resembled the *fubing* system but were nationwide, not confined to the frontier regions. After the reign of Yongle (1403–1424) the frontier defenses were allowed to decay. The garrisons lost half of their manpower and the colonies that were intended to supply the army with food sold their produce on the market instead. In 1449 the Mongols inflicted a heavy defeat on the Chinese

forces. The Ming recovered from this blow and established a system of 500 regiments, or "Guards" (*wei*), each of 5,600 officers and men. These were also encouraged to run farms wherever they were stationed.

At the beginning of the sixteenth century the military capacity and civil administration of the Ming went into a final decline that led to the dynasty's downfall in the following century. Its Qing successors started with a large and well-organized force of "Banner Armies" (see sidebar, right), but by the nineteenth century these had declined in effectiveness and were replaced by Chinese units. But the armies of the late Qing were incapable of defeating either the invading foreign forces or peasant uprisings.

The Army Board in the capital was largely an administrative body concerned with military appointments, titles, promotions, dismissals, and supplies. It also organized the military examinations. Far less prestigious than the civil service tests (see box, p.48), these contained some basic ethical papers but otherwise were largely practical, involving mastery of horse riding, archery, and swordsmanship. Those who passed became field officers and might be stationed anywhere in China.

Military strategy and tactics were the responsibility not of the Board but of the emperor's most senior officials, who in a major military crisis would raise the necessary funds and act as a general staff. Armies might be led in the field by a high official who would receive the temporary rank of general, which was removed once the campaign was over.

Troops enter the city of Jianghan in 1699 as part of the entourage of the Qing emperor Kangxi (ruled 1661–1722).

THE MANCHU BANNERS

In 1644 Manchu armies overthrew the Ming dynasty and founded China's last dynasty, the Qing. Manchu power, in spite of a small population, was largely due to their leader Nurhaci (ruled 1559–1626), who had unified the Manchus and had organized his army into eight units, or "Banners," of 300 men, each unit distinguished by its different banner. Later, every Manchu was assigned to a Banner, putting the nation on a permanent war footing. Banner heads had to provide, and provision, fighting men as the situation demanded. After conquering China the Manchus created a Banner of Chinese troops, but the Manchu Banner armies lived separately in their own enclaves outside all cities. Their military effectiveness gradually declined and by ca. 1860 the fate of the dynasty rested in the hands of Chinese troops.

FAMILY AND SOCIETY

TIES THAT BIND

CONFUCIUS THOUGHT OF THE FAMILY AS A MICROCOSM OF THE STATE. THE EMPEROR WAS THE FATHER OF ALL HUMANKIND AND EVEN THE DISTRICT MAGISTRATE WAS REFERRED TO AS THE "FATHER AND MOTHER OFFICIAL." THE WELL-BEING OF THE STATE DEPENDED ON FAMILY RESPONSIBILITIES BEING PROPERLY CARRIED OUT. THE FAMILY, OF WHICH ANCESTORS WERE AN INTEGRAL PART, WAS AN UNDYING COLLECTIVE, A LIVING ORGANISM POSSESSING A SPIRIT TRANSCENDING THOSE OF ITS INDIVIDUAL MEMBERS.

A filial son carries his parents while begging for food. A terracotta relief from a temple at Dazu near Chongqing, Sichuan province.

The traditional Chinese family, like families of most agricultural societies, was headed by the eldest male of the senior generation, who was succeeded by his eldest surviving son and so on down the generations. Within generations, the elder would take precedence over the younger. This is reflected in the Chinese language, which has separate words for "elder brother" and "younger brother" and for "elder sister" and "younger sister." The English word "uncle" can only be translated into Chinese if it is known whether he is the "father's elder brother," "father's younger brother," or "mother's brother," since these are all distinct words.

The generally recognized ideal of family life was to have four generations under one roof. Although, in practice, this was rarely achieved, it was common for several sons to inhabit the same family compound. When a son married (see p.61), his bride left her home to join her husband's family.

The family included its ancestors as present and vital members. As it thus extended into the past, so the family must also extend into the future, and the begetting of male heirs was an inescapable duty. As Confucius put it: "There are three ways of being unfilial and of these not begetting descendants is the most serious." If this could not be done in the usual way, then families could resort to adoption or, in the case of rich families, concubinage.

A family was bound together by ritual, the simplest form of which involved the burning of incense, in the morning and at night, with reverential bowing before either a portrait of the ancestor or a tablet bearing his name. The smoke of the incense floating upward was a symbolic way of contacting the ancestral spirit. More elaborate ceremonies were enacted on special days such as festivals or the anniversary of a family death. Each family member, starting with the head of the family and followed by other members in order of status, would pray and "kowtow" (bow deeply) before the ancestor's portrait or tablet. The recently deceased and the most ancient known ancestor usually received the most attention. The family would also make offerings of food, which would

he consumed following the ceremony (see also pp.142–3).

Families were grouped together into clans, which consisted of all the families of the same surname living in a particular district. Important clan ceremonies were held regularly, especially those in honor of the patriarch who had founded the family in a particular place. Such ceremonies, which included the ritual sacrifice of animals, were held in the clan ancestral temple, which housed the portraits of ancestors going back many generations. A clan would own land producing rents that helped to defray the expenses of these ceremonies and of the banquets which inevitably followed.

The corporate life of trade guilds and other social organizations followed a pattern that echoed family traditions. Instead of ancestors each guild had its own patron deity, who was honored at the annual meeting of the guild. Usually this deity was in origin a historical figure who had made an important contribution to his craft or trade. Thus the patron of builders was Lu Ban, a skilled craftsman of the third century BCE, while the medical profession honored Hua Tuo, a famous surgeon of the third century CE. Just as the moment of marriage during a Chinese wedding came when the bride bowed to the bridegroom's parents and ancestors, when an apprentice joined a guild he became bound to his master on making a ceremonial bow to him and to the patron deity.

A high-ranking official dismounts from his horse to greet an aged poor relation. This 12th-century painting illustrates a scene of filial piety.

STORIES OF FILIAL PIETY

A collection of tales called *The Twenty Four Examples of Filial Piety* was compiled in the Yuan dynasty to encourage the essential Confucian virtue of reverence for parents. Its widely known tales show the lengths to which individuals might go to please their parents. In one famous tale, Lao Laizi, aged 70, amused his mother and father by acting like a child, dancing and turning somersaults. Equally well known was Hua Mulan, who lived in the Tang dynasty. Her father was drafted into the army, but he was old and sick and her brother too young and weak. By law one male had to go, so Mulan disguised herself as a man and went off to war. For twelve years she distinguished herself in battle without anyone discovering that she was a woman.

WOMEN IN SOCIETY

FOOTBINDING

Undoubtedly the worst manifestation of the subjugation of women in traditional China was the custom of footbinding. It started at the Song dynasty court but eventually spread almost entirely throughout Han Chinese society (it was not practiced by the Hakka of the south or by most other ethnic minorities, such as the Mongols and Manchus).

Footbinding involved tightly binding the feet of girls, sometimes as young as five years old, with strips of cloth, compressing them so that the arches were gradually broken and the toes bent down under the balls of the feet. This painful process continued inexorably day and night until the feet stopped growing. The result was the "three-inch gold lilies," which were much sought after by marriage brokers, but made walking difficult and running virtually impossible.

A male sexual fetish might partly explain this practice, but its effect was to keep Chinese women tied to the home and prevent them from playing an active part in society.

In traditional China a family was organized according to two principles that were an inherent part of the Confucian way of life: the superiority of the elder generation over the younger and the superiority of males over females. If these two principles were in conflict, the first prevailed—that is, a grandmother had precedence over her grandson. But otherwise the lot of women, particularly of the younger generation, was unenviable.

Obedience to her parents before marriage was followed by obedience to her husband's parents after marriage. All marriages were arranged (see p.61) and any friendship with a young man was discouraged. If a woman was seen in the company of a man before marriage, even under completely innocent circumstances, this could ruin her reputation and render her unmarriageable. If two young people fell in love this was often taken as a reason why they should not marry, since they would be following their own wishes rather than those of their parents. Once married, a woman was at the mercy of her mother-in-law, who might become a lifelong friend, but, on the other hand, could make her life a misery.

The Sons of the Family Greet the New Year. *This Qing dynasty New Year print shows women in their traditional domestic role as home-bound nurturers of sons. The tiny pointed shoes of the woman in the left foreground indicate that she has bound feet.*

FROM CONCUBINE TO EMPRESS

China was twice ruled by women. Wu Zetian was the concubine of Tang emperors Taizong (ruled 626–649CE) and Gaozong (ruled 649–683CE). A woman of great intelligence and strength of character, she acquired a good understanding of the problems of imperial government and, when Gaozong died, she deposed his successor— her own son—and ruled as Empress Wu. Her 20-year reign was a prosperous period, during which she promoted the recruitment of new blood into the bureaucracy via the examination system.

Another concubine, Cixi, followed a similar route to power, but unlike Wu never declared herself head of state. After the death of Emperor Xianfeng (ruled 1851–1861), Cixi deposed the regents of her son, the infant emperor Muzong. He died (in suspicious circumstances) in 1874 and in 1875 Cixi secured the succession of a three-year-old nephew, Guangxu. She used her considerable talents

to increase her own power rather than to rescue the ailing Qing dynasty. When Guangxu flirted with Western ideas in the 1890s (see p.41) Cixi placed him under house arrest and purged the reformers. After the Boxer Rising (see p.105) she reluctantly agreed to some reforms (including the abolition of the examination system), but they came too late to save the dynasty. She died in 1908.

This photograph taken ca. 1900 shows the seated dowager empress Cixi ("Motherly and Auspicious") surrounded by a group of imperial concubines.

A wife's prime duty was to produce sons for her new family and if she failed she might be divorced or, if her husband could afford it, he might take a concubine. According to Confucian principles, a man's loyalty to his parents took precedence over his love for his wife. If a wife did succeed in producing sons then her status was raised, not least because in due course she would become another girl's mother-in-law.

Women managed internal household affairs, as is often still the case today. On the other hand, all matters affecting the family's relations with other families or the world outside were the prerogative of men. Only women with particularly strong personalities or outstanding ability could occasionally challenge this rule.

Women were barred from taking the state examinations and so had little incentive to study, but several talented female scholars, historians, and poets made their mark on China's cultural history. The prime example was Li Qingzhao (1084–1141), an extremely fine poet of the Song dynasty, who came from a literary background and wrote with great sensitivity and imagination about nature and human emotion.

RITES OF PASSAGE

A 20th-century print showing two ladies expressing delight in a son, a common theme of popular art. Rich families hired wetnurses from poor families, whose own children ate vegetable substitutes for breast milk (breastfeeding was always on demand and might last for two to three years).

Like most societies, traditional China marked the key stages of life with special ceremonies and rituals. There was joy at the prospect of a baby, but the process of childbirth itself was seen as unclean. Usually only a woman's mother would attend the birth, which might take place away from the house to avoid contamination. Ideally new mothers rested in bed for a month, but few families could afford this luxury. Great celebration marked the end of a baby's first month of life. On this day the child was given a "childhood name," often an unflattering one like "dog" or "cat" so that evil spirits would believe it to be unloved and leave it alone.

Marriages were entirely in the hands of parents. A prospective bride and groom were rarely even acquainted, and once their names were known to each other etiquette demanded that they avoid contact until the wedding (see box, opposite).

The most significant family events were those surrounding death. As well as giving expression to grief, funerals and mourning rites sought to commemorate the deceased and guarantee his or her safe passage to the next world. They also sought to ensure that the dead should have no reason to exert evil influence on the living. For example, the corpse would be placed into its coffin with its feet facing the door, so that if it should rise as a zombie it would walk straight out of the house. *Feng shui* experts would determine the most beneficial position for the grave.

The first funeral rite involved reporting the death to one of the gods guarding the portals of the underworld, who in turn would inform the office of Yanluo, the king of the underworld (it was commonly believed that the dead had to pass through ten courts of judgment in the underworld before going to Heaven). The living tried to ensure that when the dead arrived in Heaven they were materially well provided for. To this end, the corpse might be dressed in fine silk, and favorite possessions would be placed in the coffin. During the various stages of mourning, paper houses and "spirit money" were ceremonially burnt as a way of sending these to the deceased in Heaven.

Diviners would fix propitious times for each stage of the obsequies, during which hired Buddhist or Daoist priests might chant scriptures. Mourners were expected to express their grief openly and without restraint, but more or less in proportion to their closeness to the deceased. The chief mourner, usually the deceased's eldest son, had to wail piteously and be supported as he walked to show that his grief had made him weak.

The funeral ended with a lavish mourning feast, to which guests brought gifts of money for the family and scrolls praising the deceased.

MARRIAGE

There was no such thing as courtship in traditional China, because all marriages were arranged by the parents. As a first step, the parents of the prospective groom would commission a matchmaker to find a bride. The final choice would depend partly on the compatibility of the prospective couple's horoscopes. Next, a marriage settlement was agreed. The girl's parents might make exorbitant demands for gifts, and the matchmaker would arbitrate until the matter was settled. The gifts might include money, items of dress, and ornaments.

On the wedding day, the bride was carried from her house in a "bridal chair." She would put on a show of resistance as she climbed into the chair, her face hidden behind a veil. She arrived at the bridegroom's house to the accompaniment of loud music—this might well be the first time the bride and groom saw each other's faces.

The wedding ceremony was very simple. The couple simply bowed to the portraits or tablets of the groom's ancestors and to his parents and they were then man and wife. This ritual was followed by the wedding breakfast, to which many guests might be invited. Finally the couple entered the bridal chamber to consummate the union.

This 19th-century print of a wedding ceremony shows the bride and groom kneeling before a tablet honoring "Heaven, Earth, Parents, and Teachers."

VILLAGE LIFE

Throughout the imperial period the great majority of Chinese lived in villages, and most of these villages were spread out in the vast agricultural flatlands of the Yellow and Yangzi river basins. Village life has been the common experience of most inhabitants of China since neolithic times.

The land was divided into small parcels which on average were sufficient to support one family. This came about partly because of Chinese inheritance laws (see p.71) and partly because land could be freely bought and sold. The result was a great spectrum of rural society from wealthy landlords, who might rent out some or all of their land, to landless peasants who were reduced to the status of hired laborers. In between were peasant landowners and tenant farmers.

Nearly all peasant families lived in villages and walked or rode donkeys or buffaloes to the land which they worked. Population in Chinese villages was quite dense and there was little or no individual

The Bridge of Sacred Wind and Rain in Chengyang village, Guizhou province. The largest buildings in a village were usually temples. These were of two sorts: ancestral temples owned by particular clans (especially in south China), and temples dedicated to particular gods.

FAMILY FESTIVALS

In addition to the annual sacrifices that were held on the anniversaries of the deaths of the ancestors, all inhabitants of a Chinese village would participate in festive activities at certain fixed times of the year.

The lunar calendar was—and still is—used for most commemorative events and festivals. The most important is the Chinese New Year, a time when the whole family joins in celebration, coming together on New Year's Eve for a meal. The New Year festivities last two weeks and end with the Lantern Festival at full moon on the fifteenth day of the year, when whole villages take part in communal celebration.

Another family reunion is held at the Mid-Autumn Festival, which falls on the fifteenth day of the eighth lunar month. Later, on the twenty-third day of the twelfth lunar month, the ending of the year is marked with sacrifices to the Kitchen God, a domestic deity who is believed to make an annual report to Heaven on the conduct of the family.

The solar calendar was used to determine the correct time for planting crops. This calendar traditionally divided the year into 24 parts, or *jie* (see below). One major festival, Qingming ("Clear and Bright"), is also fixed by the solar calendar. On this day people visit their family graves, which are located outside villages and towns, often on hillsides. There they tidy the graves and make offerings of food to the deceased.

THE 24 TIMES OF THE YEAR

Beginning of Spring	Beginning of Autumn
Rain Water	End of Heat
Waking of Insects	White Dew
Spring Equinox	Autumn Equinox
Pure Brightness	Cold Dew
Corn Rain	Descent of Frost
Beginning of Summer	Beginning of Winter
Grain Full	Slight Snow
Grain in the Ear	Great Snow
Summer Solstice	Winter Solstice
Slight Heat	Slight Cold
Great Heat	Great Cold

privacy. Not all the inhabitants were farmers and there might also be fishermen, boatmen, carpenters, masons, millers, basketmakers, carters, silk spinners, weavers, and various types of fortune teller.

Villagers would generally spin their own yarn and make their own clothes, although this self-sufficiency gradually broke down after the growth of the market economy in the Tang and Song dynasties. Most villages had at least one general store, and other material needs would be met by markets held in small towns and, more frequently, at crossroads.

Every village was self-governing and had no government officials. However, from the eighteenth century onward there was a village constable (*dibao*) who was the formal link between the village and the local district magistrate (see p.50), who appointed him. The constable would transmit the demands of the government to the village. The management of communal affairs, such as flood control, poor relief, the supervision of markets, and the organization of festivals, was in the hands of the villagers themselves, who chose a village headman to oversee such activities and to arbitrate in disputes (see also pp.70–71).

TOWNS AND CITIES

Urban life was already well developed in Tang China, when the capital Chang'an was probably the largest and most prosperous city in the world. But by far the greatest growth in urban life took place between the ninth and twelfth centuries CE, following the break-up of the highly centralized bureaucratic Tang state in the eighth century CE. In terms of size and wealth, eleventh-century Kaifeng, the capital of the Northern Song dynasty, far outstripped any European city of the time.

Generally speaking there were two types of town in imperial China: the walled administrative center or *cheng* (literally "city wall") and the trading center or *shi* (literally "market"), usually unwalled. The *xiancheng* was the seat of the county government which had to be walled as a protection for the district magistrate's compound or *yamen* (see p.50). In later dynasties the *xiancheng* would also include a Confucian temple,

THE ADMINISTRATION OF TOWNS

Towns were nominally under the control of the local county, but many urban areas were too large and complicated for this to have much meaning for ordinary inhabitants. In fact, the affairs of most towns were managed by several local associations connected either with temples or particular crafts and trades. Neighborhood temple associations managed the major festivals and other events. The temples themselves were not only used for worship: they also provided schoolrooms for tutors, dining rooms that could be hired for feasts, and even storehouses for merchants' goods.

Religious associations also often concerned themselves with street markets. Craft and trade guilds worked to the benefit of the general public by upholding trading standards and providing their members security against rogue traders—as well as against officials, who persisted in the traditional Confucian attitude of hostility to trade (see p.68). Some guilds were fairly democratic, but most were hierarchical, headed by a master who exercised control over guild members much like the head of a clan or family.

Summer in Beijing, *an early 20th-century painting by Wang Daguang, shows leafy streets lined with busy traders.*

This hand-tinted photograph, taken ca. 1910, shows the Yu Yuan Garden in Shanghai. Constructed by a wealthy official called Yu in 1537, its teahouse (left) and scenic water garden remain popular to this day.

the hall for the county examinations, the temple of the city god, and the offices and residences of officials. These were all near the center of the town, where there would also be a bell tower, the chief function of which was to warn the town of the approach of hostile troops or bandits. There was also a densely populated business area.

As the population increased during the later dynasties, so the number of walled towns also grew. The demographic mix of the walled towns also changed, with many rural landowners moving into the towns, so that by the middle of the Qing dynasty very few gentry remained in the villages. In the towns they had greater access to luxuries and better opportunities for financial activity. Their main source of income was from the rents paid by their tenant farmers.

Handicraft industries also developed in the walled towns. Tailors, carpenters, apothecaries, silversmiths, embroiderers, and other specialists supplied urban needs more than rural ones, although towns were dependent on the villages for their supplies of agricultural produce.

The county towns were important as the lowest links in the chain of command leading down from the capital. Above them, during the Qing period, came the prefectural capitals, also generally walled. Above the prefectural capitals were the provincial capitals (see p.49). The locations of all the county, prefectural, and provincial capitals were determined by administrative criteria. The *shi*, on the other hand, grew to meet the commercial needs of the general population. In later dynasties they far outnumbered the county towns and in many cases came to exceed them both in size and economic importance.

THE SCHOLAR-GENTRY

A key factor in the organization of Chinese society was the gentry, or more precisely the "scholar-gentry," also collectively referred to as the *literati*. They constituted the bulk of the Chinese ruling class in both town and country and their influence was such that there was a big gap in status between them and the rest of the population. Narrowly defined, the gentry were degree-holders who had passed the state examinations (see pp.48–9). Some were very wealthy: the north Chinese landscape was once dotted with the fortified residences of gentlemen who employed gangs of retainers that amounted to private armies. The majority of gentlemen were not as rich and powerful but most came from families with sufficient resources to have their sons educated to degree standard.

The gentry included retired officials and those who for one reason or another were not attracted to a life in government service, which would necessarily have taken them away from their families. Those of a scholarly bent would concentrate on study or indulge in such gentlemanly pursuits as painting, calligraphy, and poetry (see pp.196–7).

Almost without exception, the main ambition of the gentry was to advance their family's position, and the chief means of achieving this was

Home in the Mountains, *a painting of ca. 1550 depicting the ideal setting of rural tranquillity for a scholar-gentleman's retreat. The tiny figure of a gentleman in his studio appears in the central foreground.*

THE REFORMS OF WANG ANSHI

The only serious threat to the position of the gentry before the end of the empire came during the Song dynasty, when a severe financial crisis led to higher taxes and civil unrest. The emperor Shenzong (ruled 1068–1085) turned to an experienced administrator, Wang Anshi, who instituted his "Green Sprouts Program." Under this scheme, money was loaned to farmers at a relatively moderate interest to avoid the crippling rates exacted by moneylenders, often members of the gentry. Wang also made more efficient the distribution of grain paid as tax, and a further planned measure involved organizing the population into mutual responsibility groups. This would have meant state intrusion into matters traditionally managed by families.

The reforms were well intentioned, but were repealed as soon as the emperor Shenzong died. China was not ready for such drastic changes to its traditional *laissez-faire* economic policy. The reforms extended government control beyond its traditional boundaries, antagonized the gentry who were the backbone of local order, and created enemies at court and in the bureaucracy, who accused Wang of arrogance and intolerance. The most serious defect from the point of view of the state was that Wang undermined the position of the gentry, upon whom the state relied for maintaining the supply of loyal officials. In any case, few local officials proved capable of putting the reforms into effect.

Nevertheless, Wang is still generally honored as one of China's most outstanding reformers.

to educate one or more of their sons to the point where he might succeed in passing the state exams. To this end they would hire a reliable private tutor, usually a *xiucai* graduate of proven reputation (see p.48).

The gentry usually resided in towns and maintained a symbiotic relationship with the district magistrate (see p.50), who relied on them for advice based on their local knowledge. There were many local problems with which the magistrates or other authorities needed the assistance of the gentry, such as fundraising for irrigation, flood control, and public works. Sometimes gentlemen would provide their services for a fee. They would even undertake to collect taxes and the government would grant them licenses to carry out many other functions, such as keeping government records up to date or overseeing foreign traders.

Gentlemen often met together in teahouses to discuss the affairs of the area or to agree on a common reaction to some government decree. If a government measure was seriously flawed it was often the reaction of the gentry that set in train the process by which an opinion might eventually reach the emperor via the "memorial" system (see p.50).

One of the gentry's main functions was to mediate in disputes not deemed serious enough for litigation. Such cases exceeded in number those which came before the courts. In this respect the gentry fulfilled a vital function in the dispensing of justice in a country where there was on average only one district magistrate for a population of tens of thousands. If the parties were dissatisfied with the result of such arbitration, they might still take their case to the magistrate's court (see pp.52–3).

A lively boxwood figurine from the reign of the Qianlong emperor (1736–1795) depicting a member of the scholar-gentry in relaxed posture, holding a teacup.

● CHAPTER 5 *Richard von Glahn*

THE CREATION OF WEALTH

THE FOUR OCCUPATIONS

The earliest Chinese bronze coins (5th–3rd century BCE) were cast in the shapes of metal tools such as knives (like the coin shown here) and spades.

From the time of Confucius, the Chinese divided society into four ranks, placing the warrior nobility (later replaced by the imperial officials) at the top, followed by farmers, artisans, and, lastly, merchants. While farmers, whose labor fed all others, were held in high esteem, the ruling class scorned merchants as parasites who contributed little of real value to the wealth of the realm. However, this hierarchy of occupations represented a political ideal rather than social reality. Successful merchants often amassed great fortunes, while the vast majority of peasants lived in the shadow of poverty.

The earliest empires subjected merchants to strict regulation. Trade was restricted to designated marketplaces at specific hours of the day. Local officials closely monitored merchant activities and inspected the quality of workmanship. Yet Confucian doctrine also harbored an abiding distrust of government interference in the private economy. With the notable exception of the salt industry, government monopolies on production and trade proved ineffective and short-lived. Nevertheless, merchants lacked economic independence and social solidarity. The imperial state routinely obtained the goods it needed by imposing special requisitions on merchants, who had little choice except to comply. Only from the beginning of the seventeenth century did groups of merchants form trade guilds to defend their interests. Although commercial enterprise stimulated the growth of towns and cities, most large cities served first and foremost as seats of imperial government rather than as strongholds of bourgeois autonomy (see pp.64–5).

Apart from the tribute delivered to the imperial capitals, long-distance trade did not flourish in the original Chinese heartland in the Yellow river valley. The rivers of north China generally were navigable only over short distances, and moving goods by cart was slow and costly. Intensive settlement of the Yangzi river valley from the eighth century CE onward engendered a revolution in the Chinese economy. Irrigated rice farming was far more productive than dry-land cereal crops such as millet and wheat (see pp.168–9). The rice economy could sustain much

POPULAR CONCEPTIONS OF WEALTH

Confucian philosophers condemned the profit motive as injurious to public morals and a source of social conflict. Yet ordinary Chinese typically measured happiness by degrees of material wealth. The fluid social order of imperial China enabled wealthy families literally to purchase high status by investing in the education of their sons, arranging fortuitous marriages for their children, and acquiring tangible symbols of breeding and taste, such as villas and gardens, fine silk garments, antiques, and works of art.

For Chinese of all social classes the greatest treasure was an abundance of sons to carry on the family line. During the festive New Year season, families celebrated their prosperity and prayed for continued success. New Year was a time for paying respects to the ancestors and the God of Wealth. Homes were hung with special woodblock prints depicting scenes such as a prosperous household, or the God of Wealth and his assistants hauling carts of gold and silver into the family courtyard, or a bevy of young boys collecting strings of coins from ever-bearing money trees.

The god of wealth and blessings is depicted in this popular print dressed in the raiment of a high-ranking imperial official. In his left hand the god holds a ruyi scepter, which symbolizes the fulfillment of all one's desires.

greater population densities and still yield large surpluses. Farmers in the subtropical south also specialized in cultivating cash crops such as tea and sugar, which became staples of the Chinese diet.

In addition, south China was blessed with excellent natural waterways (see pp.22–3) that facilitated the transport of bulky goods such as grain, salt, and metals. The Yangzi river delta, hub of both east–west and north–south trade routes, also became the center of the silk and cotton textile industries. The great cities of the Yangzi delta, such as Suzhou, Hangzhou, and Yangzhou, teemed with merchants and artisans who supplied innumerable types of manufactured goods to urban and rural markets across the empire. The wealth of these cities inspired the famous Chinese proverb, "Heaven above has its paradise; the world below has Suzhou and Hangzhou."

SETTLEMENT AND FARMING

The earliest Chinese states emerged on the North China Plain, an alluvial plain built up by the flooding of the Yellow river (see pp.14–17). The river takes its name from the heavy load of silt that its waters carry down from the loess region of the Ordos plateau. The Yellow river's annual spring floods draped the plain in a thick blanket of this rich silt, a boon to farmers working with primitive stone tools. Neolithic farmers on the North China Plain first cultivated millet, a sour-tasting but hardy cereal. Later, wheat was introduced from western Asia and replaced millet as the main food crop of north China.

Settlement of the Yangzi river valley was limited to river valleys and lake basins until the onset of the Iron Age, beginning around the fifth

THE YEARLY FARMING CYCLE

For farmers in the Yangzi delta, work in the fields continued year round. The widespread practice of double-cropping—rotating summer rice with winter crops such as wheat, soybeans, and rapeseed—necessitated careful coordination of agricultural tasks. Rice seedlings were grown in seed beds before being transplanted into the paddy fields in late May and early June, the crop being harvested in October. Winter crops were planted in October and November and harvested in early May. During the two-week periods between reaping one crop and sowing the next, farm families toiled virtually without rest. Preparing the fields was men's work. First the fields were plowed, and then leveled with harrows and hoes. But all members of the family were needed for the arduous task of transplanting rice seedlings.

Throughout the summer farmers worked constantly at weeding, applying fertilizer, and irrigating the rice paddies with machinery such as treadle-powered pumps (see p.169). Households engaged in sericulture used fast-ripening strains of rice that matured in three months, allowing them to delay the rice planting and devote their energies to tending the silkworms during the busy spring season.

This 13th- or 14th-century scroll painting shows various stages of rice production— threshing, winnowing, and sorting. Only at the Chinese New Year and a few other brief annual festivals could farmers cease their labors.

century BCE. Mass production of iron tools such as plowshares, axes, and saws during the Han dynasty made it possible to clear the dense forests of southern China and open new lands for cultivation. Yet settlement of south China proceeded slowly. Only from the eleventh century CE onward did the majority of China's population inhabit the southern rice-farming regions.

The Yangzi river delta, today one of the most fertile agricultural regions in the world, was originally a swampy wilderness prone to constant flooding. Painstaking labor was required to transform the swamps into productive farmland. First, farmers had to dig channels to drain the swamps, and then build dikes and irrigation networks in order to protect against flooding and deliver water to the rice paddies at the appropriate times.

By the end of the thirteenth century nearly all the land of the Yangzi delta had been reclaimed for cultivation. Every inch of ground was devoted to productive use. The embankments dividing the rice paddies were planted with mulberry trees, the leaves of which fed the ravenous appetites of silkworms. The sandy and saline soils near the seacoast were unsuitable for rice cultivation but ideal for cotton, which was introduced from southeast Asia in the twelfth century. By the sixteenth century the delta's farmers regularly planted a second crop of winter wheat or soybeans on the same fields used for rice cultivation in the summer. After trans-Pacific trade commenced in the sixteenth century, Chinese farmers quickly adopted New World crops (see p.168), which allowed China's growing population to expand into the rugged highlands of the interior provinces, where wet-rice cultivation was impractical.

A farmstead in Rongshui, Guangxi Autonomous Region in south China. The terracing, strip cultivation, and efficient use of all available land are typical of Chinese farming.

EQUAL INHERITANCE

From the Qin empire onward, Chinese law demanded that all sons inherit equal portions of their father's estate. The law aimed to prevent the concentration of land ownership in a few hands and to ensure that all adult men had an independent source of livelihood. Thus, land ownership was spread much more evenly in China than for example in medieval Europe, where the eldest son usually inherited all of his father's land. In China, possession of even a small amount of land enabled all except the poorest men to marry and raise a family, and equal inheritance and universal marriage promoted high rates of population growth.

THE RISE OF INDUSTRY

Potters at work in a factory in the great porcelain manufacturing center of Jingdezhen, ca. 1920.

JINGDEZHEN PORCELAIN
The world-renowned porcelain manufacturing center at Jingdezhen in Jiangxi province was founded in the Song dynasty, when potters in the surrounding villages began to craft fine porcelains for the luxury market. In the early fifteenth century the Ming government built an imperial factory at Jingdezhen to supply the court with as many as 100,000 pieces of porcelain each year. Subsequently the city became a thriving industrial center where skilled artisans and merchants from throughout the empire congregated. The famed blue and white porcelains of Jingdezhen achieved great popularity in the Mughal and Ottoman empires, from where they reached Europe. Jingdezhen potters responded to European tastes for highly decorated ceramics by creating the three-color and five-color enameled wares that comprised the bulk of the export trade during Jingdezhen's eighteenth-century heyday (see p.74 and also p.201).

In ancient times, bronze metallurgy was a monopoly of the nobility, and was used principally to manufacture ritual vessels and weapons rather than tools. Competition among the contending states of the Eastern Zhou period stimulated the rise of industry and trade. Among the local products that began to circulate widely were iron goods, salt, silk and other textiles, and lacquer. By the fifth century BCE metallic money had come into common use. Owners of iron foundries and saltworks (see pp. 172–3) accumulated huge fortunes that drew the attention of covetous rulers. In 119BCE Emperor Wudi of the Han dynasty enacted state monopolies on the production and sale of iron and salt, claiming that "the wealth of the mountains and marshes" properly belonged to the "Son of Heaven." Although the salt monopoly remained an enduring feature of imperial fiscal administration, it has been estimated that more than half of the salt consumed in China was contraband.

During the Song dynasty, China underwent rapid economic expansion. With the relocation of the imperial capital to Hangzhou in the early twelfth century, the center of gravity of the Chinese economy shifted from the North China Plain to the Yangzi river delta, and new industries emerged. Tea grown in the hilly interior of south China, silk fabrics woven in the cities of the Yangzi delta, celadon and porcelain from potteries across the empire, and sugar cane harvested in the tropical provinces of the far south all became major articles of trade and consumption. Cotton manufacturing boomed after new efficient techniques for ginning and spinning cotton were introduced in the late thirteenth century.

Post-Song industrial growth largely resulted from private enterprise. Although state-managed workshops probably produced the majority of finest quality silks such as damasks, satins, and brocades, they accounted for only a tiny fraction of the total output of silk cloth. Private domestic silk businesses flourished. Yet a shortfall in the supply of mulberry leaves—the basis of the silkworm diet—or a drop in the temperature of the breeding room could spell financial ruin for peasants raising silkworms, especially since most of the capital for sericulture was borrowed.

The manufacture of cotton cloth, by far the most important industrial commodity in late imperial China, was wholly in the hands of private merchants, brokers, and producers. Capital-intensive enterprises like coal mines, iron foundries, lumber and paper mills, and shipyards in some cases operated as joint-stock companies, pooling the capital of numerous investors and employing hundreds of workers.

WOMEN AND TEXTILE MANUFACTURING

Before the Song dynasty, the manufacture of silk cloth was largely confined to the North China Plain, where it served as a major item of tax payment. The early twelfth century saw the ascendancy of the Yangzi delta as the national center of silk production. Rural households concentrated on the difficult tasks of raising silkworms and reeling silk yarn, which were delegated to women and children. The silkworms required constant care and feeding during the six-week breeding period between the hatching of silkworm eggs and the spinning of the cocoons (see p.170). The weaving of fine silks, which was done in urban workshops that sometimes numbered dozens of looms, became the preserve of skilled male artisans.

The growth in the silk industry during the Southern Song period was followed ca. 1300 by the expansion of the cotton industry. Soon everyone in China was wearing cotton clothing, much of it supplied by women spinners and weavers in the countryside around the modern city of Shanghai. The increased demand for labor in textile manufacturing, coupled with a reduction in average farm sizes owing to population growth, caused women to withdraw from field work in the rice paddies, which earned them less than sericulture and cotton handicrafts.

A 17th-century depiction of women engaged in the production of silk. From this time onward, women began to reel silk or spin and weave cotton, while men took over farm work.

TRADING BY LAND AND SEA

An 18th-century porcelain vase manufactured at Jingdezhen for the European export market.

In Neolithic times people, goods, and ideas had already moved across Eurasia along the corridor of steppe grasslands and oasis towns extending from China's northern frontier to Persia and the Ukraine. By the Han dynasty the central Asian trade route had become known as the "Silk Road," after the Chinese silk that was its most valuable commodity (see map, p.28). During the Tang dynasty, Arab seafarers began to flock to the ports of southern China, and by the tenth century CE overseas commerce surpassed the caravan trade of the Silk Road. Improvements in nautical technology (see p.175) spurred maritime trade with Japan, Korea, and the Indonesian archipelago. Although the Chinese court imposed stringent controls on international trade and banned the export of goods such as iron, bronze coins, and books, smugglers abounded. In Song times China also exported silk, ceramics, sugar, and rice wine by sea, and imported aromatics, spices, silver, sulfur, and indigo, together with luxury items like ivory and coral.

The pattern of China's foreign trade changed dramatically in the sixteenth century. Silver strikes in Japan and in the New World, coupled with China's hunger for currency, created the first truly global economy,

IMPERIAL CURRENCY

The early empires based their monetary system on bronze coins (see illustration, p.68). At their peak in the late eleventh century, the imperial mints issued more than six billion coins per year, and Chinese coinage also served as the principal currency in Japan, Korea, and southeast Asia. But the heavy coins were cumbersome and ill-suited to the needs of long-distance trade. The Song dynasty therefore introduced the first paper currency as a supplement, an experiment that ended in the early fourteenth century after the excessive printing of notes provoked ruinous inflation.

Subsequently the Chinese economy increasingly depended on silver as its main currency. Silver circulated not as coins but in ingots in a wide variety of sizes and degrees of fineness. Commercial growth in the sixteenth century intensified the demand for silver at the same time as the rich mines of Japan, Peru, and Mexico vastly increased the global supply of the metal. Silver fetched a higher price in China than anywhere else, and merchants rushed to deliver silver to the Chinese market. New World silver flowed to China via Spain, the Levant, and India, or via Manila. China's massive import of foreign silver continued to the early nineteenth century.

A camel train on part of the ancient Silk Road in western China.

one based on the circulation of silver (see box, opposite). The commercial prosperity of Britain, Holland, and other European countries created markets for exotic Chinese silks and porcelains, which were imported in great quantities. Tea-drinking became a popular fashion in Holland, Russia, and above all Britain and its American colonies in the mid-eighteenth century.

A rapidly escalation in opium imports from British-controlled India eroded China's long-standing favorable balance in foreign trade. After 1825 silver drained out of China in payment for opium, and growing economic distress culminated in the Opium War of 1839–1842 between China and Britain. China's defeat resulted in the cession of Hong Kong to Britain and the forcible opening of its ports to European merchants.

Already by the time of the Opium War, China was losing its position as one of the world's leading industrial nations. Japanese and Europeans had acquired the secrets of silk and porcelain manufacture, reducing demand for Chinese products. Yet Chinese firms successfully competed with foreign rivals in many industries, notably cotton textiles. After the Opium War, Shanghai, with its superior access to China's markets and resources, quickly emerged as the country's commercial and industrial capital. By 1900 Shanghai was generating two-thirds of China's foreign trade and nearly half of its modern factory output.

Part 2

BELIEF AND RITUAL

*Priests taking part in the Da Beiba, a Daoist festival
in Taiwan. Official disapproval has adversely affected the
fortunes of Daoism in the People's Republic, but it has
continued to flourish in overseas communities. Today,
however, it is undergoing a revival on the mainland.*

OPPOSITE *Buddhism came to China from India, but
developed distinctively Chinese forms and schools. Many
Chinese Buddhist places of worship such as this one (the
Bamboo Monastery near Kunming in Yunnan province)
are wholly Chinese in their architectural style.*

CONFUCIANISM: ORDER AND VIRTUE

CONFUCIUS AND HIS FOLLOWERS

THE "THREE TEACHINGS" OF CONFUCIANISM, DAOISM, AND CHINESE BUDDHISM CONSTITUTE CHINA'S GREAT CONTRIBUTION TO THE SPIRITUAL AND MORAL HISTORY OF HUMANKIND. CONFUCIANISM PERVADED CHINESE GOVERNMENT, EDUCATION, AND SOCIAL MORES. IT WAS THE IDEOLOGY OF IMPERIAL RULE, REFLECTED IN SACRED RITES OF THE EMPEROR TO ENSURE HARMONY BETWEEN HUMAN BEINGS AND THE COSMOS, AND IN THE EXAMINATIONS THAT SELECTED HIS ADMINISTRATORS. IT ALSO UNDERLAY SOCIAL AND FAMILY ETHICS, CENTERED ON A HIERARCHY OF RELATIONSHIPS PROPOUNDED BY CONFUCIUS, AND ON THE RITES OF ANCESTOR VENERATION.

A statue of Confucius, China's greatest sage, from the temple dedicated to him in Beijing.

The founder of Confucianism was Kong Qiu (551–479BCE), better known as Kongzi ("Master Kong"). In the sixteenth century another version of his name, Kong Fuzi, was latinized by visiting Jesuits as "Confucius." He was born during the Eastern Zhou period at Qufu in the state of Lu, in modern Shandong province. Greatly disturbed by the social and political disorder of his day, Confucius traveled to various states in the hope of persuading their rulers to employ his precepts to bring about peace and social harmony. After thirteen fruitless years he returned to Lu to devote himself to teaching. It was only several centuries after his death that the rulers of the Han dynasty finally adopted his theories as principles of government.

Confucius considered himself a transmitter of ideas rather than a reformer, but his thought displays innovation as well as conservatism. He looked to antiquity for examples of practices which would bring about social harmony and benevolent government. Ancient texts revealed to him a code of ethics and morality that emphasized the complexity of the web of relationships that bound people and the virtue of attending to personal duty for the sake of the common good (see pp.56–7).

At the heart of Confucius' teachings lay a profound sense of *ren* ("humaneness"), which means acting with sensitivity to the nuances of human relationships. For Confucius, the basic relationship was that between parent and child. In his view, the child must demonstrate filial piety (obedience and duty to the parent), while the parent in return owed the child loving and attentive care. The dynamics of this fundamental relationship were echoed in other relationships, such as that between a husband and wife or a ruler and minister. Complete equality was possible only between friends. Confucius also stressed the virtues of humanity, loyalty, righteousness, and sincerity.

Confucius believed that to respond in an appropriately humane way one must study and practice the *li*—rituals and etiquette which he understood as crystallized expressions of *ren* demonstrated by the worthies of antiquity (see pp.80–81). He believed that the *li* were so powerful that the sincere practice of them would bring about a transformation of the self, which in turn would have a ripple effect that ultimately influenced the cosmos. Confucius' thought was grounded in the human realm; nevertheless, he had an abiding sense of faith in Heaven, and in the mission with which it had entrusted him—to bring righteousness to the world.

MENCIUS AND XUNZI

Confucius' ideas were expanded by Mengzi (372–ca. 289BCE) and Xunzi (ca. 310–215BCE). Mengzi, known in the West by the latinized form of his name, Mencius, asserted the imperative of virtuous government and acclaimed the natural goodness of human beings. His assertion that a king ruled only with the "Mandate of Heaven" had, literally, revolutionary implications: if a ruler did not benefit the people, it was their right to overthrow him. As a result, the rise and collapse of dynasties were interpreted in moral terms, something of which every Chinese emperor was keenly aware (see p.45). Mencius' theory of innate goodness also had far-reaching implications, for it assumed that it was possible for this goodness to be expressed, through education and effort, by all people.

Xunzi, the third of the great classical Confucians, was less well received by Chinese history. In contrast to Mencius, Xunzi assumed that human nature was inherently evil. He advocated the need for rites and etiquette and carefully defined laws and punishments to provide guidelines and encouragement for appropriate behavior. His ideas about human nature and the need for laws to control it were part of the Legalist school implemented by the First Emperor, Qin Shihuangdi, who in 213BCE took harsh steps against Confucianists whom he believed presented a challenge to his authoritarian regime (see p.84).

Mencius (center) with his mother and other women, an illustration to a Han dynasty collection of stories of virtuous women. According to the book, Mencius' greatness depended on his mother's efforts and her appreciation of appropriate behavior.

HEROES OF ANTIQUITY

Confucius looked to the Xia, Shang, and Zhou dynasties for models of exemplary behavior and inspired governance, as well as to a deeper past of divine and semidivine figures. These culture heroes, revered in Chinese tradition for bringing technology, the arts, and good government to humanity, were incorporated into early Chinese history as part of a grand narrative of the coming of civilization.

Among the most famous of the mythic heroes were the "Three Sovereigns," seen as the fathers of civilization, who established the Chinese homeland (see box, below). Their successors were the "Five Emperors," under whom humanity enjoyed a golden age of good government. The fourth of them, Yao, demonstrated his virtue and cultivation through the proper use of ritual and music, a prime Confucian concern. He deemed none of his own ten sons worthy to rule and instead chose Shun, a poor peasant of exemplary filial piety, to succeed him. Shun's father, "Blind Man" (that is, morally blind), and brother had tried to kill him three times; nevertheless Shun continued to be obedient and loving toward his parent

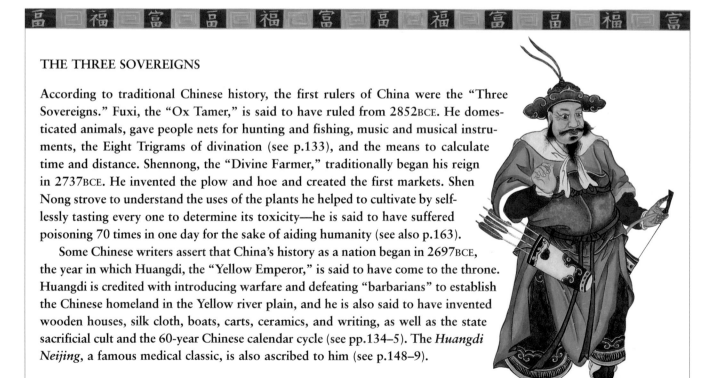

THE THREE SOVEREIGNS

According to traditional Chinese history, the first rulers of China were the "Three Sovereigns." Fuxi, the "Ox Tamer," is said to have ruled from 2852BCE. He domesticated animals, gave people nets for hunting and fishing, music and musical instruments, the Eight Trigrams of divination (see p.133), and the means to calculate time and distance. Shennong, the "Divine Farmer," traditionally began his reign in 2737BCE. He invented the plow and hoe and created the first markets. Shen Nong strove to understand the uses of the plants he helped to cultivate by selflessly tasting every one to determine its toxicity—he is said to have suffered poisoning 70 times in one day for the sake of aiding humanity (see also p.163).

Some Chinese writers assert that China's history as a nation began in 2697BCE, the year in which Huangdi, the "Yellow Emperor," is said to have come to the throne. Huangdi is credited with introducing warfare and defeating "barbarians" to establish the Chinese homeland in the Yellow river plain, and he is also said to have invented wooden houses, silk cloth, boats, carts, ceramics, and writing, as well as the state sacrificial cult and the 60-year Chinese calendar cycle (see pp.134–5). The *Huangdi Neijing*, a famous medical classic, is also ascribed to him (see p.148–9).

Huangdi, the "Yellow Emperor," the third of the mythical sovereigns who are traditionally revered as the founders of Chinese culture.

and merciful to his brother. Hearing of his great virtue, Yao took Shun into his service, giving him two daughters in marriage and his ten sons as retainers. Shun served first as a minister, then as regent, and finally became ruler on Yao's death. Shun also chose an heir whom he considered worthier to rule than his own sons. The stories of Yao and Shun illustrate how, in Confucian thought, a "golden age" was not necessarily a time of material abundance but rather one of ideal government. As well as highlighting the foundational virtue of filial piety, the legends illustrate recurrent themes in Chinese history: merit as the basis of a sovereign's entitlement to rule; and the problem of dynastic succession (see pp.44–5).

Another theme from antiquity was the need to control the floods that constantly threatened the wellbeing of the people. For Confucius, the exemplary ruler was one who strove to prevent this most frequent of natural disasters. Yu, the successor to Shun, is held up as the ideal in this regard: he was so dedicated to supervising the construction of dikes in his kingdom that for ten years he did not set foot in his own home.

Among more recent rulers, Confucius particularly admired the founders of the Zhou dynasty, kings Wen and Wu, and most especially Wu's brother, the duke of Zhou. In later tradition the duke was often held up as a paragon of virtue who appealed to the ancestors to take his life instead of his brother's when the king fell ill. It is said that the records of his appeals and divination were sealed in a metal box. Wu died, but legend has it that, rather than usurp the throne, the duke served as counselor to Wu's young son. During this time he was accused of plotting treachery, but the records in the metal box proved his loyalty.

The duke of Zhou also established rites and ritual music which Confucius saw as the outward expression of the virtue and cultivation of the Zhou dynasty's founders. For Confucius, the cause of the collapse of order in his own time was the neglect of these rites and music, combined with widespread self-serving behavior. The duke's selfless attention to duty and his ritual observance made him a worthy role model whose fame persisted throughout Chinese history—to the extent that "Duke of Zhou" was one nickname of the respected communist premier Zhou Enlai (1899–1976).

Confucians derived as many lessons from ancient tyrants as they did from heroes and sages. The last kings of the quasi-legendary Xia dynasty (traditionally founded by Yu, the controller of floods) and its successor, the historical Shang, were known for their cruelty and inhumane government. In each case, the dynasty was overthrown, with a new dynasty established by a worthy ruler who displayed virtue and benevolence.

This 2nd-century BCE painting on silk is of Fuxi, a great culture hero (see box, opposite), and Nüwa, an ancient goddess credited with creating humankind. The classical patrons of marriage, they are frequently portrayed with serpentine tails.

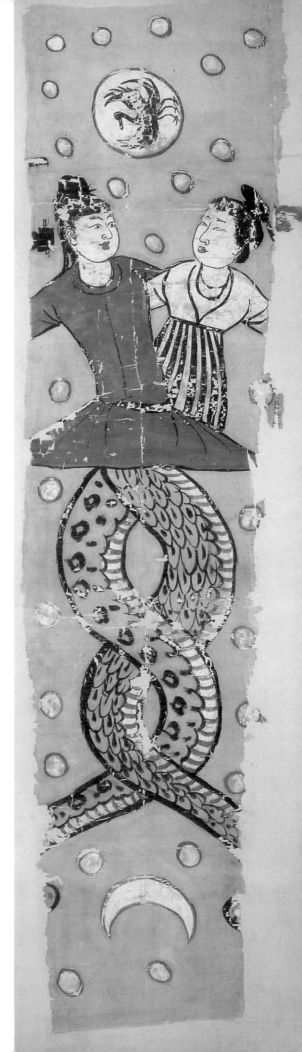

THE CONFUCIAN CANON

The Confucian classic texts form the basis of Confucian ethics, practice, and philosophical inquiry, and as the core texts for the imperial examinations they were memorized by every aspiring scholar. Many phrases and aphorisms from these works entered the common parlance and were familiar to the illiterate and highly educated alike.

At the heart of the Confucian canon are the "Five Classics" and the "Four Books." The Five Classics were the texts Confucius used to teach his students (the Chinese word translated as "classic" literally means the warp thread in weaving, on which the entire cloth depends): the *Classic of Changes* (*Yi Jing*), *Classic of Documents* (*Shu Jing*, also referred to as the *Classic of History*), *Classic of Poetry* (*Shi Jing*), *Record of Ritual* (*Li Ji*), and the *Spring and Autumn Annals* (*Chunqiu*). A sixth classic referred to by Confucius, the *Classic of Music* (*Yue Jing*), was lost by the Han dynasty. Tradition designates Confucius as the editor or compiler of these writings, but it is now thought that they were composed and altered over several centuries up to the time of the Han dynasty. The texts address divination and metaphysics, historical anecdotes and proclamations, etiquette and ritual, and include a narrative of events in Confucius' home state of Lu in the later Zhou dynasty.

Most important from the Confucian perspective were the moral lessons to be gleaned from an informed and careful reading of these texts. Confucians interpreted their diverse contents as lessons for appropriate living in general and moral government in particular. The *Classic of Changes* described the metaphysical structure of the universe and the relationship between humans and the cosmos (see p.133); the *Classic of Documents* furnished lessons and models of government from a golden age; the *Classic of Poetry* provided a map for understanding the hearts of the people (see sidebar, left); the *Record of Ritual* was a guide to appropriate actions; and the *Annals* contained Confucius' own subtly communicated judgments of benevolent leadership.

The Four Books, brought together as a group by the Neo-Confucian scholar Zhu Xi (1130–1200), are thought to sum up the teachings of Confucius. They are the *Analects* (*Lunyu*), a collection of sayings and conversations of Confucius recorded by his disciples (see examples, left); the *Mencius* (*Mengzi*), the works of his eponymous follower of that name (see p.79), and the *Great Learning* (*Daxue*) and *Doctrine of the Mean* (*Zhongyong*), each originally a chapter of the *Record of Ritual*. The *Great Learning* teaches that the first step to bring order to society is the cultivation of the individual, affirming the Confucian ideal of the

From the Analects: ABOVE *"If you know a thing, say so; if not, admit it. That is true knowledge."* BELOW *"If you desire haste, you will not make real progress and achieve success."*

morally cultivated ruler. The overarching theme of the *Doctrine of the Mean* is the interpenetration of the cosmos and human morality, the idea that humans and nature form a unity through sincerity of effort. These texts were the core works for the civil service exams from 1313 to 1905, and shaped the philosophy of Neo-Confucianism (see p.85).

Following the destruction of Confucian writings under the Qin (see p.84), Han scholars devoted great energy to restoring the canon, using some texts that had been hidden and reconstructing others from memory. An imperial academy was founded with positions established for the study of each of the Five Classics. These texts and other works from the canon were engraved on stone several times in the imperial period; the first such project began in 175 CE, the most recent was in 1803.

The content of the Confucian canon varied over time. Confucius is said to have taught his students the classics of poetry, history, music, and rites, reserving the *Annals* and the *Classic of Changes* for the very best students. In the Han, these were augmented by the *Analects* and the *Classic of Filial Piety*. Thirteen classics had been identified and standardized by the ninth century CE. They included the Five Classics and Four Books; the *Rites of Zhou* and the *Book of Etiquette and Ritual*; three commentaries appended to the *Spring and Autumn Annals*; and the *Er Ya*, a dictionary.

Basic Confucian teachings reached the masses in a variety of publications in the vernacular, or "plain," Chinese, rather than the "adorned" style of the canon. This is an illustration to The Admonitions of an Imperial Preceptress to Court Ladies, *a popular collection of Confucian cautionary tales about correct behavior and etiquette compiled in the early 6th century CE.*

IDEOLOGY AND EMPIRE

Confucianism was officially adopted by the Han dynasty after centuries of neglect and even suppression (see sidebar, left). By this time, Confucian thought had been modified by Legalist ideas of rule by law and punishment, and by the cosmological theories of Han scholar Dong Zhongshu (ca. 179–104BCE), who saw the Confucian social hierarchy as part of the natural order of the universe. The result was "imperial Confucianism," a political philosophy that emphasized the moral cultivation of the ruler, who stood at the head of a strong, unified state that was a vital part of the workings of the cosmos.

Confucianism remained the core of civil service training after the fall of the Han, but Confucian scholarship declined and Buddhism and Daoism were the focus of intellectuals and imperial patronage for nearly seven centuries. One notable voice of dissent was Han Yu (768–824CE),

THE BURIAL OF THE SCHOLARS
According to tradition, in 213BCE the First Emperor, Qin Shihuangdi, was advised by a courtier that Confucian officials were using histories and classic texts to criticize imperial policy. As a result, the emperor ordered all writings other than practical manuals on topics such as agriculture, medicine, and divination to be burned. It is said that 460 scholars who protested were buried alive as a warning to others. The actual extent of this persecution is subject to debate; however, it has remained a symbol of the tyranny of the first Qin emperor, and of the heroism of highminded Confucian scholars who did their duty regardless of the cost.

A Qing-dynasty depiction of the persecution of Confucian scholars under Qin Shihuangdi in the 3rd century BCE. *A scholar kneels before the emperor (top) while "subversive" books are burned and protesting scholars are buried (bottom).*

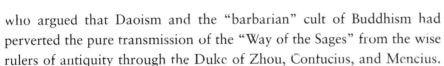

NEO-CONFUCIANISM: "DUSTING THE MIRROR"

Neo-Confucian cosmology described a world made of *li* ("principle" or "pattern," not the same word as *li* meaning "etiquette" or "ritual") and *qi* ("vital matter"). All physical and psychological phenomena are formed when *li* combines with *qi*, providing pattern and substance. Variations in form depend on varying degrees of purity of *qi*. Reasserting Mencius's belief in the essential goodness of human beings (see p.79), Neo-Confucians claimed that evil arose from impure *qi* that clouded the *li*.

According to Neo-Confucian thought, there was an essential unity to the universe through the great, undifferentiated, pure source of the Great Ultimate, which is the aggregation of all *qi* (see p.122–3). Human beings must work to reclaim their original goodness by "dusting the mirror": clearing away the impure *qi* to see their true *li* and discern their connection with the cosmos. This realization could be attained through "quiet-sitting" (*jing zuo*), a practice to focus the mind that was greatly influenced by well-developed traditions of Buddhist and Daoist meditation.

who argued that Daoism and the "barbarian" cult of Buddhism had perverted the pure transmission of the "Way of the Sages" from the wise rulers of antiquity through the Duke of Zhou, Confucius, and Mencius. Han's diatribes against Buddhism and Daoism led to his exile, but he was much admired in later centuries for his staunch defense of Confucianism.

The Song dynasty witnessed a revitalization of Confucianism. This movement, known in the West as Neo-Confucianism, was partly a response to the metaphysical questions addressed by Daoism and Buddhism, and their influence is evident (see box, above). However, Neo-Confucians rejected the Buddhist distrust of the material world and its focus on afterlife, affirming the reality of the sensory world and the need to work for the betterment of state and society.

The preeminent figures in Neo-Confucianism are the scholars Zhu Xi (1130–1200) of the Song dynasty and the Ming period's Wang Yangming (or Wang Shouren, 1472–1529). Zhu advocated intensive study into any physical or psychological matter to understand its *qi*. Zhu's recommendations, adopted after his death, remained orthodoxy until the end of imperial China. Wang's philosophy challenged Zhu's, holding that understanding *li* is a matter of clearing the mind so that one's intuitive knowledge and sense of goodness can surface, and that true knowledge lay in action rather than intellectual comprehension. Zhu's and Wang's philosophies remained the greatest influences of Confucianism from the Song into the nineteenth century, when China faced challenges from encounters with the West.

TRADITION AND REFORM

The Qing dynasty began with a reaffirmation of the state's strong commitment to Confucian orthodoxy, notably through the promulgation in 1670 of the Sacred Edict, which stressed fundamental Confucian virtues such as filiality, brotherly submission, social harmony, frugality, and also respect for learning, the law, and the payment of taxes. Officials were required to give regular recitations of, and lectures on, the Edict, which was frequently reissued in both classical and colloquial Chinese until the end of the empire.

In the nineteenth century, confidence in the Confucian order was shaken. Responses to this included the Self-Strengthening movement (see p.86) and the reform efforts of scholar Kang Youwei (1858–1927). Kang was influenced by newly available translations of European philosophical and political thought and was asked by the emperor Guangxu to spearhead the "One Hundred Days Reform" in 1898. This attempt to use Confucianism for institutional reform outraged conservatives and was quickly suppressed by the dowager empress Cixi (see p.59). Although unsuccessful, Kang's ideas are a symbolic watershed between Confucianism in traditional and modern China.

A bronze lion in the grounds of the temple of Confucius in Beijing. This is the largest such temple after that in Confucius' hometown of Qufu.

SCHOOLS AND ACADEMIES

Confucianism was seen as the primary means of social advancement and moral formation, and to this end there were a variety of public and private educational institutions from private tutors and village schools to state universities and academies. Schools were funded by the state and wealthy families, and even by some Buddhist monasteries. State support included distributing books, making schools self-sufficient with endowments of non-taxable land, and exempting students from tax and labor burdens. The wealthy had the easiest access to education and the number of learned women in the gentry indicate that it was not uncommon for girls from families of means to be educated (see p.59). In keeping with Confucius' own ideals to reward talent and effort above social position,

"SELF-STRENGTHENING"

Despite humiliating defeats in the Opium War and later nineteenth-century conflicts, almost all Chinese continued to assert the inviolability of Confucianism as the basis of civilization and government. However, the low point of Qing fortunes in 1860 (see pp.40–41) prompted a group of reform-minded officials to launch a "Self-Strengthening" movement, aimed at making China more receptive to Western ideas. As a result, the government established railroads, steamship companies, coal mines, arms factories, dockyards, and a bureau for translating Western books. It also despatched diplomatic missions to European capitals.

But China's industrial and technological development remained superficial, as its defeat by Japan in 1894 decisively demonstrated. Conservatives blamed the defeat on incompetence and corruption in the civil service and a lack of talented, upright, classically trained officials, but others saw Confucianism itself as a primary cause for Chinese weakness and demanded changes in Chinese education. By 1905, when it abolished the civil service examinations, the Qing government was taking steps to set up a modern school system, including a national system for women's education.

Examination cells, Beijing, 1873. The civil service tests lasted for several days; candidates wrote and slept in cells containing a stool and a folding bed that doubled as a desk.

most dynasties sought to make education available to exceptional students regardless of background and ability to pay. Schools were staffed by men who had received a classical Confucian education and had taken the civil service examinations, but had either failed or had passed but not taken up a government appointment, to which they were entitled. Teachers were expected also to teach matters of etiquette and protocol and to be stern disciplinarians.

As early as age four, children might practice tracing and writing simple characters. At around eight they would begin school with primers that often imparted core Confucian doctrine in jingle form for easy memorization. Students would first parrot their teachers, then practice reciting passages at their desks until they were memorized. In this way they might learn from 20 to several hundred characters of text per day. When asked to recite a text, students would stand with their back to the teacher. From around fifteen years of age, they would move on to advanced studies, which consisted of memorizing texts from the Confucian canon and learning composition. Textual analysis and comprehension skills came from studying commentaries, but only once the principal texts had been memorized.

New technologies played an important role in the availability of education. In the Han dynasty, schools were greatly aided by the invention of paper, and the advent of printing in the Song made books so cheap that families could establish their own libraries (see pp.182–3).

Academies were places of advanced learning where scholars and their disciples gathered to discuss and debate Confucian thought, and to compile, preserve, and (from the Song) publish texts. Scholars attached to an academy might be assigned a room and a stipend, and many academies had accommodation for students. Such institutions received funding from high officials, rich merchants, and often the state. The most élite and influential academy, Hanlin, was founded in the capital in the eighth century CE to train court scholars and archivists and existed throughout the imperial era. By the Ming dynasty, Hanlin accepted only the most outstanding *jinshi* graduates. From then until the end of the empire Hanlin scholars acted as imperial advisors, confidential secretaries, and high officials, and were acclaimed as national heroes.

Ideas about education began to change radically in the nineteenth century as the Qing administration struggled with the challenges of Western encroachment, and the question of the value of Confucian education in the face of superior Western technology (see box, opposite).

This soapstone statuette of ca. 1700 shows a figure who would have been familiar to Chinese students —the god of literature, Wen Chang (top), accompanied by two acolytes.

A WORLD OF RITUAL

The Kangxi emperor (ruled 1661–1722). Imperial dragons and other symbols of Heaven, Earth, and sovereignty are woven into his robe.

SACRIFICES TO HEAVEN AND EARTH

The regular sacrifices performed by the emperor—the "Son of Heaven"—to Heaven and Earth were of crucial significance for a balanced and harmonious relationship between the emperor and Heaven and Earth, and ensured the effective governance of the empire. In these rites, in which he petitioned for blessings and protection, he demonstrated his piety with an act of multiple obeisance to his divine parents. The emperor alone was permitted to prostrate himself before Heaven and Earth—anyone else who did so was considered to be committing an act of rebellion.

Also addressing Heaven and Earth, the ancient *feng* and *shan* sacrifices were among the most rare and venerated imperial rituals. Performed by the emperor at the sacred Mount Tai in Shandong province, these rites marked the founding of a new dynasty or the achievements of the emperor, who requested favor for the dynasty from Heaven and Earth.

Confucians viewed ritual and music as the ideal means to control the people, preferable to rule by force and law. Sacrifices by the emperor to Heaven and Earth ensured peace and fertility in the realm (see sidebar, left). The emperor also sacrificed to lesser powers such as the sun, moon, mountains, rivers, and natural forces. Imperial ancestors, to whom the emperor made sacrifices in accordance with his filial duty, were able to bestow blessings not only on the monarch but also on his entire realm. The emperor also made offerings to the spirits of all other past legitimate rulers as well as other important human and divine figures.

The state cult included sacrifices to protective spirits at city, county, prefectural, and provincial levels. These spirits were ranked in a formal hierarchy that paralleled the imperial bureaucracy, and sacrifices to a particular deity would be carried out by the local official of equivalent rank. In these sacrifices meat, grain, vegetables, and animals such as pigs, sheep, and bulls were offered as demanded by protocol and the rank of the deity. Participants wore ceremonial clothes and observed formal courtly etiquette. Accompanied by incense and music, and surrounded by attendants, the chief officiant would approach the altar and retreat from it in silence, bowing before the spirit tablet or image of the deity.

The Board of Rites, an imperial ministry with ancient antecedents, distributed minutely detailed guides to state rituals to all government offices. Officials of the Directorate of Sacrifices, a department within the ministry, attended to the practical side of the rituals, furnishing the necessary utensils and assisting in person at the sacrifices. Another department, the Bureau of Astronomy, was responsible for calculating the calendar and fixing the dates for the various rituals.

Sacrifices were performed at altars for the various gods and powers, at official cult temples, and at the memorial halls of great men. Temples specifically venerating Confucius and his followers were first established in the Han dynasty, and the temple at Qufu became a national shrine (see box, opposite). These buildings, called "civil temples," were dedicated to the spirits of Confucius and his most eminent followers, such as Mencius (see p.79) and Zhu Xi (see p.85). They reflect Confucian rationalism and an awareness that Confucius was a man and not a deity. Over the centuries, Confucian temples came to be built in every province of China and memorial services were held semiannually in the second and eighth months of the Chinese year. The local temple, which was open year-round, was also the place where young people traditionally went to be instructed in ancient music and rites, and where examination results were posted.

THE TEMPLE OF QUFU

Qufu, a town in Shandong province that was the capital of the ancient state of Lu, is the birthplace of Confucius and the site of a magnificent temple complex that contains superior examples of Confucian architecture. The first Confucian temple was built in Qufu in 478BCE, although no official sacrifice was made to the sage himself until 195BCE, when the Han emperor Gaodi (ruled 206–195BCE) offered the Grand Sacrifice (Daji), which included the offering of an ox, to the tomb of Confucius. Later in the Han dynasty Confucianism was adopted as the basis for the state cult.

Adjacent to the temple is the Kong family mansion, the home of the direct descendants of Confucius (Kongzi) from the first century BCE when the Han government granted the family a fiefdom and title. Later dynasties also supported the temple and family with grants of land and imperial funds.

The temple and Kong family mansion have dominated the town: at times, half the buildings in the town were associated with Confucius. Beginning in the Ming, the district magistrate's office (see p.50) was located within the walls of the Kong mansion; the only other residence also to serve as a government office was the imperial palace.

Part of the Confucian temple complex at Qufu. The most important structures of the temple are arranged in a line and facing south, echoing the plan of an imperial palace.

FOLLOWING THE DAO

THE ORGANIC UNIVERSE

DAOISM IS CONCERNED WITH THE INTERCONNECTEDNESS OF ALL THINGS, A DESIRE FOR SPIRITUAL TRANSCENDENCE, AND THE HOPE OF BODILY AND SPIRITUAL PERFECTION. ITS EMPHASIS ON COMMUNICATION WITH SPIRITS, LONGEVITY, AND A UNIVERSE IN CONSTANT FLUX REFLECTS ANCIENT RELIGIOUS SENSIBILITIES THAT PREDATE CHINA'S FORMAL TRADITIONS. DAOISM HAS HAD A RICH EXCHANGE WITH CHINESE POPULAR RELIGION, REFLECTED IN THE TENDENCY BY BOTH CHINESE AND WESTERN SCHOLARS TO LABEL AS "DAOIST" ANY PRACTICE THAT IS NOT CLEARLY CONFUCIAN OR BUDDHIST.

A gilt-copper repoussé gourd, one of a pair made for the Qianlong emperor (ruled 1736–1795). The gourd is an important Daoist symbol—full of seeds, it represents the creative potential within chaos.

Daoism encompasses a variety of ideas and practices which have permeated Chinese civilization at every level. Its concepts are expressed in meditations on cosmology and in a spiritual philosophy that provide guidelines for the ruler, as well as in a vast literature that teaches methods for pursuing longevity and immortality. It is commonly distinguished into two aspects: "philosophical Daoism" refers to the philosophical writings of the ancient masters and their commentators, while "religious Daoism" is characterized by the ritual worship of the Dao and the pursuit of immortality.

At the heart of Daoism are the teachings of the sage Laozi ("Old Master") in the book called the *Dao De Jing* (the *Classic of the Way and its Power*). Little is known about Laozi, although it is traditionally said that he was a royal archivist in the sixth century BCE and that he instructed Confucius on matters of ritual. He is said to have become disillusioned with court life and set off to the western mountains mounted on an ox. At the Chinese frontier a guard asked him for his teachings, and the result of this request was the *Dao De Jing*. Also known as the *Laozi*, the text as it now stands is thought to be the work of many authors. A relatively brief book, it is written in mystical and allusive language that is difficult to translate.

The word *dao* means "way" or "path" and is applied in many Chinese philosophical-religious traditions. In the *Dao De Jing* it is raised to a cosmic principle, the primordial and eternal aspect of the universe that underlies all creation and diversity and forms. Formless, timeless, and limitless, the Dao gives rise to *yin* and *yang* (see pp.122–3) and generates and sustains "all things." The universe is in a state of permanent fluidity in which everything begins with the unchanging Dao and returns to it in an eternal ebb and flow. Laozi

advocates drawing power from the rhythm of this cosmic force and "doing nothing" (*wu wei*) that is contrary to its natural movement. In this way all things may come about spontaneously according to nature. This subtle but inexorable power is illustrated in the *Dao De Jing* by examples of "weak and submissive" things that nonetheless overcome the "hard and strong," such as water, which will always wear down the hardest stone.

The *Dao De Jing* is also a treatise on good government. Laozi's ideal ruler is so retiring and subtle that the people are unaware of being ruled; his statecraft eradicates distinctions that cause envy and discontent so that the people have no superfluous desires.

The other great text of philosophical Daoism is the *Zhuangzi*, named for its fourth-century BCE author, Zhuangzi (Master Zhuang), otherwise called Zhuang Zhou. His work is addressed to the private individual rather than to a ruler. Zhuangzi delights in the infinite manifestations of the Dao and in its imperviousness to human values. He considers the nature of reality and reflects on the endless variations and transformations that occur in life and also in death, which he sees as a blending with the Dao. Zhuangzi speaks of Immortals—perfected individuals who live on mountains, feed on the wind, sip the dew, and experience ecstatic flight. All these ideas became central to the tradition of religious Daoism.

The Seven Sages of the Bamboo Grove, by Fu Baoshi (1904–1965). A popular subject of traditional Chinese art, the sages were a group of Daoist scholars of the 3rd century CE who eschewed the court and worldly ambition for a carefree and elegant life in pursuit of the Dao. Down the centuries a retreat from courtly life and a disregard for the niceties of etiquette, together with a love of poetry, wine, and music, all became attributes of Daoist eccentrics and sages.

RELIGIOUS DAOISM

A Yuan-dynasty painting of Genghis Khan. An important patron of religious Daoism, he asked Qiu Changchun, a famous master of the Complete Perfection school, for advice on how to attain longevity. Qiu suggested that the Khan, who had numerous concubines, try sleeping alone for one night, which "does more for prolonging life than taking elixirs for 1,000 days."

Most Chinese came into contact with Daoism through the syncretistic and amorphous popular religion. However, there was also a more formal and institutional form of Daoism to which the term "religious Daoism" is usually applied. The various schools, or sects, of this religion shared a number of characteristics: a trained literate priesthood; revealed scriptures in classical Chinese; a hierarchical pantheon of male and female deities; temples and monasteries; complex rituals; and special practices involving meditation, alchemy, magic, and therapeutic and spirit-enhancing exercises. Religious Daoism had a strong millenarian strain and in many schools women played relatively important roles.

The beginning of religious Daoism is generally dated to the foundation of the Celestial Masters sect late in the Han dynasty (see box, below). In the period of disorder following the collapse of the Han in 220CE, some Celestial Masters adepts fled south, where they adopted

THE CELESTIAL MASTERS

By the early centuries CE, Laozi had become deified as "the Most High Lord Lao," one of the Three Pure Ones, the highest divinities of Daoism. According to one text he was an omnipresent and omnipotent source of life who became manifest in the human world at crucial points in history, instructing rulers and revealing scriptures. In 142CE the Daoist master Zhang Daoling claimed to have received a revelation from Laozi prescribing a new orthodoxy to replace "degenerate" popular religious practices. Zhang founded a school called the "Way of the Celestial Masters" (Tianshi)—nicknamed the "Way of Five Pecks of Rice" for the tax that it levied on households—and established a theocratic state in western China. The Celestial Masters taught that illness was caused by sin and could be healed by confession and good works such as roadbuilding and distributing free food. Their religious practices were centered on a ritual space called the "chamber of purity" and were conducted by priests—both male and female—who were also the highest local officials. They were primarily healers, garnering celestial powers to effect cures. Other rituals included communal feasts to enhance the ties between divinities and humans, and sexual rites to strengthen vital energy.

In 215CE Zhang Daoling's grandson, Zhang Lu, ceded civil authority to Cao Cao, founder of the northern Wei dynasty. This not only ensured the survival of the school but contributed to its spread, as a hundred thousand believers were dispersed throughout north China.

ideas on alchemy, medicine, magic, and longevity articulated in the classic *Bao Puzi* (*The Master Who Embraces Simplicity*) by Ge Hong. The most fruitful result of this mix was the Upper Purity (Shang Qing), or Maoshan, school. This was based on revelations of a coming apocalypse in which evil would be destroyed and "perfected" Daoist adepts would inherit the earth. Another important southern school, the Sacred Jewel (Ling Bao), venerated "celestial worthies" in grand outdoor rituals.

Daoist sects often enjoyed imperial patronage. The Tang emperor Xuanzong (ruled 712–756CE) decreed that every family should possess the *Dao De Jing*, while Genghis Khan (ca. 1162–1227), who conquered northwest China, was fascinated by the Daoist pursuit of immortality and exempted Daoist monks from tax. The Song dynasty saw the emergence of the Complete Perfection (Quanzhen) school, one of the most dominant sects in the late empire. It proclaimed the essential unity of Confucianism, Buddhism, and Daoism and advocated a monastic life in which adepts meditated on internal alchemical processes (see pp.95; 158–61). Another important sect to appear in the late empire, the Orthodox Unity (Zhengyi) school, had a hereditary and noncelibate clergy and drew inspiration from several groups, especially the Celestial Masters.

A Sui-dynasty painting of Daoist masters presenting the emperor with a new edition of the Dao De Jing. *This central work of Daoism was augmented by the Daoist canon, whose vast corpus was first organized in the 5th century* CE *and first printed in 1120. In 1445 the emperor commissioned a new printed edition of the canon that remains in use today. Running to over 1,000 volumes and continually augmented, it includes celestial revelations and texts on ritual, self-cultivation, sacred topography, and the teachings of individual Daoist masters, as well as anthologies of various subjects.*

IN QUEST OF IMMORTALITY

THE QUEEN OF IMMORTALS
The highest goddess in the Daoist pantheon, the Queen Mother of the West (Xiwang mu), is one of the most widespread and popular figures of immortality. Daoists considered her the primal breath of Ultimate Yin—she was divine lover and teacher to humans seeking immortality.

The Queen Mother lived in the Kunlun mountains, a place that linked heaven and earth, a marvelous and frightening land beyond the western borders of Chinese civilization where pleasures, beauty, and dangers abounded. She was portrayed with a leopard's tail and tiger's teeth, disheveled hair, and a distinctive headdress, attended by jade lads and maidens and accompanied by amazing beings such as the nine-tailed fox, phoenix, the three-legged bird, the toad of immortality, and the hare of the moon (see p.134).

The Queen Mother of the West was revered for more than 2,000 years in both élite and popular cults. In the popular imagination she is most famed for growing the peaches of immortality which ripen once every 3,000 years. These are served to immortals as the final course of a celestial feast that includes such delicacies as bear paws, monkey lips, and dragon livers.

The Chinese belief in the possibility of immortality predates Daoism and is not confined to Daoists. However, it was the schools of Daoism (see pp.92–3) that systematized various techniques aimed at gaining eternal life. The assumption underlying all such practices is the correlation of the microcosmic body to the macrocosmic universe. The adept must identify and preserve the "primordial breath" (*yuanqi*) that corresponds to the life-giving, undifferentiated Dao at the beginning of creation. He or she must retain the vital bodily essences of "breath" (*qi*), "life force" (*jing*), and "spirit" (*shen*), and reverse the gradual depletion of these essences that leads ultimately to death. The reversal of ageing is accomplished by

Keepsake from the Cloud Gallery (detail). This painting of ca. 1750 shows an immortal ascending to a celestial palace.

THE EIGHT IMMORTALS

Many Chinese folk stories tell of the Eight Immortals—a group of "perfected persons" who attained immortality. They are a diverse group, associated with good fortune and the "Eight Conditions of Life" (youth, age, poverty, wealth, high rank, common rank, feminine, and masculine). Their varied experiences and status represent the accessibility of perfection to any who choose to pursue it.

A typical tale is that of Lü Dongbin, co-author of influential texts on alchemy. In the time it took him to prepare a pot of millet, Lu magically experienced an entire lifetime of worldly achievements and humiliating disasters. Awakening to his meal and to the folly of worldly pursuits, he abandoned a conventional life to become an itinerant Daoist.

A late 18th-century carved lacquer box depicting the Eight Immortals, each holding a distinctive attribute.

a range of techniques. In meditation and visualization exercises, the practitioner focuses on the Dao or on powerful astral gods residing in heaven and the body. Star gods are also invoked in therapeutic and strengthening movements. Breathing techniques aim to produce breathing that is so slow and shallow that a feather placed on an adept's nose remains motionless. Purification of the breath and body are enhanced by diet, including the consumption of foods associated with long life, such as certain mushrooms, pine seeds, and pine sap. Sexual techniques aim to control orgasm, which is believed to cause devastating depletion of vital essences. Formerly of great importance was an early practice, "external alchemy," in which adepts worked to produce a pill or elixir of immortality (see pp.144–5); this gave way to "inner alchemy," which aims to transform bodily substances into the elixir (see pp.158–61).

The coffins of those who have become immortal will be found empty except for a token, perhaps a sandal or a staff. Immortals—who have flesh as smooth as ice, snow-white skin, and strange features such as square pupils and long ears—live in remote mountains and caves, or magic places such as Penglai Island off the Chinese mainland. Masters of time and space, they walk among the stars and planets, occasionally visiting the earth incognito to grant immortality to deserving mortals.

THE EMBRYO OF IMMORTALITY
The Daoist practices that led to immortality envisioned the coalescence of purified and perfected bodily essences—such as sexual fluids, saliva, spirit, and *qi*—into a "holy embryo," or "embryo of immortality." Also called the "Red Child," this embryo was nourished in the belly of the adept, where, properly nourished and instructed through correct practices, it would develop into a perfected body, an immortal "real" self that would completely replace the adept's old, corruptible one.

HEALERS, MAGICIANS, AND EXORCISTS

The work of Daoists in the community was in large part directed toward healing and renewal, protecting the people from malign forces, and summoning the power of benevolent spirits. Although the early schools of religious Daoism warned against popular forms of magic, many Daoist priests engaged in such practices. They would be called upon to provide protective amulets, talismans, potions, and cures, or to perform magic spells and exorcisms.

For the Chinese, writing has always been a powerful means of communication with the spirit world, and Daoist magic also relied greatly on the written word. Characters were inscribed on charms, amulets, and talismans to imbue them with magical power, and texts in classical Chinese which were believed to have been revealed by the gods were read, memorized, and chanted in spells. Some Daoist charms were written in the form of official documents ("memorials"; see p.50) issued by the gods as part of their bureaucratic duties—the gods of the popular

THE *FANGSHI*

The *fangshi*, or "gentlemen with techniques," were specialists in the arts of magic from the Qin dynasty until the early part of the Six Dynasties period. Also called "gentlemen of the Dao," they formed an official group at court that was generally distinct from the aristocracy and *literati*.

The *fangshi* were the emperor's official magicians and performed a wide range of functions. These included communicating with ghosts and spirits, performing exorcisms, and practicing various forms of divination (see p.133). As healers, the *fangshi* performed acupuncture and moxibustion (see pp.156–7) and prescribed special regimes of hygiene, diet, and medication, in addition to suggesting techniques for sexual vitality. They were also skilled in predicting cosmic phenomena,

which was considered essential for demonstrating the ruler's ability to harmonize the human and natural realms. However, they were prized most of all for their knowledge of the means to prolong youth and attain immortality.

Under imperial patronage many *fangshi* acquired great influence and wealth. But their rustic manners, lack of classical learning, and willingness to address occult matters put them at odds with the Confucian scholarly class. Court *literati* took every opportunity to expose incidents of *fangshi* incompetence, dishonesty, and abuse of privilege. Their prestige at court declined in the final decades of the Han dynasty.

A pottery model of an exorcist or fangshi. *Eastern Han dynasty, 1st or 2nd century* CE.

pantheon were organized in a hierarchy that paralleled the imperial bureaucracy on earth. By memorizing esoteric scriptures, Daoist priests acquired the ability to summon and direct supernatural forces, including divinities and spirits, and to fight demons.

Daoists also employed special paper talismans to control spiritual beings. Widely used by all Daoist sects, but especially associated with the Upper Purity and Sacred Jewel schools (see pp.92–3), such talismans were symbols of cosmic power and order and conferred the protection of spirits. They bore symbolic representations of the natural order and cosmic energy, such as the hexagrams (see pp.132–3) and the Luo Shu—a magic square of nine numbers positioned so that every line adds up to fifteen. In traditional Chinese numerology, nine represents heaven and six represents earth, and fifteen (nine plus six) represents heaven and earth in harmony.

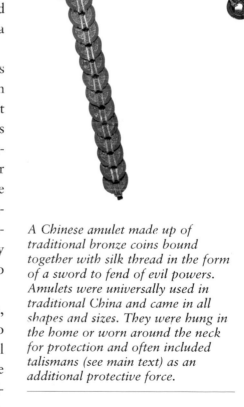

Talismans were commonly used by Daoist healers. A widespread cure for physical or mental distress consisted of drinking water mixed with the ashes of a talisman, and one early Han recipe for repelling a curse recommends taking a bath containing talisman ashes.

Related to this were the practices of other specialists, such as diviners and mediums who bridged the human and divine realms. From the Song dynasty, mediums were commonly employed to practice "spirit writing," whereby deities would transmit messages to the living, such as fortunes, medical prescriptions, and predictions of results in the civil service examinations. In later centuries, mediums would also deliver longer sermons or morality texts from the gods. The medium would write the divine message in character-like forms on paper or in the sand, and a specialist—who was not necessarily literate—would interpret it. Spirit writing and many other magical arts originated in the late Zhou and early imperial periods and drew on the tradition of female shamans (*wu*) who mediated between the human and spiritual worlds (see box, opposite).

Daoist priests were commonly employed as exorcists—for example, to appease earth spirits inhabiting the site of a planned new building, to remove ghosts haunting the place where they had died, or to dispel demons causing mental or physical distress. A priest would summon the spirits through which he would perform the exorcism by making magical gestures and reciting chants and scriptures. Holy water and sometimes flaming alcohol were also used, either sprinkled or sprayed through the mouth over a written spell. Other exorcistic techniques included the "Dance of Yu," a dance patterned on the pacing of the legendary ruler Yu as he roamed China controlling floods (see p.81).

A Chinese amulet made up of traditional bronze coins bound together with silk thread in the form of a sword to fend of evil powers. Amulets were universally used in traditional China and came in all shapes and sizes. They were hung in the home or worn around the neck for protection and often included talismans (see main text) as an additional protective force.

MEDITATION AND RITUAL

In philosophical Daoism, meditation is a process of "un-knowing," described by Zhuangzi as "sitting and forgetting," wherein the adept dissolves distinctions between the self and the eternal flux of the Dao. Through meditation one might perceive the nameless entity which dissolves all opposites and hence move from a one-sided, ego-centered perspective to a holistic, non-discursive vision of the self-generating and self-completing cosmos. The rituals of religious Daoism served a similar purpose of connecting with the Dao. They might be performed for individuals—for example, exorcisms and rituals for the expiation of sin—or to promote the spiritual renewal of the community. Daoist priests were ranked according to the number and types of rituals they memorized and performed. In the later empire these rites took place in temples of the Chinese popular religion.

Many Daoist rituals were established by the earliest Daoist schools. The rites of the Celestial Master school (see p.92) formed the basis for subsequent developments, and included ceremonies to cure disease through the expiation of one's own sins and those of one's ancestors. They also included a sexual rite adapted from an ancient folk tradition which took place at every new moon and entailed men and women having intercourse as an expression of the joining of *yin* and *yang*. Later schools dropped the ritual itself but continued to meditate on its symbolism. The Upper Purity school combined the structures of Celestial Masters ritual with alchemical practices, emphasizing inner cultivation (see pp.158–161). The Sacred Jewel school, by contrast, established the format for communal rituals, which often involved great feasts and elaborate liturgies. Such rituals emphasized the communion of disciple and master, and of the heavenly powers and humankind.

At court, Daoist rituals were performed in private for members of the imperial family, some of whom—including emperors—might themselves be ordained as Daoist priests. A court priest (not to be confused with a *fangshi*; see p.96) might pray for divine blessings to be bestowed on the dynasty, or perform rituals asserting the emperor's mandate to rule. There are also some accounts of emperors commanding rain-making rituals during times of drought. These rites sometimes took the form of competitions between Daoists and Buddhists.

An 18th-century boxwood carving of three astral deities, who played an important role in Daoist ritual and meditative practices. Star gods were called down from the heavens into the body of the adept to renew the power of the organs and revitalize qi.

THE *JIAO* RITUAL

The great *jiao* ceremony represents the pinnacle of Daoist ritual practice in China. Dating in part to the fifth century CE, the *jiao* is known for its beautiful vestments, elaborate altarpieces, and powerful music. It is usually performed around the time of the winter solstice, when the creative *yang* force is believed to be on the verge of renewal.

In the sacred space created for the *jiao*, the priest first paces out the world in miniature. In the ceremony itself the energies of the cosmos are realized in the high priest's body. The Daoist theme of returning to the origin in order to achieve renewal is central to the *jiao*: the priest aims to bring about the replenishment of the forces of light, life, blessing, growth, and *yang* for the whole community, both living and dead.

The *jiao* is offered to the Three Pure Ones, remote and abstract beings that are the highest gods of Daoism: the Venerable Celestial of the Primordial Beginning, the purest manifestation of primordial *qi*; the Venerable Celestial, the Lord of Dao, the mediator between the primordial beginning and the gods; and the Venerable Celestial Laozi, disciple and messenger of the first two.

A Daoist priest's silk robe. The yellow area, adorned with cloud motifs, represents heavenly powers. The border bears other celestial symbols, such as dragons.

PRIESTS AND TEMPLES

The Daoist clergy followed a variety of paths. Some withdrew from the community to live as hermits or monastics and practice self-cultivation, while others were "fire dwellers" and "libationers," who married and lived with their families, performing rites of healing and exorcism in the community. Monastic centers, where Daoist priests trained and monks and nuns lived and practiced, could be found scattered throughout China. However, temples with Daoist priests were established in every village and neighborhood.

Most Daoist monastic temples were effectively under the control of one of the Daoist schools (see pp.92–3). Typically, a novice joined the monastery between the ages of twelve and 20 and began his or her monastic life with menial labor, in addition to the daily practice of devotions. Every year the novice was promoted to other work. At the ordination rite, the novice's hair (which had been allowed to grow since entering the monastery) was combed into a topknot, and he or she was crowned before taking the vows of priesthood. Some monasteries were open to monastics and priests of all schools, as well as to individuals

Daoist priests take part in an outdoor festival at a temple in Taiwan.

GUANDI

Thousands of temples, many under imperial sponsorship, were dedicated to Guandi, one of the most popular of all Chinese gods. Guandi originated as Guan Yu, a historical folk hero who was captured and executed in 219CE. Known for his ferocity, courage, and unswerving loyalty to his bloodbrothers and to the Shu Han dynasty, one of the three successor states to the Han in the Three Kingdoms era (220–263CE). His story is told in the *Romance of the Three Kingdoms*, a famous novel of the Ming dynasty.

Later dynasties deified Guan Yu and promoted him through the ranks of the celestial bureaucracy—by the Ming, he possessed the title of "Faithful and Loyal Great Deity, Supporter of Heaven and Protector of the Realm." Guandi is the god of war, but also a god of merchants, literature, and bean-curd sellers (one of Guan Yu's early professions), among many others. His temple housed the local executioner's sword, for it was thought that no felon's ghost would be brave enough to enter the fierce and just Guandi's residence.

A soapstone statuette of ca. 1700 depicting Guandi. By the end of imperial times he had 1,600 state temples and thousands of smaller ones.

who wished to pursue Daoist practices of self-cultivation.

Monks and nuns of later schools, notably the Complete Perfection School, practiced celibacy, but there is evidence of communal sexual rites in earlier mixed sex monasteries. In the later empire, ordained Daoists were exempt from taxation, military conscription, and labor duty.

"Daoist" neighborhood temples were sponsored by the local community and run by laypeople. They housed images of deities from remote heavens, such as the Three Pure Ones (see p.99), as well as other popular spirits, including the Eight Immortals (see p.95), Guandi (see box, above), tutelary gods, and figures from the Confucian and Buddhist traditions. Some Daoist temples were situated by natural features of spiritual significance, such as holy mountains. These often became important pilgrimage centers, notably those at Mount Tai and Mount Wudang.

Many temples and abbeys received imperial patronage, particularly under the Tang emperors, who shared Laozi's family name (Li) and claimed him as an imperial ancestor. The Tang established shrines and monasteries on 46 sacred peaks and on sites where famous Daoists had "obtained the Way." One monastery, called the Tower Abbey, was founded on the site where Laozi is said to have revealed the *Dao De Jing*—it became a dynastic cult center, and was renamed the Abbey of the Holy Ancestor.

DAOISM AND POPULAR RELIGION

DIVINE PROMOTION
If a local god or goddess became highly popular, the emperor would order an official investigation into the deity's performance and miracle-working powers. To those divinities deemed worthy, the emperor would grant a title and erect an inscription written by the Imperial Secretariat. A famous case was the goddess Mazu, who started as a protector goddess among south Chinese fishing communities. She was steadily promoted up the celestial hierarchy until she became Tian Hou, the Empress of Heaven.

Most Chinese did not consider themselves as "Daoist," "Buddhist," or "Confucian"—each of these terms designated a trained specialist, such as a priest, a monk, or a bureaucrat who had passed the imperial examinations. The average person engaged in a composite religion that was called simply "worshipping the gods" or the "religion of the gods." This amorphous and eclectic popular religion is often referred to loosely as "Daoism," but in fact it reflected the general concerns and ethical teachings of Daoism, Buddhism, and Confucianism—such as filiality, loyalty, respect for authority, good deeds, compassion, longevity, and preparation for the afterlife—and included a variety of indigenous religious practices that predated the formal traditions. The popular pantheon embraced figures and deities from all three traditions, as well as characters from legend and literature.

Two distinguishing characteristics of the popular religion are its lack of defining scriptures, and its basis in autonomous local cults. Unlike orthodox Daoism and the two other highly literate traditions, the popu-

PRACTICE IN THE HOME

The two venues for the practice of popular religion were the community temple and the home. When moving into a home, a family hired a *feng shui* practitioner (see pp.130–31) and an astrologer to ensure that the building harmonized with natural forces and that the family would therefore live in peace and prosperity. If some disharmonious element was discovered, the family might hire a Daoist priest to sort out the problem, for example by exorcising any malevolent spirits.

Whereas the community temples were generally led by men, religious activity in the home was largely the responsibility of the women of the household. They would ensure that regular offerings were made to the "spirit tablets" representing deceased family members and the family's favorite deities. These tablets were kept on the family altar in the focal room of the house (often the kitchen). Women had sole charge of the upbringing of infants and this included propitiating certain domestic deities who were believed to care for children, such as the Bed Mother. Other family members ignored this low-ranking deity, but a mother of young children would see that she was regularly propitiated in order to ensure the health, growth, and sound sleep of her children.

lar tradition was not based on scriptural authority, but rather on the reciprocal relationship cultivated between the human realm and the world of spirits and ghosts (see chapter 10). Many practices date from the Zhou and Han dynasties; by the Song dynasty, the popular tradition had taken on a more or less stable form and was common to all levels of society, although the educated élite were scornful of a number of practices.

Popular temples functioned independently of one another and were supported by the local community which they served both as places of worship and as centers where people could meet for a variety of purposes. Communual festivals such as the annual celebration of a god's birthday or a *jiao* ritual of renewal (see p.99), were overseen by the temple leaders, who in turn would hire Daoist or Buddhist priests to perform specific rituals.

A worshipper in a popular "Daoist" temple in Taipei, Taiwan. To this day, worship in the temples of the popular religion is generally performed on an informal and individual basis.

SECTARIAN MOVEMENTS AND SECRET SOCIETIES

A 17th-century painting showing Daoist deities associated with long life, wealth, and good fortune with a yin-yang *banner. The veneration of such popular celestial beings expressed the idealistic aims of many followers of sectarian groups.*

Daoist ideas and practices were influential in an array of eclectic and syncretistic sectarian movements, brotherhoods, and secret societies that were based on voluntary association. Sectarian groups performed charitable acts for the destitute, travelers, and monks; they also printed and distributed religious tracts and contributed to public works. Some had their own revealed scriptures and simple rituals. These were often combined with practices such as martial arts and breathing techniques aimed at enhancing strength and even helping the adept to acquire magical powers. Vegetarianism and a faith in divine beings were other common features.

The moral and ethical teachings of such groups generally mirrored those of Daoism and the other two formal traditions. Unusually, women often occupied leadership positions and served as preachers and tract distributors. Sectarian groups could be both messianic and millenarian, predicting a coming cleansing apocalypse that would be followed by a time of peace and prosperity. Unorthodox attitudes toward women, together with an emphasis on voluntary membership rather than family blood ties or local affiliations, and the periodic revolts by some groups, made even peaceable sects and societies suspect in the eyes of China's imperial authorities.

One of the first sectarian movements was the Way of Great Peace (Taiping Dao), also known as the Yellow Turbans, which fostered a great rebellion near the end of the Han dynasty. Adherents believed that the dynasty had lost the Mandate of Heaven and would fall in 184CE. Led by Zhang Jue and similar in many respects to the contemporaneous Celestial Masters sect of Daoism (see p.92), they organized rituals of communal confession and expiation, declaring the imminent advent of a new regime of equality and peace led by a deity related to the deified Laozi. However, imperial troops crushed the uprising and Zhang was executed in 184CE.

The apocalyptic, antinomian, and syncretic nature of such groups is evident in similar movements throughout the imperial period. In the later empire, the figure of Maitreya, the *buddha* of the future, became a focal point for many messianic groups, notably the White Lotus Society (see p.111). In the nineteenth century, the Taipings combined Christian and Chinese millenarianism in a fourteen-year revolt in the name of "great peace" that seriously undermined the Qing government. This was followed a few decades later by the devastating Boxer Rising, which incorporated Daoist-type practices and beliefs (see box, opposite).

Different from such sectarians groups were the secret societies and brotherhoods. These groups were primarily political and fraternal rather than religious in nature, but they often performed religious rites to gain assurance of divine support. Complex initiation rituals included blood covenants, elaborate secret codes, gestures, and writing which bound members together and helped them recognize each other in public. Secret societies like the Triads pledged themselves to uphold moral values such as filial piety and humanity, some modeling oaths on those sworn by Guan Yu and his bloodbrothers Liu Bei and Zhang Fei (see p.101). Members were to exhibit the degree of loyalty of those three heroes as well as the 108 rebels of the novel *All Men are Brothers*. The name "Triad" refers to the great trinity of heaven, earth, and humankind (see pp.120–21).

OVERLEAF *A Daoist shrine in the Huangshan mountains, southern Anhui province. Mountains are traditionally revered in China as places of special power; in Daoism they are also where immortals reside (see p.95).*

THE BOXERS

The Boxer Rising of 1899–1900 was a violent revolt by members of a secret society called the "Righteous and Harmonious Fists," which had a distant connection with the White Lotus tradition (see p.111), although its members worshipped a number of popular folk deities and drew their beliefs from many sources, including novels and street plays. They practiced Chinese therapeutic and *qi*-strengthening movements (dubbed "boxing" by Westerners) that were reputed to confer supernatural powers, notably the ability to fly and an invulnerability to bullets and swords. Boxers wore distinctive yellow, black, or red turbans, red leggings, and white charms (representing purity) on their wrists for further protection.

The Boxer Rising was principally an attack on foreign presence and influence in China. Christian converts were vilified for not obeying traditional family customs and refusing to worship Chinese gods. Westerners were accused of destroying the fabric of society and of perverse sexual practices, and their railroads were blamed for cutting the "dragon lines" that ran through the earth, causing the devastating droughts and floods affecting the peasants who made up the majority of Boxers. Brutal massacres of Chinese Christians and attacks on foreign legations led to the invasion of Tianjin and Beijing by troops of eight nations. The devastating terms imposed by the foreign powers hastened the collapse of the ailing Qing dynasty.

A Boxer, photographed in 1900. A violently antiforeign movement, the Boxer rising adopted slogans such as "Support the Qing, destroy the foreigner."

● CHAPTER 8 *Jennifer Oldstone-Moore*

THE WAY OF THE BUDDHA

BUDDHISM CAME TO CHINA FROM INDIA, AND WAS REGARDED BY THE CHINESE AS THE "FOREIGN" RELIGION. YET IT WAS PATRONIZED BY SEVERAL RULING HOUSES AND BUDDHIST IDEAS ALSO EXERTED A PROFOUND INFLUENCE ON INDIGENOUS CHINESE RELIGIOUS THOUGHT. OVER THE CENTURIES, TOO, BUDDHISM DEVELOPED NEW AND UNIQUELY CHINESE FORMS AND MODES OF EXPRESSION.

A monumental rock carving of the Buddha at Leshan, Sichuan province.

THE BUDDHA AND HIS TEACHINGS

The founder of Buddhism, Siddhartha Gautama (traditional dates 566–486BCE), was born a prince of the Shakya clan (hence he is also known as Shakyamuni, the Sage of the Shakyas), which ruled a small kingdom in present-day Nepal. According to legend, his conception and birth were marked by auspicious portents, which were interpreted to mean that the prince would become a *chakravartin* ("wheelturner"), literally a revolutionary—either a great political leader or a great sage.

As a youth Siddhartha was surrounded by courtly pleasures and shielded from life's miseries. In time he married and had a son. It was only when he was in his thirties that he first witnessed human suffering in the forms of an old man, a sick man, and a corpse. To the Indian mind, these were not merely examples of human misfortune—the law of *karma* teaches that all suffering is earned by negative actions in this and previous lifetimes. The effects of *karma* are apparently inescapable, with every sentient being condemned to an eternity of worldly suffering in *samsara*, the unending cycle of birth, death, and rebirth.

Inspired by the sight of a mendicant sage who had forsaken worldly attachments and gained spiritual peace, Siddhartha renounced his princely life to pursue enlightenment, a supreme knowledge of the nature of existence which would be accompanied by a simultaneous release from all suffering. After a long period of meditation at Bodh Gaya, near Varanasi in northern India, he attained enlightenment to become a *buddha*, or "awakened one."

The Buddha's teachings, or Dharma, began with the "Four Noble Truths" and the "Middle Way" (see sidebar, right). The Buddha taught for some 45 years to the growing Sangha (Buddhist monastic community) until his death, or "final *nirvana*," at the age of 80.

THE "FOUR NOBLE TRUTHS"

The Buddha began to teach soon after his enlightenment. Before a small group of ascetics in a deer park at Sarnath, near the Indian city of Varanasi, he expounded the "Four Noble Truths": that suffering exists; that the root of suffering is desire; that suffering may be ended by attaining *nirvana*; and that the way to attain *nirvana* is to follow the "Noble Eightfold Path" centering on wisdom, ethical behavior, and meditation. *Nirvana*, often translated as "liberation" or "enlightenment," is a blissful, detached state in which all effects of *karma* have ceased, and with them *samsara*. Beyond this, *nirvana* is almost impossible to describe—it is not annihilation, but something beyond both existence and non-existence.

In his "First Sermon" the Buddha also advocated his doctrine of the "Middle Way": that those on a spiritual quest should adhere to a lifestyle that lay between the extremes of asceticism and self-indulgence.

Over the centuries, the teachings of the Buddha developed into several distinct traditions. The Mahayana tradition, which spread to China and other parts of north and east Asia, is distinguished by its cult of quasi-divine *buddha*s (the Buddha Shakyamuni is said to be one of countless *buddha*s who have appeared through the eons) and *bodhisattva*s (enlightened beings who delay their own *nirvana* in order to assist others). *Buddha*s and *bodhisattva*s (Chinese *fo* and *pusa*) who acquired particular importance in China include Amitabha (Amituo), the *buddha* of the Western Paradise or Pure Land, a region of bliss where devotees go after death in order to pursue enlightenment away from the stresses of the world; Maitreya (Mile), the future *buddha* of our world; and Avalokiteshvara (Guanyin), the *bodhisattva* of great compassion. These and many other celestial beings became integrated into the Chinese religious tradition together with such fundamental Buddhist concepts as *karma* and reincarnation. This led to the establishment of new practices and ideas and the transformation of old ones.

THE DHARMA IN CHINA

Tradition has it that the emperor Mingdi (ruled 57–75CE) of the Han dynasty foresaw the coming of Buddhism in a dream of a flying golden figure. Certainly, Mingdi's rule was roughly contemporaneous with the oldest Chinese evidence of the new religion, which was transmitted along the Han-controlled trade routes linking northwest India and central Asia with China (see p.28). The collapse of the Han in 220CE heralded three centuries of political instability in which Buddhism was established as a religion of salvation and began to evolve distinct forms reflecting the unique culture and outlook of China.

During this period, north China was ruled by central Asians who employed Buddhist monks as ritual specialists and political aides. In south China, monks became a part of a cultured Chinese élite who had

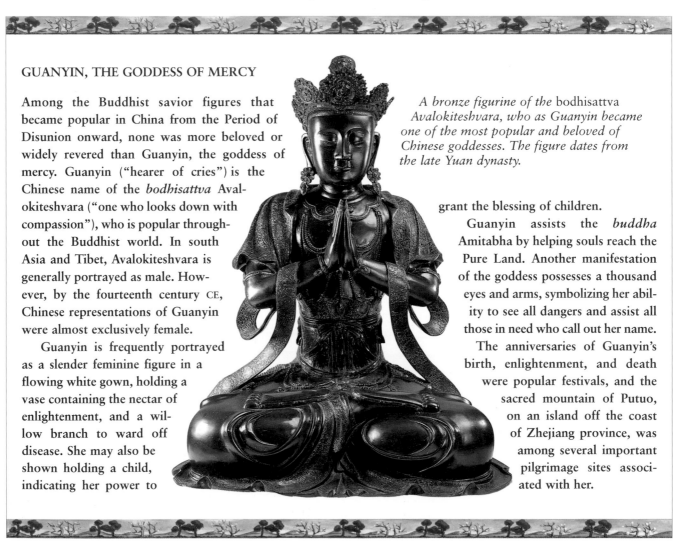

GUANYIN, THE GODDESS OF MERCY

Among the Buddhist savior figures that became popular in China from the Period of Disunion onward, none was more beloved or widely revered than Guanyin, the goddess of mercy. Guanyin ("hearer of cries") is the Chinese name of the *bodhisattva* Avalokiteshvara ("one who looks down with compassion"), who is popular throughout the Buddhist world. In south Asia and Tibet, Avalokiteshvara is generally portrayed as male. However, by the fourteenth century CE, Chinese representations of Guanyin were almost exclusively female.

Guanyin is frequently portrayed as a slender feminine figure in a flowing white gown, holding a vase containing the nectar of enlightenment, and a willow branch to ward off disease. She may also be shown holding a child, indicating her power to

A bronze figurine of the bodhisattva *Avalokiteshvara, who as Guanyin became one of the most popular and beloved of Chinese goddesses. The figure dates from the late Yuan dynasty.*

grant the blessing of children.

Guanyin assists the *buddha* Amitabha by helping souls reach the Pure Land. Another manifestation of the goddess possesses a thousand eyes and arms, symbolizing her ability to see all dangers and assist all those in need who call out her name.

The anniversaries of Guanyin's birth, enlightenment, and death were popular festivals, and the sacred mountain of Putuo, on an island off the coast of Zhejiang province, was among several important pilgrimage sites associated with her.

fled the invasions of the north. Despite occasional persecutions—at times encouraged by Daoists and Confucians—Buddhism flourished and by the end of this period had permeated all classes of Chinese society, with monasteries acquiring great material wealth and social prestige. Buddhism was widely embraced as a religion with teachings and practices that had no counterparts in indigenous traditions. The Buddhist faith supplied highly articulated ideas of the afterlife, together with quasi-divine savior figures (see box, opposite), devotional and healing practices, intricate intellectual and philosophical traditions, powerful meditation techniques, and an active and evangelistic clergy. It also provided a meaningful vocation outside the family and the state.

China was reunified under the Sui (581–618CE) and Tang (618–907CE) dynasties, which were a golden age for Chinese Buddhism. Under the Sui Buddhism was a state religion that expressed the renewed ideological unity of China. Tang emperors claimed descent from Laozi, the great sage of Daoism (see p.90), but they were also avid patrons of Buddhism, establishing state control over monasteries and ordination.

Confucians and Daoists commonly accused Buddhist monastics of being unfilial, antisocial, and parasitic. The Buddhists countered with the claim that monks observed a higher form of filial piety and contributed to the welfare of the empire through their prayers for the imperial family, the state, and ancestors. This claim was reinforced by the popular Buddhist tale of Mulian who, following the instructions of the Buddha, accumulated sufficient merit through prayer and offerings to rescue his mother and other souls from hell.

Monasteries under the Tang acquired tremendous wealth from donations of land, grain, and precious metals. They also enjoyed exemption from land taxation and were often used as tax shelters by landowners who remained in control of tax-exempt land nominally "donated" to monasteries. This practice exacerbated a growing resentment to Buddhism felt by many Confucian bureaucrats, which culminated in 845CE with an imperial decree ordering the destruction of more than 40,000 temples and the return to lay life of 260,500 monks and nuns. Although short-lived, this persecution resulted in the permanent disappearance of several Chinese Buddhist schools, and while Buddhism recovered it never regained its former power and influence.

Chinese religion was (and is) notably syncretic and Buddhism in late imperial China became thoroughly sinicized, permeating many aspects of popular tradition and sectarian movements (see sidebar, right). It was also evident in aspects of Neo-Confucianism, such as the practice of "quiet-sitting." Buddhist practice became increasingly laicized, expressed in the reading of sutras (Buddhist teachings), chanting the name of the Buddha, and the performance of good works.

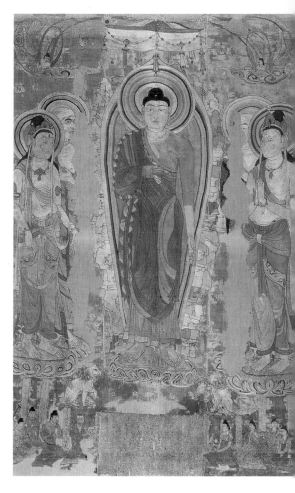

An 8th-century banner of the Buddha from the Buddhist caves at Dunhuang on the Silk Road in Gansu province.

THE WHITE LOTUS
The White Lotus Society and related sects were among the most powerful religious groups in the late empire. Originally devoted to practices aimed at attaining the Pure Land of the *buddha* Amitabha (see p.109), White Lotus became a millenarian movement with a mix of Buddhist and indigenous ideas proclaiming salvation through Maitreya (the *buddha* to come) and a deity called the Eternal Mother. White Lotus sects were not always subversive, but in the mid-fourteenth century one of them, the Red Turbans, mounted a full-scale revolt in anticipation of the apocalypse. Other White Lotus uprisings rocked the Ming and Qing dynasties periodically until the end of the empire.

PATHS TO ENLIGHTENMENT

The Ox-Herding Sequence (detail).
This series of ten paintings, by the
15th-century Japanese Zen (Chan)
monk Shubun, articulates the
transformation from ignorance to
enlightenment—the boy represents
the person on the path to enlightenment and the ox represents one's
true buddha-nature. The picture
on the right is entitled "Searching,"
and illustrates that one must first
be motivated to follow the Buddhist
path. The central image, "Seeing the
Traces," represents the individual
becoming aware of, and harnessing,
the efforts and example of others
who have already traveled the path.
The left-hand image, "Seeing the
Ox," shows that, through meditative
experience, one can glimpse true
reality, or one's buddha-nature.

The earliest Chinese schools of Buddhism either were simply imported from India without alteration or sought to emphasize similarities between Buddhist and native Chinese thought. However, the most enduring schools were those which adapted and altered the "foreign" religion to its Chinese context, establishing new practices and scriptures.

Buddhism arrived in China as a rich and well-established cultural tradition that had generated a wealth of often contradictory scriptures. The teachings of many Chinese Buddhist schools reflect efforts to synthesize these diverse writings. One strategy was to develop a scheme of "graded revelation" in which each sutra (a discourse attributed to the Buddha) was ranked according to the degree of spiritual advancement it represented. The varying degrees of profundity found in the sutras was believed to reflect the Buddha's skill at addressing people at their own level of ability. Another strategy favored practice and experience over scripture, resulting in distinctively Chinese methods for attaining enlightenment.

Chinese Buddhists were particularly concerned to show that the transmission of the Dharma, the Buddha's teachings, remained unbroken, however distant the connection between the Buddha and the Chinese patriarchs; there was much emphasis on lineages of teachers. For example, the line of patriarchs who presided over Chan Buddhism was initiated by Bodhidharma, the First Patriarch, who in turn was the twenty-eighth in a direct line of Indian patriarchs stretching back to the Buddha.

Schools generally focused on the study and interpretation of a particular text or group of texts. Monks might study with different masters and hence appear in several different lineages of teachers, while adherents of different Buddhist schools might live together in one monastery. Distinctions between schools had meaning only for professional clerics and were of no interest or import for the average Chinese.

The earliest important schools of Buddhism in China were imported from India without significant alteration. The two most notable schools—Three Treatise (Sanlun) and Mind Only (Faxiang)—were founded respectively by Kumarajiva (344–413CE) and Xuanzang (602–664CE), the two greatest translators of Indian texts into Chinese (see p.117). The Three Treatises school introduced the teachings of Middle Doctrine (Madhyamika) Buddhism, which taught that in reality there is no difference between being and non-being: all that truly exists is the void, or "emptiness" (Sanskrit *sunyata*, Chinese *wu*). The Mind Only school (also called Yogacara or Vijnanavada) established by Xuanzang asserted that all things exist only in the mind of the perceiver. Both schools engaged in philosophical argument, a practice that was at odds with the Chinese love of resolving opposites and their conviction that a cultivated person did not argue. As a consequence, perhaps, neither school flourished after the Tang persecutions of 845CE.

The two most lasting schools of Chinese Buddhism, Chan (see box, below) and Pure Land (Qingtu), adapted most completely to the

CHAN BUDDHISM

Traditionally founded in the sixth century CE by the Indian patriarch Bodhidharma, Chan arose from a creative combination of the central Buddhist practice of meditation (Sanskrit *dhyana*, whence Chinese Chan and Japanese Zen) with Daoist concepts such as the importance of intuition, the inability of words to convey profound truths, and a love of the absurd and unexpected.

Chan claimed that its teachings were transmitted without speech or writing —a theory inspired by an incident in which the Buddha responded to a question by simply picking up a flower and smiling. It advocated intuition over rational discourse and sought to break down the stubborn mind through meditation, conundrums (*gong'an*; see p.117), and "shock tactics" such as shouting at adepts to spur them on to the "lightning-bolt" experience of enlightenment.

Chan practice centers on communal monastic living and group meditation. The master closely monitors the progress of monks. Appealing to intellectuals, Chan's influence is evident in Chinese art and calligraphy.

A Song-dynasty mural of Huineng (638–713CE), the uneducated and illiterate woodcutter who became the Sixth Patriarch of Chan Buddhism.

THE TIANTAI AND HUAYAN SCHOOLS

Two Chinese schools sought to harmonize Buddhist scriptures by creating a hierarchy of progressively more sublime and difficult texts, culminating in a particular *sutra*. For Tiantai Buddhism—organized by Zhiyi (538–597CE) and named for its headquarters on Mount Tiantai in present-day Zhejiang province—this supreme text was the *Lotus Sutra*, in full the *Sutra of the White Lotus of the True Law* (*Saddharma Pundarikha Sutra*), a collection of sermons, allegorical writings, and poetry which stressed that salvation was open to all through the eternal compassion of the Buddha. Tiantai claimed that the *Lotus Sutra* contained the essence of Buddhism and reconciled the divergent views that had emerged on central questions, such as whether the way to enlightenment lay in meditation and good works or in erudite philosophical inquiry.

The Huayan school is named from its own core text, the *Flower Garland Sutra* (*Avatamsaka Sutra*, Chinese *Huayan Jing*), which taught the emptiness and interpenetration of all phenomena. A highly intellectual approach given definitive form by its third patriarch, Fazang (643–712CE), Huayan claimed that few could ever follow its teachings, for which the doctrines and methods of other schools served only as a preparation.

Both Tiantai and Huayan declined after the Tang persecutions of 845CE.

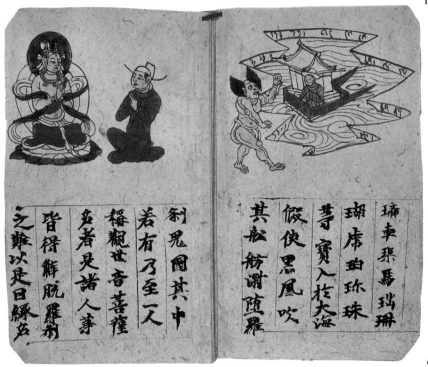

A Chinese manuscript of the Lotus Sutra *found at Dunhuang and dating to ca. 1000CE. The* sutra *became the most popular and influential* sutra *in east Asian Buddhism.*

Chinese sensibility, creating distinctly Chinese forms of Buddhism. The devotional Pure Land school had by far the greater number of followers. It was founded on the vow of the *buddha* Amitabha (Amituo Fo) to use the boundless merit he had created over eons of self-perfection to save those who called out to him, causing them to be reborn in his paradisial realm, the Pure Land, also known as the Western Paradise (Sukhavati). The faithful chanted Amitabha's name in the simple phrase "*namo Amituo Fo*" ("hail to Amitabha Buddha"), repented of their sins, and relied on the grace of Amitabha and his assistant Guanyin (see p.110) as a simple and painless means of attaining salvation. The Pure Land was not *nirvana* but a place of beauty and bliss beyond *samsara* (see pp.108–9), where Buddhist law was constantly expounded; from here even the least sophisticated follower would find the ideal conditions to attain *nirvana*. Pure Land adherents recounted stories of people on their deathbeds experiencing signs of their imminent rebirth in the Pure Land—such signs included music or sweet fragrances emanating from the heavens, multicolored clouds, and visions of Amitabha's attendants.

Masters of the Pure Land school, such as Tanluan (476–542CE) and Daochuo (562–645CE), stressed the need to acquire Amitabha's grace by doing good works, the only means to salvation in an age when human beings had become degenerated and the world was in "the Latter Days of the Law" (*mofa*). The faithful engaged in recitation marathons —one monk set a record by reciting the *Namo* chant a million times in one week. Despite Confucian disapproval of such practices, by the twelfth century Pure Land Buddhism had followers from all walks of life and at all levels of Chinese society. By the late empire Pure Land practices were even to be found in Chan monasteries.

Tibetan Buddhism was another important school in China in the imperial period under the rule of the Mongols (the Yuan dynasty) and Manchus (the Qing dynasty), whose empires included Tibet. Also referred to as "Lamaism," from the *lama*s (religious teachers) who play a prominent role in the Tibetan schools, it is a form of Mahayana Buddhism with a strong Tantric element which incorporates native Tibetan magical, exorcistic, and healing rituals. While it was never popular among the mass of Chinese, Tibetans came to dominate the Chinese Buddhist hierarchy after the conversion to Tibetan Buddhism of Khubilai Khan, the Yuan dynasty founder. Under the succeeding Ming dynasty, although Tibet was not part of the Chinese empire it remained a tributary state and Tibetan Buddhism continued to be influential in China. Numerous Tibetan-style monasteries were built, especially in Beijing (see pp.221–2).

The Qing emperors also adhered to the Tibetan form of Buddhism, even considering themselves to be the reincarnations of the *bodhisattva* Manjushri, who was greatly revered in Tibet. In 1720 Tibet became a Chinese protectorate and from then until the end of the empire the Dalai Lamas, the heads of the Tibetan theocracy, came under the official tutelage of the imperial government.

An elaborate cloisonnée enamel Buddhist reliquary made for the emperor Qianlong (1736–1795) exemplifies Sino-Tibetan styles of Buddhist art that evolved under the Yuan and Qing dynasties.

SACRED WRITINGS

The body of Buddhist scripture is not fixed, nor is there one single canon accepted by all regional, sectarian, and linguistic traditions. However, all Buddhists accept as core scripture the *Three Baskets* (*Tripitaka*), which are the earliest texts to survive in an Indian language (Pali, a close relative of Sanskrit). Its three parts, or "baskets," consist of *sutra*s (discourses attributed to the Buddha), texts on monastic discipline, and scholastic works. The Chinese Buddhist scriptures—which run to nearly 100,000 printed pages—contain, in addition to the Chinese version of the *Three Baskets*, biographies of eminent monks, travelogues, histories, and apologetics.

The scriptures of most lasting importance in China were those that reflected particularly Chinese concerns. The *Vimalakirti Sutra* holds up the devout layman as the ideal being to attain enlightenment; this resonated

Part of a 19th-century copy of the Jade Book of the Prajnaparamita (Heart Sutra), *engraved in gilded characters on jade tablets.*

XUANZANG'S PILGRIMAGE TO INDIA

One of the most famous figures in Chinese Buddhism, Xuanzang (602–664CE), was a monk, scholar, pilgrim, translator, and the founder of the Mind Only school of Chinese Buddhism (see p.113). By the age of 20 he had studied all the Buddhist texts available in China and in 629CE he left on a pilgrimage to India to find more scriptures. In India, Xuanzang visited Buddhist sites, mastered Sanskrit, and studied Indian philosophy and sciences. He was acclaimed on his return to China in 645CE and was later honored by the Tang emperor Gaozong. Xuanzang spent the rest of his life translating the 75 Buddhist *sutra*s that he is said to have brought back with him.

Record of the Western Realms, Xuanzang's account of his long and perilous journey, is still valued by historians for its detail and precision. Chinese were fascinated by the world beyond China, and Xuanzang's adventures were retold and embellished in popular plays and story cycles that culminated in Wu Chengen's irreverent and much-loved novel *Xiyou ji* (*Journey to the West*), published in 1596.

This figure from the novel Journey to the West *at the ancient Buddhist site of Bezeklik in Chinese Turkestan commemorates Xuanzang's famous pilgrimage to India.*

with the traditional Chinese emphasis on family life, which sometimes conflicted with Buddhist monasticism on the grounds that it was unfilial to leave home and seek ordination. The *Lotus Sutra* appealed to the Chinese love of synthesis by claiming to contain the essence of the thousands of scriptures that had reached China (see p.114). Attractive to the majority of Chinese were scriptures associated with popular devotional practices. These included writings that described the Pure Land of Amitabha (see pp.113–15) or the mercy of the popular goddess Guanyin (see p.110).

New forms of scripture also developed in China, such as the recorded discussions between Chan masters and their disciples. These "public cases" (*gong'an*, the origin of the *koan* of Zen) were used in meditation and were typified by paradoxical conundrums or apparently impossible questions such as "What is your face before your parents' birth?" (see also p.113).

Another important group of texts were the "precious scrolls" (*baojuan*) of various sectarian groups. Drawing on all of China's religious traditions, these sects were often strongly Buddhist in influence, preaching the coming of Maitreya and a new order that would establish peace, prosperity, and immortality for believers (see p.111).

TRANSLATING THE DHARMA
The difficulties of translating scriptures from Sanskrit and other Indian tongues were daunting. Translators could use existing terms for foreign words, which might obscure important differences, or they could render foreign terms phonetically, for example *man te le* for *mantra* and *pusa* for *bodhisattva* though such terms often sounded crude or outlandish. The most famous translators were Kumarajiva (344–413CE), an Indian whose work remains unsurpassed for elegance and accuracy (see also p.113), and Xuanzang (see box above).

WORSHIP AND MONASTICISM

A Ming dynasty gilt bronze figure of the Buddha. He is depicted in the moments after he emerged from the long meditation that culminated in his enlightenment, his right hand reaching down to the earth to attest to his merit.

The monastic life of renunciation lay at the heart of Buddhist teachings. The Buddha himself set the example in his own quest for liberation from existence and suffering. In China, established monasteries were more socially acceptable than the Indian tradition of the wandering mendicant, and monastic communities were usually supported by landholdings worked by peasants or, in some cases, by the community members themselves. Monasteries differed greatly in size and wealth, and were often built in honor of important figures, such as great teachers, or celestial beings identified with the area, and became important sites of pilgrimage.

The growth of monasteries is one indicator of the rapid spread of Buddhism. In the Period of Disunion, they were refuges from constant warfare and social upheaval. By the end of the fifth century CE there were more than 1,700 monasteries in south China; in the northern Wei kingdom alone there were more than 30,000. In the reunified period of the Tang dynasty, monasteries were great landowners and they developed commercial enterprises and other functions. Although during this time Buddhist institutions came under, and were to remain subject to, imperial supervision, they became very wealthy and often boasted magnificent and massive architectural structures.

Monasteries came to play an important role in the Chinese economy. Contributions from devout laypeople often allowed them to acquire considerable surpluses. They loaned money and grain at interest, as well as mills and oil presses that processed agricultural products for farmers, and operated bathhouses and hostels for travelers.

Life in the monastery was regulated by the Buddhist monastic code, the Vinaya, with local modifications. The community was ruled in paternalistic style by an abbot who was elected by the monks and nuns and approved by the state, which also controlled ordination. Novices found a teacher at a monastery under whom they would study, and after their training they would take vows. As a faith of universal salvation, Buddhism had particular appeal to Chinese women; the first Buddhist convent was established in 312CE, and the female monastic order remained unbroken beyond the imperial era.

Of the various schools, Chan developed the most distinctive communal living structure. By the seventh century, Chan monks had established a monastic life centered on communal meditation, manual labor, group discussion, and private meetings with the abbot.

SACRED MOUNTAINS

Sacred mountains form a major part of the Chinese religious landscape, and some of the most important serve as sites of Buddhist pilgrimage. Four mountains, each associated with a particular *bodhisattva*, were particularly important in this respect: Mount Wutai in the north, Jiuhua in the south, Emei in the west, and Putuo in the east. These were linked respectively with Manjushri (Chinese Wenshu), Ksitigarbha (Dizang), Samantabhadra (Puxian), and Avalokiteshvara (Guanyin). Pilgrims venerated these figures at the various monasteries that were built in their honor on the slopes of the mountains.

Of the four mountains, Mount Wutai has the richest history. By the sixth century CE it had more than 200 monasteries, and Japanese visitors in the ninth century reported huge crowds of pilgrims. Its most famous structure is the Great Hall of Nanchansi, built in the seventh and eighth centuries CE and the oldest standing wooden structure in China. As a cult center for Manjushri, who was a significant figure in both Chinese and Tibetan Buddhism, Mount Wutai was perhaps the most celebrated pilgrimage site in Asia outside India.

A Buddhist nun meditating in the snow at Jinding temple on Mount Emei in Sichuan province.

THE HARMONY OF HEAVEN AND EARTH

THE GREAT TRINITY

SINCE ANCIENT TIMES, THE CHINESE HAVE ORGANIZED THE WORLD INTO VARIOUS CATEGORIES. THUS THE UNIVERSE IS A TRINITY OF "HEAVEN, EARTH, AND MAN," AND MATTER WITHIN THE UNIVERSE IS COMPOSED OF "FIVE ELEMENTS." HOWEVER, BECAUSE THESE CATEGORIES ARE NOT REGARDED AS EXCLUSIVE BUT AS OVERLAPPING AND INTERPENETRATING, THE TRADITIONAL CHINESE WORLDVIEW ALSO EMBRACES THE REALITY OF A UNIVERSE IN A CONSTANT STATE OF CHANGE AND EVOLUTION.

The Chinese have always been inclined to view the world in terms of categories. But all the myriad categories derive from just three realms, expressed in the phrase *tian di ren* ("heaven, earth, man"). One of the earliest accounts of the invention of culture describes Fuxi (see pp.80) modeling the human world on the natural world. This same description goes on to say that Fuxi's purpose was "to penetrate the virtue of spiritual brightness and to categorize the real characteristics of the 10,000 beings," meaning that the three realms of *tian di ren* are joined together, if humans can but perceive their unity. Confucius, for one, perceived it when he urged his students to study poetry so as "the better to recognize the names of birds and animals, plants and trees": since the realms of earth and humankind were interpenetrated, knowing the features of the earth would help his students understand the features of humankind.

One does not have to look far to see the implications of this grand union of heaven, earth, and humankind—which has been called "The Great Trinity"—in Chinese history, mythology, philosophy, religion, or any other field. Just over 500 years before Confucius was born, a spectacular conjunction of the five visible planets (Mercury, Venus, Mars, Jupiter, and Saturn) was interpreted as the signal for the rise of a new dynasty, which indeed occurred when the Zhou overthrew the Shang. Similar events have been recorded throughout Chinese history in the standard dynastic annals (see pp.126–7). The most recent event to receive such notice was an earthquake that occurred in the vicinity of Beijing in 1976, the year in which Mao Zedong died.

Chinese mythology provides a narrative context for some of these natural phenomena. One story tells

A Han-dynasty bronze censer with gold inlay. It represents a miniature version of the universe, with water below and the mountains of earth reaching to the heavens.

A throne room in the Forbidden City, Beijing. It is in microcosmic form, with the square platform representing the earth and a round ceiling adorned with the celestial dragon, representing heaven. Between the two is the throne of the emperor, who linked the worlds of heaven, earth, and humankind.

THE WAY OF THE KING
Dong Zhongshu (ca. 179–104BCE) was for a time the most influential minister to the emperor Wudi (ruled 141–87BCE) of the Han dynasty. Dong was responsible in part for the establishment of Confucianism as the state orthodoxy. In an essay entitled *How the Way of the King Joins the Trinity,* he looked to the character for "king" (illustrated below) to provide an etymological rationale for how the sovereign unites heaven, earth, and humankind: "Those who in ancient times invented writing drew three lines and connected them through the middle, calling the character 'king.' The three lines are heaven, earth, and humankind, and that which passes through the middle joins the principle of all three."

how, in ancient times, a minister named Gong Gong tried to overthrow the legitimate ruler, but failed. Gong Gong angrily struck one of the four mountains that held apart heaven and earth. It collapsed, causing heaven to slope down toward the northwest and earth to slope down toward the southeast. This is said to be why the sun, moon, and stars move across the sky from east to west, and why China's rivers flow from west to east. For those attuned to mythic language, it also has many meanings for human institutions: in one reading, it marks the beginning of time; in another, the legitimacy of imperial rule—as much a concern to ancient Chinese rulers and their philosophers as it still is to their modern counterparts.

YIN AND YANG
AND THE FIVE ELEMENTS

The "egg of chaos" represents the opposing but complementary forces of yin and yang. Each flows into, and contains the seed of, the other.

The Chinese notion that is probably best known in the West is that of the *yin* and the *yang*, the opposing but necessarily coexisting aspects of all being. The words originally meant respectively "shady" and "sunny," but in their philosophical usage they have been extended to include a wide range of opposing pairs such as dark and light, wet and dry, female and male, weak and strong, dead and living, and so on (but not necessarily bad and good). Although the earliest written examples of this usage seem to be no earlier than about the fifth century BCE, there is at least some evidence of a similar principle of duality as early as the fifth millennium BCE. A Neolithic tomb discovered in 1988 at Puyang in Henan province revealed a corpse lying between two animal figures modeled from clam shells. The animals have been interpreted to represent a dragon and a tiger, precursors of the Azure Dragon and the White Tiger, the mythical embodiments of *yang* and *yin*.

The Azure Dragon, at least, was not just a mythical animal. It was very visible, appearing in the night sky as a constellation of stars. At the time that Chinese myths were being systematized, the Dragon constella-

THE FIVE ELEMENTS: TABLE OF CORRESPONDENCES

	WOOD	FIRE	EARTH	METAL	WATER
SEASONS	Spring	Summer	–	Autumn	Winter
DIRECTIONS	East	South	Center	West	North
TASTES	Sour	Bitter	Sweet	Acrid	Salty
SMELLS	Goatish	Burning	Fragrant	Rank	Rotten
NUMBERS	Eight	Seven	Five	Nine	Six
PLANETS	Jupiter	Mars	Saturn	Venus	Mercury
WEATHER	Wind	Heat	Thunder	Cold	Rain
COLORS	Green	Red	Yellow	White	Black
ANIMALS	Fishes	Birds	Man	Mammals	Insects
GRAINS	Wheat	Beans	Panicled millet	Hemp	Millet
VISCERA	Spleen	Lungs	Heart	Kidney	Kidney
BODY PARTS	Muscles	Veins	Flesh	Skin and Hair	Liver
ORGANS	Eyes	Tongue	Mouth	Nose	Ears
EMOTIONS	Anger	Joy	Desire	Sorrow	Fear

tion appeared in the night sky from March. It was probably because of this that the Dragon was associated with spring and with the east. The Tiger, by contrast, was associated with autumn and the west. Eventually two other animals, a Red Bird and a Black Turtle, became associated with summer/south and winter/north respectively.

At about the same time that the notion of *yin* and *yang* was being extended to include all being, another development was taking place that would have even greater implications for the Chinese worldview. The earlier categorization of the world into four parts—Azure Dragon, White Tiger, Red Bird, and Black Turtle; east, west, south, and north; spring, autumn, summer, and winter—was transformed by the early third century BCE into a grand scheme dividing all matter into five parts. This transformation was probably originally achieved by the addition of the "center" to the four cardinal directions, but its standard representation came to be as five "elements" or "phases" (*wu xing*): wood, fire, earth, metal, and water. These elements, conceived not as inert substances but rather as sorts of constantly evolving energy, were thought to be elemental to all matter. Over time, every aspect of life came to be categorized under one of the five elements. The table of correspondences, which could be extended considerably, gives just a few of the correlations (see box, opposite).

The notions of yin *and* yang *and the Five Elements have given rise to some of China's most profound metaphysical thinking. They have also made their mark on neighboring religious and philosophical systems. Here, the* yin-yang *symbol (see illustration, opposite) is painted on a door of a Buddhist monastery at Sera in Tibet.*

MAPPING THE HEAVENS

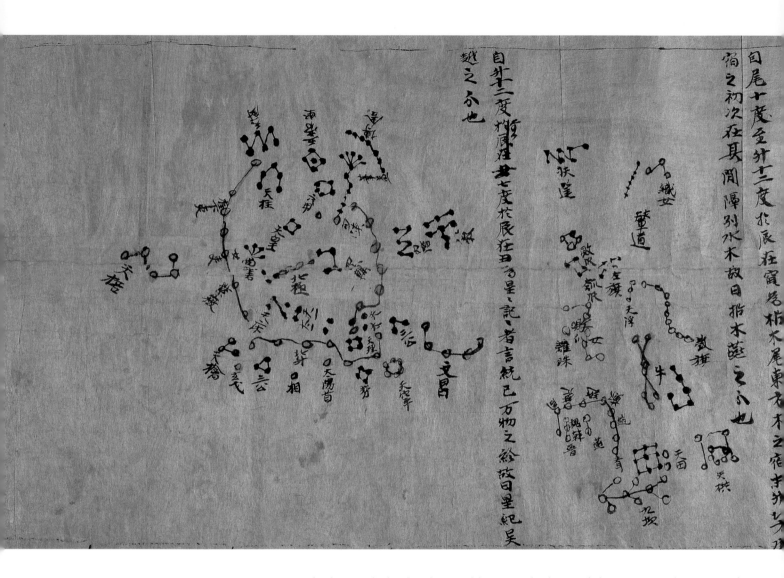

A star map of ca. 940CE showing constellations including the Big Dipper (Plow). In the later centuries BCE, as official record-keeping became more routine, Chinese astronomer-scribes produced the most complete record of unusual celestial phenomena of any civilization, including lunar and solar eclipses, comets, supernovas, and even sun spots.

The heavenly bodies loomed large in the lives of the ancient Chinese, and played a crucial role in China's political history, mythology, and religion. From the earliest written records down to China's first encounter with the West, comprehending the heavens was a primary goal. While departures from the celestial norm were important (and almost always interpreted as omens), astronomers were also careful to observe the usual state of the heavens—the regular positions and motions of the stars (*hengxing*, or "constant stars") and planets (*xingxing*, or "moving stars").

The earliest Chinese conceptions of the heavens—traditionally attributed to the culture hero Fuxi—are called *gai tian* ("covering heaven") and *hun tian* ("englobing heaven"). The *gai tian* theory, the more primitive of the two, depicted heaven as a hemisphere hovering over a square earth, and turning like a millstone. The earth itself was stationary, floating on a watery abyss into which the waters of the earth drained. The *hun tian* theory, which developed later but was certainly current by ca. 350BCE, envisioned heaven as a sphere totally encompassing the earth.

While Greek astronomy measures the positions of stars along the ecliptic (the apparent path of the sun as it moves around the earth), Chinese astronomers have always viewed the heavens relative to the celestial equator (the line of the earth's equator projected onto the heavenly sphere). The heavenly sphere is divided into *xiu* ("equatorial star groups," or "lodges"). To use Joseph Needham's analogy, it is as if the sphere of the heavens consisted of segments like those of an orange. From at least the fourth century BCE (see box, below), there were considered to be 28 segments, each associated with a particular star (see illustration, p.127). The number of *xiu* seems likely to be derived from the motion of the moon, which "stopped" each night of the lunar month in one of the "lodges."

The 28 *xiu* were fundamental to Chinese astronomy, but were by no means the totality of it. The earliest catalogs and maps of stars, probably dating from the fourth or third century BCE, list a total of 1,464 stars grouped into 284 asterisms or constellations. For each asterism, the catalogs indicate its name, the number of stars in it, its position with regard to neighboring asterisms, and measurements of its determinative star in terms that Western astronomers could describe as right ascension (celestial longitude) and declination (celestial latitude).

Part of a famous observatory at Nanjing, which was originally built by the astronomer Guo Shoujing in 1270 at Linfen in Shanxi province, but was moved to Nanjing, the southern imperial capital, under the Ming. While preserving the beautifully constructed bronze instruments, the move ruined their accurate alignment so that they were no longer functional.

THE TOMB OF LORD YI OF ZENG

In 1978 the tomb of Lord Yi of Zeng, a minor state of the Eastern Zhou period, was discovered at Suixian in Hubei province. The earliest tomb of a ruler yet discovered in China, it was certainly furnished as extravagantly as one would expect for a head of state. Among Yi's burial goods was a lacquer clothes hamper that is of little material value, but of tremendous importance in terms of the history of astronomy. It is decorated with a design of the Celestial Dipper (the Big Dipper or Plow), around which are written the names of the 28 *xiu* or heavenly lodges (see main text). It is the earliest complete record of the *xiu*.

Beneath the name of the lodge *Gang* (Neck) there is the notation "*jiayin* third day of the fifth month." *Jiayin* is a day in the Chinese cycle of 60 days (see p.134) and the third day of the fifth month fell on a *jiayin* in 433BCE. According to other evidence in the tomb, this was apparently the year in which Lord Yi died. It is possible, therefore, that the diagram on the clothes hamper depicts the night sky on the date of his death.

INTERPRETING THE HEAVENS

King Wu, the founder of the Zhou dynasty, whose rise was said to have been heralded by celestial portents.

In premodern China, as in the premodern West, there was no categorical distinction between astronomy and astrology. Beginning with the premise that the universe was intelligible—a premise that is key to the traditional Chinese worldview—then it stood to reason that the heavens were especially intelligible (*tian*, "the heavens," is the same word often translated as "Heaven" and understood as a divine power that was able to control events). Heaven was understood to express itself by the changes that came across its face. Chinese of all social and intellectual backgrounds and of all periods spared no effort in trying to interpret these changes.

The mapping of the heavens was never just a scholastic exercise. It took little observation to see that the appearance of the heavens was generally constant; the relative positions of the stars were fixed, and the sun and moon and planets moved through them at regular intervals. Yet there were aberrations: the paths of the sun and moon could intersect, causing one or the other "to be eaten" (that is, eclipsed); and the planets' motion brought them into different positions not only with regard to the stars, but also each other. There were comets and meteors, of which Chinese astronomers have left the world's longest and most complete record. Stars

THE ASTROLOGICAL BOOKS OF MAWANGDUI

In 1973 archaeologists at the important site of Mawangdui in Changsha, Hunan, discovered the tomb of the son of Li Cang, a local governor. The son, who died in 168BCE, was buried with a complete library that included two astrological almanacs referred to as *Prognostications of the Five Planets* and *Miscellaneous Prognostications of Astronomy and Meteorology*. The first correlates the five visible planets with the Five Elements (see pp.122–3), and includes omens for each planet as well as an annual record of their positions from 246–177BCE. The second text illustrates various phenomena including clouds, solar and lunar halos, rainbows, and comets.

A detail of the Miscellaneous Prognostications. *The text below each drawing names the celestial phenomenon and sometimes explains its astrological significance.*

could also apparently change colors or appear to "shake," while supernovas could appear suddenly. Finally, the picture of heavenly activity also included events much closer to earth such as clouds, rain, thunder, lightning, rainbows, and other atmospheric phenomena—meteorology, like astrology and astronomy, did not exist as a distinct discipline.

Unique apparitions of the heavens would be linked with unique events on earth. Heavenly portents were seen especially at the time of great political events, such as the fall of dynasties. One of the earliest such phenomena with a claim to historical validity occurred on May 28, 1059BCE, toward the end of the Shang dynasty, when there was a remarkable conjunction of the visible planets: Mercury, Venus, Mars, Jupiter, and Saturn. Within fifteen years, King Ji Fa of Zhou overthrew the Shang king and established the Zhou dynasty. Ji Fa, better known as King Wu, is still regarded as one of China's greatest culture heroes. Another conjunction of the five planets on May 29, 205BCE was linked with the fall of the Qin dynasty and the rise of the Han, and the *shi* (astronomer-scribes) who kept records of these event inferred from the similarity of the two conjunctions of 1059BCE and 205BCE that future conjunctions would have a similar meaning.

Other heavenly phenomena were also observed to have regular meanings, and these were compiled into systematic digests (see box, opposite). An example of the historical use of celestial "precedents" occurred in 620CE, two years after the formal establishment of the Tang dynasty but before all other claimants had been suppressed. On November 29, a meteor landed in the city of Luoyang. Court astrologers explained to the Tang emperor, Gaozu, that according to precedents the falling star portended the death of a villain where it fell. Luoyang was the base of Gaozu's rival Wang Shichong, and in 621CE the prediction was proved true when Gaozu's forces besieged Luoyang and killed Wang.

Chinese manuals of all sorts, histories as well as occult sources, are full of such stories. They were all based on the same belief: that heaven, earth, and humankind were all united, and that what happened in one realm would necessarily have an effect on the others.

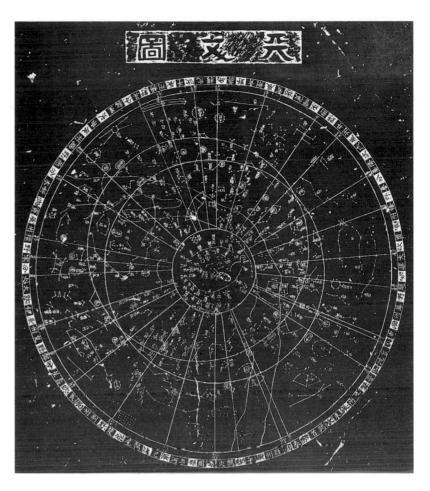

A rubbing of a Chinese planisphere, or chart of the heavens, that was engraved in stone at Suzhou in 1247CE. It shows around 1,400 stars as well as the division of the night skies into 28 "lodges" (xiu; see p.125).

MAPPING THE EARTH

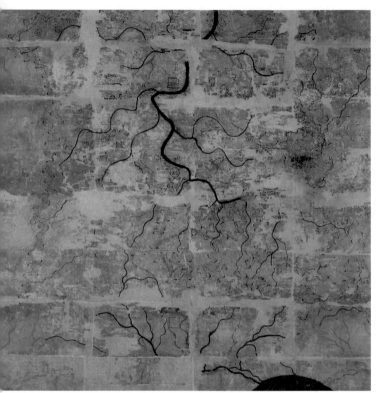

A silk map discovered in Tomb 3 at Mawangdui (168BCE). It is probably of the southern region of the ancient state of Changsha and shows rivers, military bases, and other features.

THE FANGMATAN MAPS
The earliest true maps in China were unearthed in 1986 at Fangmatan, Gansu province, in the tomb of a Qin dynasty officer who probably died in 239BCE. The seven maps, drawn in ink on four wooden boards, all depict the ancient administrative district in which the tomb was located, and show cities, army camps, rivers, mountain passes, transportation checkpoints, and forests. Like many traditional Chinese maps they are oriented with south at the top and north at the bottom: in Chinese cosmology, south is associated with summer and the sun and hence it is above; conversely, north is associated with winter and water and thus is below.

Westerners interested in China have tended to be focused on topics with universal significance; hence their great interest in Chinese notions of moral philosophy and metaphysics. However, with respect to the union of heaven, earth, and humankind, a unifying theme of this chapter, the emphasis on heaven and humankind should by no means be taken to mean that earth was unimportant. Earth was more than just the ground of all activity; it too was alive with powers and meaning.

The earliest references to geographic concepts in China are on the Shang dynasty oracle bones (see p.132), in which *si fang* ("four quarters") are routinely mentioned. These are sometimes specified as referring to the four cardinal directions. Other aspects of the earth, such as the winds, also came in sets of four and it is probably only the scarcity of written sources from the period that prevents scholars from saying that all of the world was conceived quadrilaterally. In any event, by the Eastern Zhou period, there was a great impulse to organize the earth.

Several texts dating from between the fifth and third centuries BCE attempt to order the earth and particularly its regions. The most important of these is probably the "Yu gong" or "Tribute of Yu" chapter of the *Shu Jing* (*Classic of Documents*). This earliest geography of China divides the realm into nine regions, more or less according to their natural features and characteristics. Later, more encyclopedic attempts to organize the world tended to render the nine regions more schematically, drawing them on a grid—the *Record of Rites*, one of the Confucian classics, even remarks: "within the four seas there are nine regions, each a 1,000 *li* squared [about 330 square miles/550km²]."

The adaptation of a four-directional arrangement of the earth to an arrangement in nine parts—the four cardinal directions (north, east, south, west), the four ordinal directions (northeast, southeast, southwest, northwest), and the center—is one of the most interesting transformations in Chinese intellectual history. It stood at the center of Chinese statecraft in the form of the *Ming tang* (Hall of Light), one of the most important ritual sites in the imperial capital (and the forerunner to the *Tian tan*, or "Altar of Heaven," that still stands in Beijing). The Hall of Light had a cruciform shape, with four outer chambers surrounding a central hall. The ruler was to proceed from one chamber to

the next in accordance with the seasons, returning also to the center at prescribed moments. In this way, he could regulate both space and time.

A royal procession also stands behind the earliest Chinese reference to a map. A bronze inscription of the Western Zhou period describes King Kang (ruled 1005–978BCE), before setting out on a royal procession, examining maps of processions made by his two predecessors, kings Wu (ruled 1049–1043BCE) and Cheng (ruled 1042–1006BCE). Bronze inscriptions from later in the dynasty refer to other sorts of maps and indicate that there was a Map Chamber in the royal palace.

It is not surprising that practical concerns should lie behind the need for maps. Indeed, some of the oldest maps yet discovered in China seem certainly to derive from a military use (see sidebar, opposite), and the most frequent mentions of maps in later periods are in military treatises.

The ceiling of the Temple of Heaven in Beijing, the most important enclosed ritual space in imperial China. Deriving from the ancient Hall of Light (see main text), its square base represents the earth and its round ceiling represents heaven. The emperor moved through this space in performing sacrifices (see p.88).

FENG SHUI

Feng shui, literally "Wind and Water," is the art of geomancy or the interpretation of the earth with the purpose of selecting auspicious sites for human structures. It is one of the most popular features of Chinese civilization in the West, owing perhaps to the intuitive appeal of some of the principles shared by all schools of *feng shui* in China. It is not difficult to appreciate the allure of the ideal site, or "dragon's lair," for a home—a spot nestled amid mountains to the rear and on either side, open to the south (the front), with a stream flowing gently before it. *Feng shui* is essentially just another manifestation of the unity of heaven, earth, and humankind, and interpreting the earth is in many ways similar to interpreting the heavens.

The roots of *feng shui* are certainly ancient in China. It is likely that some geomantic considerations were responsible for the siting of the last capital of the Shang dynasty at Anyang, or at least of the royal tombs to the north of the royal city. The east–west division of the tombs into two groups may reflect some social distinction among the various kings that cannot be attributed to geomancy, but the north–south orientation of the tombs does suggest great care in their placement: they are all directed toward true (astronomical) north, six degrees east of magnetic north.

With the establishment of the Zhou dynasty came the first documented city planning. The Zhou, a power based in the western Wei river valley in present-day Shaanxi province, were determined to build a new capital in the center of their newly conquered lands. Choosing a general location that is said to have been revealed in a dream to the dynastic founder, King Wu (see p.126), the Zhou dispatched the Grand Protector Shao Gong Shi to examine the site at the confluence of the Luo, Jian, and Chan rivers in what is today northern Henan province, just south of the Yellow river. The *Classic of Documents* describes the Grand Protector as laying out the

A modern copy of a traditional geomantic compass. Experts in feng shui *required a thorough grounding in almost all forms of Chinese divination, as well as a general understanding of the organization of the universe.*

RESPECTING THE DRAGON: SCHOOLS OF *FENG SHUI*

Only since the beginning of the Song dynasty has it become possible to discern some of the theories that underlie traditional Chinese geomancy. At that time, two schools emerged: the Compass School (or Directions and Positions School), and the Form School (or Forms and Configurations School).

As its name suggests, the Compass School emphasized the geomantic compass (see main text). Adherents of the Form School claimed to be more attuned to the life forces inherent in the earth itself. They examined the landscape, especially the shapes of hills and streams, to determine underground currents that were said to be the veins of a dragon. Members of this school advised clients against obstructing these veins or otherwise cutting too deeply into the earth. Especially in south China, this had the effect that buildings tended to fit into the natural environment rather than overpower it, and structures featured curving designs rather than severe angularity. In the flat plains of north China, however, it was harder for these theories to take root.

A grave in southern China near Hong Kong. In accordance with feng shui *theory, it is ideally positioned facing down a valley with a gentle hill behind.*

city of Luo (present-day Luoyang) according to divinations that he performed on the site. This canonical pedigree has made the Grand Protector the patron saint of geomancers.

During the Han dynasty geomancy was so popular that it was criticized as a "common belief" by the renowned Han skeptic Wang Chong (27–ca. 97ce). In this period, the imperial library kept copies of geomantic treatises known by the term *kan yu*, translated by Joseph Needham as "the canopy of Heaven and the chariot of Earth," which emphasizes the unity of heaven and earth in this type of divination.

From this same period there have also been discovered several examples of what is usually referred to as a *shi pan* ("Diviner's Board"), in two parts: a square, stationary bottom board, supposed to represent the earth, and a round, revolving top board that bears astronomical notations. Although it seems that this Diviner's Board had more immediate uses for astrologers than for geomancers, it was clearly the precursor of the later geomantic compass (*luo pan*), an instrument with a magnetic needle at its center, around which there are concentric rings with various astronomical, calendrical, and spatial indications (see illustration, opposite). These indications included aspects of the heavens such as the 28 lunar lodges (see p.125), the Five Elements (see pp.122–3), and the *Yi Jing* (see p.133).

DIVINATION

A turtle plastron used in Shang dynasty "oracle-bone" divination, excavated at the ancient Shang capital of Anyang in present-day Henan province. The earliest extant oracle bones date to the reign of the Shang king Wu Ding (ruled ca. 1215–1190BCE). Turtleshell divination continued as late as the Han dynasty and is mentioned in all of the Chinese classics.

Divination, the attempt to interpret omens in the world and through them to determine the future, was one of the most important fields of knowledge in traditional China. The earliest Chinese bibliography, which purported to catalog the Han dynasty imperial library, categorizes works on divination under the heading "Number and Skill," which in turn is divided into six subcategories: "Astronomy-Astrology," "Calendrics," "The Five Elements," "Milfoil and Turtleshell," "Miscellaneous Prognostications," and "Topography" (geomancy, or *feng shui*). Four of these subcategories are treated elsewhere in this chapter. Of the remaining two, turtleshell and milfoil divination are the most significant.

In 1899 "dragon bones"—an ingredient used in Chinese medicine—bearing incised characters began to appear in pharmacies in Beijing. Wang Yirong (1845–1900), a renowned expert on early writing, recognized these characters as a form of Chinese script even more archaic than that found on ancient bronze vessels, until then the oldest type of writing known in China. When the source of the bones—actually the plastrons (lower shells) of turtles and the scapulas (shoulderblades) of oxen—was traced to the city of Anyang in Henan province, the site of the last capital of the Shang dynasty, it became clear that the bones were over 3,000 years old.

Through comparison with later Chinese writing, scholars subsequently identified several thousand of the characters on the bones. As the inscriptions were deciphered, it became clear that they were the records of divinations performed on behalf of the Shang kings. For this reason these bones are now usually called "oracle bones." They also show vestiges of the act of divination itself: the bones were burned by putting red-hot brands into specially prepared sockets on the bone, causing cracks to appear on the surface. The cracks were interpreted by the royal diviners, who recorded the divination and its outcome on the bone.

"Oracle-bone" divination preceded virtually every aspect of royal government. The great affairs of state—sacrifices (including human offerings) to the ancestors, wars, harvests, and so on—of course feature prominently. But many aspects of the king's daily life also appear: for example, if he had toothache, he would seek to determine which of his ancestors was causing it (see also p.148).

Turtleshell divination was gradually supplanted by other types of divination, including most especially divination by milfoil, or yarrow, a type of plant with long, slender stalks that were sorted numerically. The dominant tradition of milfoil divination is associated with the text of the *Yi Jing* (see box, opposite).

THE *YI JING*

The *Yi Jing*, or *Classic of Changes*, is the most widely known of the ancient Chinese classics. It is organized around "eight trigrams" and "64 hexagrams," symbols (*gua*) consisting of respectively three and six solid or broken lines (see illustrations) obtained by the counting (sortilege) of yarrow stalks. For each line of each of the 64 hexagrams the *Yi Jing* provides a short cryptic statement open to different interpretations. These statements are used as the basis of divination.

The text of the *Yi Jing* took shape in the first millennium BCE. The earliest stratum, perhaps dating to ca. 800BCE, was probably a simple manual giving the results of milfoil divination. But in the Eastern Zhou period, the *Yi Jing* was transformed into a great repository of wisdom, largely owing to the *Da Zhuan* (*Great Commentary*), composed probably ca. 300BCE. This work provides a philosophical rationale for the *Yi Jing*, whereby changes in the hexagrams and lines are seen to replicate the process of the world's changeability. Unlike other books, the texts of which are fixed on the page, through divination the *Yi Jing* becomes alive, changing with each new reading.

This late-Qing charm and the Hong Kong lion dancer's mask (below) bear the Eight Trigrams and the yin-yang.

THE CALENDAR

A Chinese dragon embroidered on a late imperial silk robe. Above it is a representation of the moon. The "hare in the moon"—equivalent to the "man in the moon" in the West—is shown grinding the elixir of immortality.

The oracle-bone diviners of the Shang dynasty (see pages 132–3) took great care to indicate the day, and often the month and sometimes also the year, on which a divination was performed. Time would prove to be a continuing concern throughout Chinese history. One of the first responsibilities of any new dynasty was to regulate the calendar: if time were ever allowed to become disordered, the consequences would be dire.

As the oracle bones show, the fundamental Chinese conceptions of time were already in place in the Shang dynasty. The basic unit of time (at least for most record-keeping purposes) was the day, probably counted from midnight to midnight. Days were enumerated in a cycle of 60, produced by combining a set of ten *tiangan* ("heavenly stems") with another set of twelve *dizhi* ("earthly branches"). Although this could theoretically produce 120 different days, only 60 of them were actually used. (This same cycle of 60 was later used to number consecutive years.)

The ten *tiangan* apparently derive from the ten suns which, according to Chinese mythology, took turns crossing the daytime sky from east to west: while one sun was in the sky, the sun that had just completed its passage would be returning from west to east by swimming through the watery abyss under the earth to the Fusang Tree beyond the far eastern horizon, where the other eight suns awaited their turns (as depicted in the upper right section of the Mawangdui silk banner; see p.141). The twelve *dizhi* correspond to the twelve moons that usually appear in a year; indeed, these same designations were later routinely used to number the months of a year.

The 60-day cycle was divided into six "weeks" of ten days. Although in later times there were also seven- or eight-day units of time linked with the phases of the moon, these never displaced the ten-day week. However, the moon was the basis of the month (indeed, the same word, *yue*, means both "moon" and "month"). Months alternated between "long" months of 30 days and "short" months of 29 days to account for the 29.53-day mean period of a lunar cycle. Since this produced a year lasting only 354 days, it was necessary roughly every three years to add an extra month to bring the lunar year into line with the solar year. This is why the Chinese New Year fluctuates between late January and late February of the Western calendar.

While the mechanics of the Chinese calendar are reasonably simple, the importance of time in the worldview of traditional China cannot be stressed too greatly. In the Shang dynasty, ancestors were given posthumous names according to the days on which they received sacrifices. Also in the Shang, certain days were apparently already regarded as lucky or unlucky, which explains both why some day names were never given to ancestors and also why activities such as hunting only took place on particular days. In later times, almanacs indicated what to expect from certain activities conducted on specific days (see box, below).

ALMANACS

Almanacs, or *ri shu* ("day-books"), have become a pervasive and are very much a daily feature of Chinese life, and they were among the earliest printed books in China. To this day, the almanac remains almost certainly the single most widely distributed genre of book in China.

Ancient day-books have been discovered buried in tombs throughout China—the oldest, found in 1942 at Changsha, dates from ca. 300BCE—and various early texts also describe the activities of "day-men," experts at divining which days would be auspicious and which not. For instance, here is part of the section on "Clothing" in an almanac of the third century BCE from Shuihudi in Hubei province: "If you tailor clothes on *dingchou* [day fourteen of the Chinese cycle of 60 days], they will seduce others; on *dinghai* (day 24), they will be appealing to the spirits; on *dingsi* (day 54), they will be comfortable on your body; and on *guiyou* (day ten), there will be many clothes. Do not start wearing any new clothes on the day *jiwei* (day 56) of the ninth month, and in clothing the hands [on this day], one will certainly die."

Part of a modern New Year almanac. Even today, almanacs are found in almost every Chinese household.

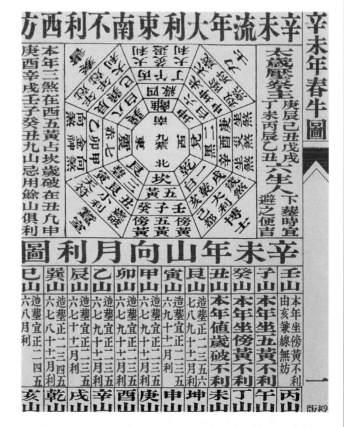

● CHAPTER 10 *Edward L. Shaughnessy*

THE REALM OF GHOSTS AND SPIRITS

A WORLD OF SPIRITS

IN TRADITIONAL CHINA, LIFE DID NOT END WITH DEATH. PEOPLE WERE THOUGHT TO LIVE ON IN VARIOUS WAYS. THOSE WHO HAD LIVED EXEMPLARY LIVES BECAME SPIRITS (*SHEN*), WHILE THOSE OF LESSER ACCOMPLISHMENTS BECAME GHOSTS (*GUI*). BOTH GHOSTS AND SPIRITS CONTINUED TO INTERVENE IN HUMAN EVENTS, AND HUMANS DID ALL THEY COULD TO INFLUENCE THE GHOSTS AND SPIRITS, IN ORDER TO ENSURE AS FAR AS POSSIBLE THAT THEIR INTERVENTIONS WERE BENEVOLENT.

The popular door god marks the entrance to a temple of the Chinese community in Penang, Malaysia.

Although many Europeans' first impression of China was of a highly rationalistic people (after all, it was said of Confucius that he did not speak of spirits and ghosts), anyone familiar with traditional China will appreciate the following description of the Chinese people by the great French Sinologist Marcel Granet (1884–1940): "They experienced the presence of a tutelary power whose sanctity sprang from every corner of the landscape, blessed forces which they strove to capture in every way." Spirits (*shen*) were everywhere. The heavens, of course, were filled with spirits: each of the stars had an identity and a power; Heaven itself was the greatest of the spirits. The earth too teemed with spirituality, each mountain and stream was imbued with spirit and inhabited by spirits, each animal and plant potentially a part of the religious system of the Chinese people. And the realm of man was not without its spirits; people—at least some of them—could be spirits too. Usually, to enter the realm of spirits one had to relinquish mortal life, but this was not always the case. Sometimes, especially in later periods, the living could engage with the spirit world by visualizing miniature spirits inhabiting the organs and viscera of the body.

China's earliest written records, the oracle-bone inscriptions of the Shang dynasty (see pp.132–3), record that sacrifices were made to sacred beings of all sorts, but especially to the ancestors. Curiously, the Shang high god, Shang Di (God on High), was never the recipient of sacrifices; apparently he could be approached only by intermediaries in the spirit realm. Apparently, too, at this time a competing religion was beginning to develop: that of the Zhou people with its high god Tian (Heaven). There are later stories of a Shang king who filled a leather pouch with blood and then shot it with an arrow, mockingly claiming to have killed Heaven. This magic did not work—the Zhou overthrew the Shang and Heaven became the god of all under it.

Not only did Heaven—a deity which, if not quite personified, was at least individualized (it certainly had a will of its own)—become the god of all, it also became the abode of almost all the other gods and

The moon (left) and the sun (right) are personified in this 11th-century handscroll as respectively a female and male deity. On her headdress the goddess bears an image of the hare which, according to tradition, lives on the moon and pounds the elixir of immortality (see also p.134). The image of a bird on the headdress of her consort represents the sun.

The god Tai Yi (top, with splayed legs), as depicted in the Diagram for Repelling Weapons, *a text discovered in 1973 at Mawangdui in Hunan province. Tai Yi is assisted by other gods, two of whom are identified as Rain Master and Thunder Lord.*

spirits. Some of these were easy enough to see. Tai Yi (Grand One), the god of war during the Han dynasty, was depicted sometimes as a spirit with legs splayed, sometimes as a spear; this depiction derives both from his name—written with a character shaped like a spear—and his appearance in the night sky as a group of stars in the shape of a triangle just above the Big Dipper (Plow). As time went on and the heavens were mapped in ever greater detail, diagrams of the spiritual pantheon also became ever more detailed: in later Daoist sources, 36,000 different gods are elaborated in an intricate hierarchy.

Spirits also resided within the human body. In highly allusive language, the *Huangting Jing* or *Classic of the Yellow Court*, one of the earliest and most important scriptures of Daoism, describes these spirits and how they can be cultivated so that one can ultimately escape one's mortal body entirely. The complete text shows the bodily spirits to be a perfect microcosm of the spirits in the universe, and refers to the body in terms such as "celestial court" and "earthly barrier" (the areas between the eyebrows and the feet respectively) and "numinous terrace" (the heart).

WANDERING SOULS

Virtually everyone in traditional China believed in spirits and ghosts. Some spirits found their place in the heavens (see pp.136–7); those that did not became ghosts, often referred to as "those with no place to return." Ghosts were not usually as longlived as spirits, who in theory were immortal, but they could certainly cause trouble for some time after the death of their human body.

Perhaps the earliest discussion of ghosts in China tells of Bo You, a nobleman of the state of Zheng in the Eastern Zhou period, who was killed in 543BCE in a conspiracy led by Si Dai and Gongsun Duan. Eight years later, in 535BCE, Si Dai and Gongsun Duan died and terror spread throughout Zheng in the belief that Bo You's ghost had returned. The hero of this story, Zi Chan, ended the panic by promoting Bo You's son to an official position, with the responsibility of maintaining his father's tomb. As Zi Chan explained: "When ghosts have someplace to return,

A Tang dynasty illustration to a Buddhist text showing sinners being punished before an official of the underworld. According to Buddhist and Daoist conceptions of the afterlife, almost everybody lives as a ghost for a time, being taken to purgatory to atone for their sins on earth. To control such ghosts, these religions established hierarchies of officials in the underworld as elaborate as those on earth.

then they do not cause evil; I have given him a place to return."

Zi Chan subsequently gave the earliest description of the Chinese notion of the human souls. He said that life first begins, apparently in the womb, with what he called a "moon-soul" (*po*). Then, at birth, it is infused—presumably on taking its first breath of air or *qi*—with what Zi Chan called a "cloud-soul" (*hun*). If properly nurtured, these souls could become strong and could even attain "spiritual brightness," evidently the state of an immortal. But if a person died a violent death, the two souls would still remain reliant on others and if they were not cared for, the deceased would create trouble. The more prominent the person was in life, the more trouble could be caused after death.

One of the most important Chinese funerary rituals, "Summoning the Cloud-Soul," was performed just before burial. It was thought that at death the *hun* floated off, returning to its original place in the heavens. Every effort was made to bring it back to the body so that it did not roam aimlessly but could be nurtured by the offerings in the grave. When the ritual was successful, a jade plug was put into the corpse's mouth, the door of the body, so that the *hun* would not get out again.

GHOST TALES

The ghost story has been one of most popular forms of literature throughout Chinese history. In 1986 at Fangmatan in Gansu province, archaeologists unearthed in a tomb what is perhaps the earliest ghost tale yet found. The story is cast in the form of an official report on a case that happened in 300BCE. A man named Dan committed suicide after stabbing a neighbor. The villagers buried Dan, but three years later the village headman petitioned the gods to let him come back to life, arguing that Dan had taken his own life before he was fated to do so. The gods sent a white dog to dig up the tomb and release Dan, who bore the scar where he had slit his throat and his four limbs were "useless."

Demons fighting with each other, painted on the wooden tomb of Lady Dai (died ca. 166BCE), excavated in 1972 at Mawangdui in Changsha, Hunan province.

Dan described the realm of the dead and also offered some advice to the living: "The dead do not want many clothes. People think that wrapping offerings in white cogon-grass makes them auspicious, but ghosts think offerings are auspicious no matter how they are wrapped. But those who offer sacrifices ought not to spit. If they spit, the ghosts flee in fright."

DEATH AND BURIAL

ZHUANGZI AND FATE
The great Daoist philosopher Zhuangzi (ca. 365–285BCE), whose eponymous book stands today as one of the great treasures of both Chinese thought and literature, was criticized by a friend for singing just after the death of his wife. Zhuangzi admitted that he had grieved when she died, but then had thought better of it. He realized that "in the midst of the jumble of wonder and mystery, a change took place and she had a spirit. Another change and she was born. Now there's been another change and she's dead. It's just like the progression of the four seasons ... If I were to follow after her, bawling and sobbing, it would show that I don't understand anything about fate."

Whether destined to be ghost or spirit, all humans were understood to share the common fate of death. Attitudes toward death could vary widely. In a letter to an acquaintance condemned to death, Sima Qian (ca. 145–86BCE), the imperial Grand Astronomer-Historian, defended his own decision to choose the shame of castration instead of the honor of suicide when he himself had been condemned some years before, because "some deaths are heavier [that is, more significant] than Mount Tai, while other deaths are lighter than a goose feather." According to Sima, the suicide of a mere historian would be trivial. What is more, continuing to live, even in a reduced state, allowed him to complete his *Records of the Historian (Shi Ji)*, the first great history of China.

On the other hand, the Daoist mystic Zhuangzi could almost dismiss death entirely (see sidebar, left). However, few could face death with such nonchalance, perhaps especially the death of loved ones. The Shang dynasty king Wu Ding (ruled ca. 1215–1190BCE) had the tomb of his favorite consort, Fu Hao, furnished with incredible riches: excavated in 1976 at Anyang in Henan province, the tomb contained over 440 bronzes, 590 jade carvings, and nearly 7,000 cowrie shells, among other treasures (see p.24)—not to mention sixteen human sacrifices. Fortunately for the excavators, Fu Hao's tomb was preserved by the foundations of a temple that Wu Ding had built over it. Many other tombs, including that of Wu Ding himself and the other Shang kings who reigned at Anyang, did not lie in peace for nearly so long.

The prevalence of grave robbing already in antiquity touched off a debate that lasted from the time of Confucius to at least the end of the Han dynasty, and doubtless well beyond that: what sort of burial was most appropriate? This was an especially vexing question among the followers of Confucius, many of whom seem to have earned their living as professional undertakers. Given that one's emotional response to the death of a loved one is deeply felt and sincere, simply throwing the corpse into a ditch would be emotionally unbearable.

A pair of glazed pottery qitou (guardian spirits) of the Tang dynasty. Such fierce figures were placed in tombs to ward off evil influences.

It was a filial son's responsibility to bury the dead properly—the grave should be neither so shallow that animals could dig up the corpse, nor so deep that underground water would seep into the tomb. On the other hand, furnishing a tomb with too many riches would be an invitation to robbers to plunder it. Already by the mid-third century BCE, the *Lüshi chunqiu*, a sort of encyclopedia compiled for a prime minister of the state of Qin, criticized the ostentatious burials of the time: "Extravagance is considered glorious, frugality demeaning. [The people] are not motivated by what is of convenience to the dead but simply devote themselves to what the living might praise or blame. These are not the feelings of a loving parent or filial child."

The text goes on to describe how contemporary tombs were furnished: "As states grow larger and families richer, burials become more elaborate. Such a burial includes a pearl put in the mouth of the corpse, a jade shroud that covers the body like fish scales, silk cords and bamboo documents, trinkets and treasures, bronze goblets, tripods, pots, and basins, horse-drawn carriages, clothes and coverlets, as well as halberds and swords—all too numerous to count. Every utensil required to nurture the living is included." Even this did not suffice for the tomb of Qin Shihuangdi, the First Emperor (ruled 221–210BCE), in whose reign the *Lüshi chunqiu* was compiled. His tomb was designed to be a perfect model of the universe, including not only all the types of artifact described above, but also rivers and seas of mercury, with the patterns of heaven painted on the ceilings and all the configurations of earth on the floors.

The magnificent terracotta army buried near the tomb (see p.187) forms only a tiny portion of the whole site. The tomb itself has not yet been excavated, although it was almost certainly robbed at least twice in antiquity. Archaeologists have been busy all over China, opening tombs of all periods and of individuals of all different social backgrounds. Their discoveries of how the dead were buried have transformed our understanding of how people lived—and died—in traditional times (see also p.60).

A funeral banner painted on silk, from the tomb of Lady Dai at Mawangdui (see p.139). It depicts the lady in old age (middle), in death (below), and resurrected as a young woman again (above).

SERVING THE ANCESTORS

SUMPTUARY LAWS

During the Eastern Zhou dynasty the sets of ritual vessels placed in burials became so elaborate that laws were decreed limiting private expenditure on the goods that could be provided for one's ancestors. Called "sumptuary laws," they stipulated that kings could have sets of nine caldrons and eight tureens; lords of states seven caldrons and six tureens; great officers five caldrons and four tureens; and gentry three caldrons and two tureens. Archaeological evidence does reflect a system of this sort, and archaeologists often rely on the number of vessels found in a tomb to determine the status of their owner. However, it is sometimes clear that owners commissioned more than the number to which they were entitled.

Death and burial did not end the responsibilities of the living toward the dead, who continued to exist and to require sustenance. Some of this sustenance was already buried with the deceased in the tomb, but much more was provided in the way of offerings and sacrifices in the ancestral temple. Already in the oracle-bone inscriptions of the Shang dynasty (see pp.132–3), there are numerous divinations that seek to determine what would be an auspicious offering: oxen, pigs, or even humans. By the end of the dynasty, five types of offerings to the royal ancestors had been developed into a sacrificial system that filled every day of a 360-day year.

The following Zhou dynasty developed a system of ancestor offerings that would define the relations between living and dead throughout China's traditional period. Sometime in the middle of the Western Zhou period, there was a radical transformation in the way Zhou society was organized. A government that had been characterized by patriarchy was now bureaucratic, and families that had been close-knit were now extended to lineages and sublineages. Thanks to recent archeological discoveries, it is now possible to see—quite literally—another manifestation of this social transformation. Whereas in the early Western Zhou vessels used to make offerings to the ancestors were made in relatively small individual sets that were placed in the tombs of the deceased, around the middle of the dynasty (ca. 900BCE) ever more elaborated sets

HUMAN SACRIFICE

The Shang oracle-bone inscriptions and the archaeological excavations at the Shang capital of Anyang revealed considerable evidence of human sacrifice. Scholars were not surprised, since there was some mention of ancient human sacrifice in the traditional literary record, and Confucius' complaint against the use of pottery figurines in burials instead of human victims was well known. (In Confucius' view, even though no blood was let, the practice still reflected a sense that humans were disposable.)

Confucius lived not long after the death of Duke Mu of the state of Qin in 621BCE, whose burial is said to have been accompanied by 177 human victims, three of whom were noblemen of Qin celebrated in a song of the

Classic of Poetry (*Shi Jing*). In 1977 archaeologists thought that they had found Duke Mu's final resting place when they discovered an enormous tomb—1,000 feet (300m) long by 80 feet (24m) deep—containing 166 human victims at Fengxiang in Shaanxi province, the heartland of the ancient Qin state.

However, further study revealed that the Fengxiang tomb was not that of Duke Mu, but that of his great-great grandson, Duke Jing (ruled 576–537BCE). Jing died when Confucius was fifteen years old, so perhaps Confucius objected even to pottery sacrificial victims because real human sacrifice itself was still widespread in his own day.

A lord of the underworld, where a register is kept of all humans, living and dead. He is portrayed during Hong Kong's annual Tin Hau festival. Tin Hau is the Cantonese name of the goddess Tian Hou (see p.102).

This strange antlered bird was buried with Lord Yi of Zeng at Leigudun, Hubei province, in the 5th century BCE. Five feet (1.5m) high, it stood next to the coffin and was perhaps intended to protect it (see also p.207).

were produced that were kept in the ancestral temples. Still later, the number and types of vessels that one could make for one's ancestors came to be regulated by laws (see sidebar, opposite).

Beginning around the time of Confucius (551–479BCE), Chinese social practices came to have an explicit philosophical underpinning, and responsibilities to one's ancestors were certainly no exception. Confucius emphasized that ancestor rituals must be meaningful and not mere show; one's internal feelings would determine their efficacy. He also referred to an important ritual practice that would continue throughout traditional Chinese history: the need for a son to mourn the deaths of his parents for three full years. This mourning period, which required complete retirement from public life for three years, was criticized as excessive even in antiquity, but Confucians regarded it as an emotional necessity.

ARTS OF TRANSFORMATION

A Ming-dynasty portrait of the First Emperor, Qin Shihuangdi (ruled 221–210BCE), the earliest imperial patron of alchemy.

秦始皇

Given a worldview that saw heaven, earth, and humankind as intimately related, with each of the three realms but another dimension of the other two (see pp.120–21), and given also the notion that the human body replicated this macrocosm in miniature, it was perhaps natural that China should have developed a long tradition of alchemy—the attempt to transform the common into the precious. While alchemists in other parts of the world often aimed to attain riches by producing gold from base metals, in China they more often had spiritual goals. True, the earliest form of Chinese alchemy involved attempts to produce gold. However, the goal was not to become rich but immortal; gold was considered the one incorruptible element in nature, and it was thought that ingesting gold in sufficient quantities could also make the human body incorruptible. This came to be known as "external alchemy" (*wai dan*). A second form of Chinese alchemy, known as "internal alchemy" (*nei dan*), shared this goal of immortality but attempted to transform only the elements within one's own body. Internal alchemy was an integral part of many different meditation practices and was also intimately related to the theory and practice of traditional Chinese medicine (see pp.158–61).

One of the earliest references to alchemy involves the First Emperor, Qin Shihuangdi, who united all of China in 221BCE. He went to great lengths during his life to try to avoid death. A polemical Confucian text of the succeeding Han dynasty says that at the time of the First Emperor people throughout the empire "set aside their plows and hoes and competed to make themselves heard on the subject of immortals and magicians. They asserted that the immortals had eaten gold and drunk pearls, so that their lives would last as long as heaven and earth."

The oldest extant alchemical treatise in China is the *Can tong qi*, a very ambiguous title but probably meaning something like *The Compound of the Three Communions*. It is attributed to Wei Boyang, who is said to have lived in the second century CE. The "three communions" of the title seem to refer to the three major topics of the text: the *Zhou Yi* or *Changes of Zhou* (that is, the *Classic of Changes*, or *Yi Jing*), external alchemy, and internal alchemy. The *Can tong qi* has never been successfully translated, and perhaps never can be, since the theory and practice of the text are completely integrated: the theory is that these three different fields share the same principles and "commune with" each other. This is reflected in the elusive and ambiguous language of the work, which make the *Can tong qi* one of the great puzzles of world literature.

Recent years have brought a renewed study of external alchemy in China. During most of the twentieth century, alchemy, and particularly external alchemy, was dismissed in China as a superstition. However, after attracting the interest of Western historians of religion and science, it is now seen as an important offshoot of science and the scientific method.

CINNABAR

Despite the Confucian disapproval of both the First Emperor and his fondness for alchemy (see main text), the ingestion of gold—or, rather, of transformed gold—appears to have remained quite popular throughout the Han dynasty. However, most Han dynasty alchemists worked with cinnabar, sometimes with fatal results. Cinnabar (mercury sulfide) is an ore of mercury that is a deep vermilion in color. When heated, cinnabar produces liquid mercury, and further heating and combination of mercury and sulfur will in turn reproduce cinnabar (a cyclical transformation that particularly intrigued Chinese alchemists). Mercury was further amalgamated with other metals (gold and lead in particular) producing elixirs to be ingested.

While cinnabar itself was non-toxic—indeed it still maintains a prominent place in traditional Chinese medicine—the mercury amalgams, especially with lead, could be lethal when ingested. There are accounts of a number of emperors and other devotees of immortality cults who died as a result of their alchemical practices. This may have been a catalyst for the subsequent development of internal alchemy, although not everyone necessarily regarded this sort of death as a failure. Some alchemists explained these deaths as "corpse release," the sloughing off of the mortal body and allowing the soul or souls (see pp.138–9) within to become immortal, flying off to take their place among other immortals.

This 18th-century cinnabar-lacquer table screen depicts scholars playing chess under a pine tree as their attendant looks on.

Part 3

CREATION AND DISCOVERY

One of the most useful navigational inventions was the magnetic compass, developed in China by the early centuries CE. *This late imperial example forms part of a portable sundial and compass*

OPPOSITE *The pagoda of the monastery of the Ten Thousand Buddhas in Hong Kong. Bearing little resemblance to the ancient Indian* stupa *from which it is derived, the pagoda is a distinctively Chinese contribution to Buddhist architecture (see pp.222–3).*

● CHAPTER 11 *Vivienne Lo*

HEALING AND MEDICINE

THE SOURCES OF MEDICAL TRADITION

UNTIL RECENTLY, MEDICAL HISTORIANS FAMILIAR WITH THE RECEIVED CANONS OF CHINESE MEDICINE TENDED TO PRESENT THE TRADITION AS A SINGLE AND INTERNALLY CONSISTENT BODY OF KNOWLEDGE THAT WAS UNCHANGING THROUGH TIME. FRESH APPROACHES TO CLASSICAL WORKS COMBINED WITH NEW SOURCE MATERIAL HAVE EXPOSED THE RICH VARIETY OF MEDICINAL PRACTICES THAT ALWAYS EXISTED SIDE BY SIDE IN CHINESE SOCIETY.

Chinese patients often made use diagnostic dolls, such as this ivory female figure of ca. 1800, to indicate the part of the body that was causing them discomfort or pain, thus avoiding the need to undress in front of the doctor.

Countless scholars have devoted themselves to interpreting the canons of Chinese medicine over the ages. Newly discovered archaeological evidence, and studies of individual physicians' records of their patients' case histories, reveal a long trend of innovation and diversity in Chinese medical practice. Regional differences, as well as political and social factors, have had distinct influences on the way individuals and groups have constructed and interpreted classical medicine. While most Chinese written sources give limited descriptions of an élite and male-dominated medical profession, some texts throw new light on popular and female medical history.

Our knowledge of Chinese medical practice during the Warring States and Han periods is gleaned mainly from anonymous technical or philosophical treatises. Authors and compilers tended to attribute their work to the early revelations of legendary teachers or sage emperors and their ministers. As students of medicine, early imperial physicians often copied sections of manuscripts and arranged them in an order that reflected a succession of teachers from different medical lineages or families. This accounts for the existence of four large collections of short treatises on acupuncture and moxibustion, which are collectively known as the *Huangdi Neijing* (*The Yellow Emperor's Inner Canon*). The legendary Yellow Emperor, Huangdi (who is said to have lived 2697–2597BCE), is known as the "Father of Medicine." Much of the medical theory contained in *The Yellow Emperor's Inner Canon* (compiled around the turn of the Common Era) is revealed in dialogue form between the emperor himself, represented as a patron of natural philosophy, and his minister Qibo, a specialist in acupuncture and other esoteric matters.

The value that educated people placed on such medical manuscripts may explain the presence of early collections

of similar material in Han-dynasty family tombs, such as the three found at Mawangdui in Changsha, the capital of modern Hunan province. Among the texts found in Tomb 3 at Mawangdui (see p.126) were seven medical manuscripts that reflect the theories of *yin* and *yang*, magic, ritual incantations, sexual practices, meditation, and prescriptions made up of every conceivable herb, animal, and household substance.

The rapid expansion of commerce in general and of the printing industry, in particular, during the Ming period, brought about a popularization of medical knowledge. Direct contact between master physician and disciple became less important as essential texts were distributed more widely than before. In families of hereditary physicians, the later generations would publish and promote their forefathers' writings, no doubt to recount successful treatments, prove theoretical points, and demonstrate new techniques. Case histories, which also became popular, give us an impression of how medical theory was put into practice.

Finally, literature, and especially novels from the Ming and Qing periods provide us with a colorful impression of the complexity of the Chinese medical world. It is arguable that these images of everyday life are no more or less distorted than physicians' own accounts of their work.

A traditional qigong *practitioner uses ancient healing techniques to assist a patient in Guangzhou.*

HEALERS AND THEIR ART

Research into the history of medical care in China reveals an elaborate system of competing and complementary practitioners: at any one time, scholar-physicians, religious healers, wise women, and healing programs run by millenarian cults may all have coexisted. However, the work of individual scholar-physicians are best documented, and they sometimes influenced the development of Chinese medical theory. For example, after an epidemic had decimated his town, Zhang Zhongjing (142–220CE) wrote two much-quoted treatises on febrile diseases. His pharmacological work was continued in the Song, Jin, and Yuan periods by a new breed of scholar-physicians who wrote innovative treatises, often hailed as schools of thought in their own right. Some respected physicians, such as Sun Simiao (ca. 581–682CE), were later deified as medicine gods.

During the Shang dynasty, divination may have been essential to appease an offending ancestor, but at other times divinatory and calendrical calculations were applied to determine the course and outcome of an illness. Religious practitioners, often women, also carried out medical work

This set of Chinese surgical instruments in a folding leather case dates from the 18th century.

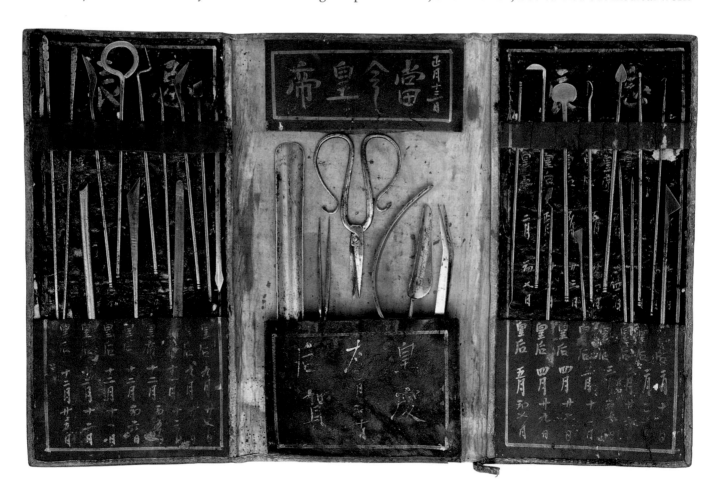

TALES OF SEX AND MEDICINE

Jingpingmei is a late-Ming erotic novel, set in the twelfth century CE, which charts the sexual exploits of a minor official named Ximen Qing, his six wives, and numerous maidservants. The novel arguably provides a fair representation of the complex medical practices of the late sixteenth-century world in which its author lived.

The largest group of practitioners attendant on the fictional family are literate, male doctors who practice classical medicine—they take the pulse and write detailed prescriptions. There are also male religious specialists who prescribe pills, make divinatory calculations, and communicate with spirits. The women tend to prefer the informal ministrations of Granny Liu—who takes the pulse and prescribes drugs, but also leads spirit possession rituals—and of midwives and Buddhist nuns who provide charms, potions, and spiritual consolation.

A 19th-century watercolor by Zhou Pei Qun shows a doctor taking a female patient's pulse using the tips of his index, middle, and ring fingers to apply pressure in three different positions on her wrist.

that was closely related to their spiritual duties. They were experts in divination—which they used to diagnose illness—and were able to invoke the honorific titles of deities, and summon spirits and ancestors to aid in healing, as well as manipulate effigies of the patient to heal (or harm) them.

Technical literature testifies that both religious and magical medicine were at one time integral to the scholarly medical traditions. However, by the mid-second century BCE those practicing medicine based on natural philosophy certainly regarded themselves as the guardians of a sacred, text-based medical tradition.

While the development of pharmacology was an integral part of Daoist alchemy, with the arrival after the first century CE of Buddhism, monks began to prescribe drugs and dietetic measures, meditative routines, and breath-control exercises. Amulets, incantations, and introspection were a cure for illnesses caused by demons and evil gods.

In the late nineteenth and early twentieth centuries, repressive measures were taken to marginalize superstitious practices. Nevertheless, traditional Chinese medicine continued to flourish at a local level, and its status was partially restored after the communists came to power.

THE CASEBOOK OF CHUNYU YI

Chunyu Yi was a professional Han physician who, like government advisors since the time of Confucius, traveled from one court to another selling his services. In Sima Qian's account of Chunyu Yi's life, Yi is said to have been arraigned on an unknown charge and his education, professional competence, and therapeutic successes are called into question. In his defense he lists his teachers and methods of learning, his medical skills, and the books he owns. His description of 44 case histories from his mostly well-to-do clientele provides us with a great deal of evidence about the social history of medicine, as well as its theory and practice in second-century BCE China.

QI AND HUMAN PHYSIOLOGY

The essential elements of traditional Chinese physiological theory, considered central to health and well-being, were *shen* (the spirit that resided in the heart), *jing* (its finest manifestation), and *qi* (the all-pervasive energy that powers the universe). The earliest references to *qi* from Shang and Zhou inscriptions are associated with food and sustenance. These perhaps anticipate the life-giving and revitalizing qualities that eventually came to be associated with *qi*. References dating from the middle of the Warring States period tend to use the term *qi* to describe atmospheric and environmental conditions, especially moist vapors—clouds and mists—and, by analogy, formless, clustering qualities such as smoke, or ghosts.

By the mid-fourth century CE the term *qi* was being used to describe the fundamental stuff in nature which both promoted and indicated vitality in the phenomenal world. It was also often employed to describe an intensification of sensation experienced within the body—one of heat, pain, pleasure, or passion. There had already been an important transition in the concept of *qi* from those environmental qualities which one could observe and to which the body was subject, such as the passing of the seasons, to *qi* as a body constituent over which individuals were able to exercise control.

On the whole, inner-body *qi* was thought to be invisible, and could be sensed only by the individual or perhaps by a physician through the demeanor and complexion of the patient or the quality of the pulse. One exception was the convergence of signs of redness, burning pain, and fever which were visible as "red *qi*," a correlate of pathological heat. In the earliest times, *qi* was thought to travel from above to below. Rising *qi*, like heat, was believed to be almost always related to a pathological condition, often associated with breathing difficulties. Emotions, both normal and pathological, were also seen as a "fullness of *qi*"—particularly in relation to martial valor, anger, and belligerence. A man who loved to fight was said to be *hao qi* "tending to *qi*" and even today *sheng qi*, literally "producing *qi*," means "to be angry."

In the centuries following the unification of the empire, *qi* became the fundamental unifying principle of Chinese medical theory, which differentiates many grades of *qi*. Normal *qi* could be polluted by perverse, even evil emanations, and in the inner organs *qi* takes on particular characteristics. Liver *qi*, for example, has a tendency to rise and cause havoc, heat, pain, and bad humor.

The character for qi *includes the particle for "cloudy vapors" (below) and may refer to rising steam.*

THE "FLOOD-LIKE *QI*"

The swell and fall of the waters of the Yellow and Yangzi rivers have been both a source of life and also the cause of large-scale annihilation to the Chinese people. Water itself came to be an analogy for moral strength, for life, and for the passage of time, and the water metaphor informed the Chinese medical conception of the human body.

According to the sage Laozi, the ruler—like the rivers and oceans—should seek the lowest position in order to establish the most natural and heavenly authority. For Mencius, human nature spontaneously moves toward the good, just as water flows downward. He consciously cultivated "flood-like *qi*," which is said to bring in its wake courage, calm, and sturdiness.

In the same way that controlling and directing the flow water is seen as one of the first steps to a civilized world, so channeling *qi* into routes around the body marks a significant stage in bringing the body—conceived of as a natural process—under human control. Thus the metaphor of water for *qi* pervades *The Yellow Emperor's Inner Canon* (see p.148), most remarkably when it matches the natural waterways of China to the acupuncture channels.

A mist-covered landscape in the Huangshan mountains, Hunan province. The banks of low cloud call to mind the "cloudy vapors" of the character for qi *(see opposite). Scholars often translate* qi *as "vapor" and, in doing so, underline the amorphous, watery qualities of steam and mist.*

THE STRUCTURE
OF THE BODY

Chinese perceptions of the various structures and functions of the human body mirrored China's philosophical, political, and religious realities, replicating every aspect of the natural and human worlds in anatomical and physiological form. Chinese medical texts have described the body as containing the entire universe: the sun and moon, stars and constellations, mountain ranges, waterways, animals, and plants all find emblematic representation. Patterns of human organization, administrative, and architectural plans are also thought to be reflected in the body's structures.

It was thought that in the physical space of the viscera there dwelt various spirits and souls, such as the *shen*—the spirit that resided in the heart and determined a person's radiance and acuity. Han-dynasty medical texts describe how a weakness of the *hun* and *po* entities, or the souls that lived in the blood and lungs respectively, could cause an individual psychological distress and dream-disturbed sleep. After death, some believed that the deceased's *hun* and *po* might remain around the gravesite where, if unattended, they would cause trouble (see p.139).

During the late Warring States period the rise of *yin* and *yang* theories led to descriptions of the body that were based on dualisms such as interior and exterior, up and down, and hot and cold. Early imperial political philosophers adopted and expanded a complementary conceptual framework that was governed by the proper interaction of the Five Elements: wood, fire, earth, metal, and water. When applied to illness within the body, these agents matched specific seasons, colors, emotions, viscera, and physiological functions, as well as the acupuncture channels. For example, the lung or great *yin* channel, which began in the lungs and traveled to the thumb, was associated with the autumn, white, and grief; it also generated the skin and hair, breathing, and the transformation of *qi*.

Each individual could be assessed according to how the special characteristics of their symptoms and constitution revealed a disruption in the

A 16th- to 18th-century bronze figure illustrating the points that can be treated to influence the bodily "channels" fundamental to acupuncture and other traditional therapies (compare illustration on p.156).

interaction of these five agents. By stimulating one of the acupuncture channels just under the surface of the body, a practitioner was able to adjust the whole spectrum of a person's organic, physiological, emotional, and spiritual being.

After the political unification of China under the authority of a single emperor, medical literature came to mirror the theme of unification in a new concept of the body. All aspects of human physiology were drawn together under the unifying influence of *qi* (see p.52). As if to stamp imperial power at the core of each individual, every organ of the body was also believed to play a role in the administration of the "empire," just as a state official took charge of various ministries.

The earliest datable references to the acupuncture points are those in manuscripts excavated from a tomb at Wuwei, which was sealed in the first century BCE. The points had names that reflected the structure of the imperial palace, the natural world, and the heavens. *Tianshu* ("heavenly pivot"), *riyue* ("sun and moon"), and *shangxing* ("upper star") reflect the cosmic order of the universe; *shenting* ("spirit hall"), *shenzhu* ("body pillar"), and *neigong* ("inner palace") represent the imperial architecture of the body; and Kunlun shan ("Kunlun mountains"), *zhaohai* ("illuminated sea"), along with many springs, streams, and marshes, chart the topography and watercourses of the natural

PANGU

A recurrent theme in Chinese medicine is that the body and its physiology are a microcosm of the universe and its movements. In what amounts to a reversal of these images, the body of Pangu, the cosmic giant who holds heaven and earth apart in the Chinese creation myth, literally transforms into the features of the universe:

"His breath became the wind and clouds; his voice became the thunder. His left eye became the sun; his right eye became the moon. His four limbs and five extremities became the four cardinal points and the five sacred mountains. His blood and semen became the water and rivers. His muscles and veins became the earth's arteries; his flesh became fields and land. The hair on his head and his beard became the stars; the hair on his body became plants and trees. His teeth and bones became metal and rock; his vital marrow became pearls and jade. His sweat and bodily fluids became streaming rain. All the mites on his body were touched by the wind and were turned into the black-haired people [=the Chinese]."

An 18th-century depiction of Pangu (see p.122). He is often shown clothed in leaves; sometimes he also has horns on his head and holds the sun and moon.

ACUPUNCTURE
AND MOXIBUSTION

According to Chinese mythology, the legendary Yellow Emperor was the earliest patron of acupuncture and moxibustion. In *The Yellow Emperor's Inner Canon* (see p.148), the body is described as being divided into twelve distinct *jingmai*—the "vessels" or "channels" through which *qi*, the fundamental vitality of life, was thought to move rhythmically around the body. The texts describe ten of these channels as linking specific internal organs to the skin where, at certain locations, burning moxibustion or inserting one of nine types of needle could stimulate *qi*. These locations came to be known as *zhenxue*, literally "needle pits," or acupuncture points. Fine metal needles were thought to be most subtle and effective for influencing the flow of *qi* and *jing* (the finest manifestation of *qi*).

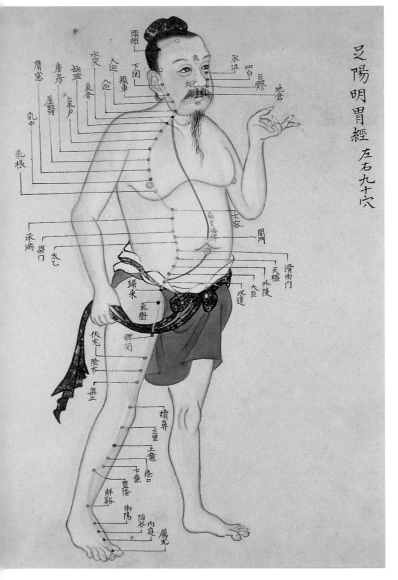

This 19th-century painting of a male figure is labeled with acupuncture points.

Acupuncture and moxibustion (see box, opposite) were first linked in Han times, although the procedures used were quite unlike the treatments known today. The biography of the semimythical physician Bian Que mentions the use of *zhen* (needle) and *shi* (stone) to treat the blood, and *mai*, an early form of the channels. Acupuncture and moxibustion arose from a synthesis of early medical practices with new ideas about physiology that flourished in the culture of self-cultivation (see pp.158–9).

With the imposition of imperial authority, existing medical traditions began to be re-invented. Recent archaeological discoveries from the Western Han period help us to piece together that process. Two manuscripts describe the body as having eleven *mai*, the names of which are similar to those of the channels of classical theory. A small, black-lacquered wooden figurine (buried no later than 118BCE) with ten red-lacquer lines painted on its surface has also been found. The manuscripts and figurine—which chart lines and pathways reflecting superficial aspects of skeletal, muscular, and arteriovenous structures, and give no evidence of acupuncture points—are thought to be attempts to formalize ideas about the experience and relief of pain.

Before the discovery of the Western Han figurine, the earliest extant medical models of the human body were cast bronze figurines dating from the Northern

MOXIBUSTION AND OTHER HEAT THERAPIES

Moxibustion is a healing technique related to, and sometimes combined with, acupuncture. It uses moxa, a substance prepared from the dried and ground leaves of *Artemisia vulgaris* (Chinese or common mugwort). In the earliest records, moxa was hung around the door of the family home and on the clothes to ward off demons. Modern practitioners of traditional Chinese medicine burn ready-prepared rolls of moxa or numerous cones of the herb on or over acupuncture points and/or painful areas of the body. Sometimes moxa balls are burnt on the needle handle in order to conduct the heat further into the body.

Moxibustion arises from the most fundamental medical observation that heat relieves pain. Cautery was one of the earliest therapies to be applied to the channels and was said to stimulate the flow of blood and healing *qi*. Early heat treatments included pressing burning cords, mugwort rolls, and heated stones or tiles to the body to relieve anything from lizard bites to aching muscles.

A Song dynasty painting depicting a country doctor performing moxibustion treatment on a patient's back.

Song period. These teaching models clearly display the circulation network, and label the acupoints. When the model had been covered with a layer of yellow wax and filled with water, medical students had to locate the required acupoint exactly with a needle, causing water to gush out of the model through the hole.

Early acupuncture and moxibustion formed part of an élite medical tradition. It was popular at court during the Tang period and was on the curriculum of the Song Imperial Medical College. However, there were times when physicians slandered acupuncture as dangerous, or as the work of "women" and non-professionals. By 1822 it was banned at the imperial college and with the increasing hegemony of Western medical ideas in the early twentieth century the practice of acupuncture reached an all-time low. However, it was never entirely eliminated. During Mao Zedong's campaign of the late 1950's to promote national treasures, acupuncture began its modern revival with the establishment of new training centers, clinics, and hospitals.

"DEATH POINTS"

The knowledge of acupuncture points belongs to a more general culture of strategic body points in China. Dating from Southern Song times are a number of comprehensive specialist charts of points on the body where a criminal might inflict a fatal blow without fear of easy detection. These documents demonstrate a sophisticated knowledge of how the inner body and its vital systems react to stimulation at the surface of the skin—albeit for the purpose of murder rather than for cure. Such knowledge was naturally of value in the practice of the martial arts.

SELF-CULTIVATION

A reconstruction of a silk chart of 168BCE excavated at Mawangdui. It shows 44 figures engaged in the therapeutic movements known as daoyin ("guiding and pulling"; see main text).

In China the idea of self-cultivation, or *yangsheng* ("nurturing life"), embraces many practices aimed at strengthening the body, mind, and spirit. At the one end of the spectrum, self-cultivation might mean toning the musculature through a form of therapeutic exercise known as *daoyin* ("guiding and pulling"), but there was usually a higher ideal. In the philosophical texts of the Warring States period, the term *yangsheng* is often found in discussions about human nature. The great Confucian thinker Mencius (372–ca. 289BCE) believed in nourishing the seeds of goodness that grew within every heart (see p.79). For him, cultivating courage and morality meant nourishing "the flood-like *qi*" (see pp.152–3) with proper breathing techniques. The earliest extant description of such *qi*-enhancing practices, aimed at bringing heavenly influences into the body, is inscribed on a block of jade that dates to this time.

In the following centuries, a range of scholarly writings were sponsored and collected by élite families and these testify to a wide range of more esoteric, inner practices aimed at strengthening and preserving the body by refining its most fundamental essences, *jing* (see p.152) and *qi*.

At one extreme, this led certain groups to believe in the possibility of attaining physical immortality (see pp.94–5).

Common to many traditions of self-cultivation, and probably retained from earlier religious ideals, is the perception that the body is a crucible for transformations of its essences and spirits. One of the earliest texts to set out the advantages of breath cultivation systematically is the "Inner Training" chapter of the *Guanzi*—a politico-philosophical text attributed to Guan Zhang (died 645BCE), but probably compiled between the fifth and first centuries BCE. The *Guanzi* recommends stilling the heart and the breath in order to establish the triad of *qi, jing,* and *shen* ("spirit") and thus to ensure *shenming,* "illumination of the spirit." Once *shenming* occurs, the body is strong and sturdy, there is an acuity and clarity of the senses, and the skin shines with inner radiance.

Many of the concepts generated by self-cultivation practices left

A TEMPLE OF THE MARTIAL ARTS

Founded in 495CE, Shaolin temple in Henan province was one of the earliest Chinese centers for the translation of Buddhist texts and developed into a large, wealthy monastery. Bodhidharma, revered as the founder of Chan (Zen) Buddhism, may also have resided here ca. 530CE. He is also credited in legend with establishing the practice of martial arts for which Shaolin—sometimes nicknamed the "Kung Fu monastery"—is famous.

The first mention of "fighting monks" at Shaolin dates from the early seventh century CE, when the emperor Gaozu was aided in battle by thirteen of its monks. It is difficult to gauge to what extent and in what form martial arts were practiced there, but by the Ming dynasty Shaolin was a renowned fighting center. It was especially famous for the practice of martial arts using a staff.

In the late Ming and Qing dynasties, Shaolin fighting techniques spread throughout China. In 1553, some Shaolin monks helped defend Fujian province against the

incursions of Japanese pirates, although in 1561 one general, Yu Dayou, was highly critical of a sword style he saw demonstrated at the temple. Many styles of martial arts that emerged during the late Qing, often among secret societies, claimed to trace their lineage back to the fighting monks of Shaolin.

Two of the main halls at Shaolin survive. They contain murals depicting monks at martial arts practice.

THE GENTLE MARTIAL ART: *TAIJIQUAN*

Taijiquan, commonly called just *taiji* (*t'ai ch'i*) in the West, is remarkable among the Chinese martial arts (*wushu*) because of its deceptively slow pace and yielding form. However, most of the individual movements that make up its sequences are also found in other, more visually combative martial arts. *Taijiquan* movements were first outlined in *Quan Jing* (*Classic of the Fist*) by a Ming general, Qi Jiguang (1528–1587). Rather than simply undertaking physical fitness training, adepts of *taijiquan* concentrate on building inner strength and developing a heightened awareness of *qi* and its dynamic between two opponents. Only in the mid- to late nineteenth century were the theory, postures, and sequences of *taijiquan* fully defined. In the wake of the breakdown of imperial authority in this period, *taijiquan* flourished as élite organizations sought effective means of defense against widespread banditry and rebellions.

Taijiquan draws on the breath cultivation and *daoyin* traditions. Its repetitive cycles, measured rhythm, and circular movements—alternately pushing forward and yielding—mirror the ceaseless transformations of *yin* and *yang*. In the progression of movements a symbolic journey can be detected: they begin with small circles, but grow as "the stork spreads out its wings," and progress to "riding the tiger" as one's inner nature is harnessed.

In an attempt to demilitarize the martial arts and prevent the growth of cults as centers of political resistance, the communist government has actively promoted the peaceful, meditational qualities of *taijiquan*.

Today the gentle therapeutic qualities of taijiquan *make it popular with the elderly and infirm, who gather to practice every day at dawn and dusk in courtyards and parks.*

A late Qing-dynasty painting illustrating sexual techniques. The legendary patron of sexual practices was Ancestor Peng, who was said to have lived for 700 years. A self-cultivation regime attributed to him and promoted in the 2nd century CE recommends adapting one's hygienic routines, diet, exercise, breathing, and "entering the chamber" (a euphemism for sexual relations) to the dynamic of the passing seasons. For the most part, sexual cultivation was aimed at strengthening the male partner through the practice of absorbing female jing and through semen retention, achieved through anal constriction. Peng's longevity also made him the patron of other health-care regimens, such as daoyin.

an enduring impression on the medical ideas formed in early imperial times. By taking the inner realm of the body as its focus for improvement, the self-cultivation tradition naturally developed concepts of physiological process: the gross material of the body was invigorated and rejuvenated by the movement and passage of *qi*. Self-cultivation refined *qi* and concentrated its essence, bringing physical and mental illumination. This, in sum, was the cultivation of *yin*.

One important lesson that medicine learnt from self-cultivation was that the most enlightened physicians were those who treated the body before it became sick. While this refers to aspects of preventive medicine such as proper diet, exercise, and sexual relations, it also came to signify the detection of patterns of illness before they manifested as gross pathology in the body.

Also derived from self-cultivation was the ability to use the power of intention to direct *qi* within the body. The visualization of "centers of transformation" in the body, such as the *dantian* ("cinnabar field") was common in breath meditation. Ultimately acupuncture and moxibustion borrowed this technique in order to move a patient's *qi* by manipulating the needle "with intention." Classical Chinese medical treatises regularly customize the tenets of self-cultivation for their own purposes. While in meditation the emphasis was more on refining *qi*, medical practice stressed the balancing of *qi*, *jing*, and *shen*. This is seen in the techniques of *daoyin*, which have been popular throughout Chinese history and are retained in modern times in various *qigong* and calisthenic exercises.

DRUGS AND
HEALING FOODS

A stall in a modern Chinese market displays ingredients to be ground up for medical use, including snakes (bottom left) and seahorses (bottom center). Seahorses are an endangered species and attempts are now being made to discourage their use in traditional Chinese medicine.

The earliest extant collections of Chinese pharmacological remedies were excavated at Mawangdui (see p.149) and provide evidence of the wide variety of substances that were used for medical purposes during the late Warring States and early imperial periods. Everything from foodstuffs and common herbs to human and animal excreta, ground insects, and household objects were combined in a rich variety of approaches to healing the human body. Substances were prepared fresh or dried, pounded or chopped. Some were made into tinctures and decoctions with liquor or vinegar, while others were applied as hot compresses.

Although an estimated 156 of the 224 or so substances identified in the largest collection from the Mawangdui tomb have been compared to those used in the later applications of traditional medicine, there are almost no references in the material found in the tomb to the tenets of classical Chinese medicine. Rather than being linked to the *yin-yang* and Five Elements (*wu xing*) correspondences (see pp.122–3), the remedies are matched directly to symptoms. Many are intended to exorcize the demons of disease or depend for their effectiveness on sympathetic magic.

The Mawangdui burial took place in 168BCE. Nearly 700 years later, Tao Hongjing (452–536CE) compiled *The Divine Farmer's Canon of Materia Medica*, in which he listed the medical properties of drugs and compared them using the analogy of administrative posts in the empire. There were three classes of drug—upper, middle, and lower—and each one was assigned a function, such as ruler, minister, or aide. Drugs for promoting strength and longevity were classed as "rulers," whereas drugs with medicinal and curative powers were "aides" to the body.

The Treatise on Cold Damage by Zhang Zhongjing (142–220CE) is the earliest known text to establish an aetiology of illness based on the phases of *yin* and *yang* together with integrated pharmacological prescriptions. His work had a huge impact on medical theorists working much later and particularly on the Japanese pharmacological tradition.

Competing schools of thought, which built on Zhang Zhongjing's work in different ways, proliferated a thousand years later during the late Song, Jin, and Yuan periods. Individual scholar-physicians typically concentrated on reducing and simplifying descriptions of disease to those

DRUG ADDICTION

Drugs were not always designed to cure the body. By Wei and Jin times (3rd–4th centuries CE) a substance known as *wushi* ("five stones") had become fashionable as a stimulant. *Wushi* was a warming drug that probably contained arsenic. It seems to have had a pleasant and exciting effect that served to blind the addict to its effects—a slow and insidious degeneration of the body. The deaths of a large number of scholars of the period are consistent with long-term arsenic poisoning (symptoms included fever, dryness, scabbing of the skin, nerve poisoning, lapses in consciousness, weakness, heart paralysis, delusions, and diarrhea).

THE DIVINE FARMER

Shennong (the "Divine Farmer") was one of the mythological bearers of culture at the beginning of civilization (see p.80). Han historians and mythmakers describe his most fundamental task as having led humanity out of a state of hunting and savagery, away from eating raw flesh, drinking blood, and wearing skins, toward an agrarian utopia. One second-century BCE source (*The King of Huainan*) reads:

"In ancient times people ate grasses and drank from rivers; they picked fruit from trees and ate molluscs and beetles. At that time there was much suffering from illness and poisoning. So the Divine Farmer taught the people for the first time how to sow and cultivate the five grains."

Later accounts describe how nine magical wells spontaneously appeared around Shennong at his birth, and how he used their water to nurture grains that had fallen from heaven. He is said to have revealed the essential tastes and smells of all plants, and then classified those that were fit for consumption and those suitable for medical use. From this tradition of empirical testing his name was evoked in the title of *The Divine Farmer's Canon of Materia Medica* (see main text).

A 19th-century ivory statuette of Shennong. As here, he is usually portrayed wearing a robe decorated with leaves from medicinal plants.

caused, for example, by fire and heat, or those that had an internal or external origin, as well as finally creating a pharmacology that was systematically based on classical Chinese medical theory.

Bencao gangmu (*Materia Medica, Systematized Monographs*) by Li Shizhen (1518–1593) is a richly illustrated encyclopedia which gathers together and augments the wisdom of 952 earlier sources in the fields of medicine, pharmaceuticals, mineralogy, metallurgy, botany, and zoology. In each monograph Li Shizhen refers to historical treatments of each herb, animal, or mineral, and its appearance, cultivation, and preparation, as well as many different properties, including affinities with other drugs, *yin* or *yang* nature, and its degree of efficacy. This painstaking and comprehensive work is still held in very high esteem among traditional Chinese medical practitioners and schools today.

PRESERVATION OF THE CORPSE

From as early as the ancient Longshan culture (which flourished ca. 2000–1500BCE), high-status Chinese families commonly used certain minerals in their burial practices with the aim of preserving the body after death. Members of the Han-dynasty élite even ingested such minerals while they lived, both for bodily preservation and possibly also as recreational drugs. Traces of lead, mercury, cinnabar, and arsenic were found in the almost perfectly preserved corpse of Lady Dai, buried at Mawangdui in the early second century BCE. She had taken all of these minerals for a long period during her lifetime, and her clothes had been soaked in cinnabar.

Another well preserved corpse excavated at Fenghuangshan had been filled with cinnabar after death. Cinnabar clearly helped prevent decomposition (see p.145).

Certain stones were also believed to possess the power to preserve the body. Jade seems to have been particularly important in this regard. Prince Liu Sheng, who also died in the second century BCE, was buried within many layers of jade and enclosed in a magnificent jade suit (see illustration).

Prince Liu Sheng's burial suit was made up of jade plaques linked together with fine gold wire.

However, the seventh-century CE scholar-physician Sun Simiao recommends treating illnesses with food as the primary medical intervention: "A good doctor first makes a diagnosis, and having found out the cause of the disease, he tries to cure it first by food. When food fails, then he prescribes medicine."

Abstention from grain had long been a requirement for lightening the body in the pursuit of a longer life or even immortality. Other contaminants variously avoided by Buddhist and Daoist devotees included meat, alcohol, and spicy, pungent foods. Among the earliest attested dietary traditions is food for strengthening the body, which was frequently chosen according to the resonances of sympathetic magic. Eating dog, deer, and donkey penises was believed to increase sexual vigor; walnuts, being kidney-shaped, were thought to nourish the kidneys. Equally, many high-protein foods such as wild game were believed to increase strength. The rarer and more difficult to obtain the food, the more highly it was prized.

Eventually every foodstuff was embraced within the *yin-yang* and Five Elements system of correspondences, although *yin* and *yang* themselves are considered less significant than equivalent polarities, such as heat and cold. The five thermostatic qualities of food are "hot," "warm," "neutral," "cool," and "cold." There is evidence of widespread empirical work by Chinese physicians, from simple observations (for example, that chilli and ginger burn the palate) to knowledge of the effect of food on body temperature.

Food is also classified according to the five flavors: "sour," "bitter," "sweet," "acrid," and "salty." According to the tenets of traditional Chinese medicine, the flavor assigned to a food is linked to its therapeutic effect. "Bitter," for example, is the most *yin* of flavors. It causes contraction, reduces fever, and enters the heart channel, clearing heat and calming the spirit. "Acrid," or "pungent," on the other hand, is believed to be the most *yang* of flavors: it stimulates the flow of *qi* and blood, normally heats the body, dries fluids and clears mucus. In general, medical priorities demand moderation and restraint—too much strong meat, spice, oil, and fat create excess heat, while raw vegetables and cold food and water are indigestible and harm the stomach.

An early 19th-century boxwood model of a Chinese medicine shop. Such shops sold drugs that were categorized according to their different qualities—their ability to heat or cool the body, their taste, their nature according to the yin-yang *and* wu xing *system, and their ability to stimulate upward or downward movement in the body, or to enter a particular channel.*

The mechanism of Su Song's clocktower from his description published in 1088, which included nearly 50 illustrations. These, together with the accompanying text, have enabled modern scholars to propose detailed reconstructions of just how the mechanism worked.

● CHAPTER 12   *Peter J. Golas*

TECHNOLOGY AND SCIENCE

THE INQUIRING SPIRIT

In the modern world, science and technology are closely linked, and technology is frequently viewed as applied science. In earlier societies, things were quite different. For most of human history, technology and science—in the sense of non-religious efforts to understand and explain nature—largely developed separately. Scientific knowledge (or speculation) was of little assistance in solving technological problems.

Nevertheless, the Chinese drew no sharply defined line between technological and scientific pursuits. Indeed, the very concepts of "science" and "technology" as they are understood in the West did not exist in traditional Chinese thought. It is therefore not difficult to find examples of instances in which at least partly "scientific" concerns stimulated technological responses. The desire to discover order in the universe by means of astronomical and astrological observations, for example, prompted the invention of many instruments over the first millennium CE, eventually culminating in the eleventh-century clocktower inveneted by Su Song, which represented the crowning mechanical achievement of

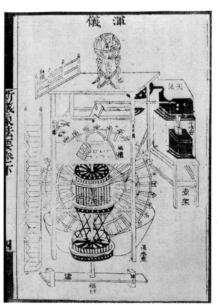

traditional China. The clocktower's escapement system—which consisted of pouring water into successive cups on the periphery of the driving waterwheel—allowed a slow and regular rotation of the wheel and of the armillary sphere, celestial globe, and timekeeping jackwork that were linked to it.

Similarly, the Chinese fascination with and understanding of magnetism, including the knowledge of magnetic declination by the eighth or ninth century CE, led to the invention of the compass. Alchemical experiments were crucial for discovery of the combination of ingredients that made up gunpowder. Stimuli, of course, also often went the other way—the Han invention of the seismoscope, for example, undoubtedly stimulated speculation about earthquakes.

Both the achievements and the limitations of technology and science in traditional China owed much to their dependence on state support. The government had sole command of the country's natural resources and had the power to promote research into whatever technologies it deemed important. State workshops designed and produced the weapons needed to maintain China's military strength. Gifts of silk were often an effective means of diplomatic persuasion, as under the Song dynasty. The spread of cotton production throughout China owed much to its promotion by the Mongol government during the Yuan dynasty. The desire to strengthen imperial legitimacy by bringing human affairs into harmony with the cosmos led to more than one hundred government-sponsored calendar reforms in the course of Chinese history. Government officials were also perennially concerned to improve or at least maintain the economic basis of the state—their efforts inevitably had a significant effect on the technology used not only in agriculture but in other important areas as well, including mining and textile production.

On the other hand, the very structure and values of the Chinese state often worked to inhibit scientific and technological advance. This was perhaps nowhere more apparent than in the government's tendency, especially in the last thousand years of the imperial system, to co-opt the majority of the most talented individuals in the country for service as officials in the bureaucracy and to assure a preeminent status for officials that could not be challenged by any other occupation. The strongly literary bias of the educational and examination systems— which required students to memorize philosophical classics and to write with style and flair—effectively diverted most, although not all, officials from any serious personal engagement with complex scientific ideas or mechanical details.

A Qing-dynasty astronomical clock, built in 1790.

FARMING AND FOOD

No greater technological challenge confronted the Chinese than the need to produce sufficient food for a large and densely settled population. By the early Shang dynasty, farming in what is now north China already generated a surplus, which made the emergence of a distinctively Chinese civilization possible. Moreover, alongside the dry-field millet/wheat agriculture of north China, there arose in central and south China the entirely different wet-field rice agriculture that would eventually prove even more productive.

Highly labor-intensive cultivation and a varied repertoire of agricultural tools and techniques accounted for much of Chinese agriculture's high productivity. In the middle of the first millennium BCE tools with iron tips or blades came into widespread use, making farming more efficient and contributing to China's first great population explosion. Among examples of more complex Chinese agricultural machinery—often the best in the world at the time—were a variety of plows designed to work different soils: multitube seed drills for faster and more regular

This Qing-dynasty painting shows the emperor (left of center, in yellow ceremonial robes) driving an iron-tipped ox plow during a spring agricultural festival in Beijing.

planting; winnowing fans that made use of a mechanically produced air blast; and various kinds of mills powered at first by humans, and later often by animals or by water (see pp.178–81). The invention of the breast harness and then of the collar harness (probably by the first century BCE) led to the earliest efficient use of horses and mules as draft animals.

Chinese farmers borrowed and adapted new crops from beyond their country's borders. Wheat, for example, arrived from the West—probably not long before ca. 1000BCE—and soon became the characteristic grain of north China. Near the end of the first millennium CE, new early-ripening rice strains from what is now Vietnam opened the way to double- and even triple-cropping on an unprecedented scale.

Experimentation with planting and cultivation methods was common. As early as the Han dynasty, many Chinese farmers had switched from scattering seeds to spot sowing in rows, opening the way to better tending of the growing plants, systematic crop rotation, and even the simultaneous cultivation of different crops in alternate rows.

Pasture animals played a minor role in the Chinese agricultural system, depriving farmers of an important potential source of fertilizer. Instead, they fertilized their fields with "night soil" (human excrement), river mud, ashes, lime, weeds, leaf-mold, chaff, and straw.

FOOD PROCESSING

The distinctiveness of Chinese cuisine owes much to the processes by which the ingredients are prepared. Two very early innovations had a great impact: the frequent use of mold ferments and the widespread, often large-scale, milling of grain. From at least the fifth millennium BCE, the Chinese used pottery steamers to cook the soft grains of millet and rice either for consumption or to produce fermentations that were vital ingredients of alcoholic drinks and a number of important foods, such as pickles and steamed bread. Wheat grain, harder and less easily cooked than millet and rice, was ground into flour to make dough from which a variety of a foods are produced—above all, noodles and bread.

IRRIGATION TECHNOLOGY

A very high percentage of China's rural labor was expended on water control and irrigation projects. The ubiquitous square-pallet chain-pump (often called the "dragon's backbone" in Chinese) was an extremely versatile machine that could be powered by hand, foot, draft-animal, or waterwheel. The pump could raise water up to fifteen feet (4.5m). A lighter version of the machine could be dismantled easily and carried on a person's shoulder, to be reassembled where needed. Waterwheels were also used for irrigation purposes. By ca. 1850CE, as a result of the widespread use of these various irrigation techniques, China had, by percentage, almost ten times more irrigated land under cultivation than India.

A Yuan-dynasty painting depicting a square-pallet chain pump, or "dragon's backbone."

SPINNERS AND WEAVERS

Chinese theory maintained that "Men till while women weave." The reality of life in China, of course, was never quite that straightforward, but the Chinese felt strongly that these separate but complementary male and female responsibilities formed the foundation of social order.

Although, in many people's minds, the Chinese textile industry is especially associated with silk (see box, below), two other kinds of cloth, ramie and cotton, also played key roles in the history of the country's textile production. Ramie (also called China grass, a member of the nettle family) is a perennial that produces a white, glossy, light, and durable fiber that is up to ten times longer and stronger than cotton. The plant itself is hardy and often continues to produce new fibers for many decades, even up to a century.

FROM WORM TO SILK

Silkworm cocoons are made up of a single filament which, if carefully unwound, can be as long as 2,400–3,000 feet (730–915m). This can be woven to produce material that is soft, lightweight, strong, durable, and ideal for dyeing. However, the raising of silkworms was a labor-intensive and precarious activity. During the 25–30 days when the very delicate worms were growing to full size, they required constant attention and needed to be fed several times a day on fresh mulberry leaves. At exactly the right time, the fully-grown worms were placed either on an inclined frame or more spacious trays so that they could begin spinning their cocoons. Finally, just before the moths were ready to emerge (which would break the delicate filament), the silk had to be reeled from the cocoons. If there were insufficient reeling machines or labor to do this in the short time available, the moths would have to be killed by boiling or smoking and the silk reeled at a later time, although this usually resulted in inferior quality silk.

It was probably the complexity of silk production that delayed its spread to other parts of the world—for example, silkmaking did not become well-established in Europe until the tenth century CE.

A painting dated ca. 1830 depicting people involved in the process of silk manufacture.

Production of both ramie and silk can be traced back to China's Neolithic period. Together with silk, ramie and hemp achieved a predominance among textiles that went unchallenged until the Song and Yuan dynasties, when they were largely displaced by cotton. In early times, ramie was often a vigorous competitor to silk, able to rival it for sheen, absorbency, warmth in winter, and coolness in summer.

In order to make cloth, the short, individual plant fibers must first be twisted together to form thread. Originally this was done without tools simply by rolling the raw fibers between the hands or between hand and thigh. However, by at least 5000BCE, the Chinese were beginning to use spindle whorls—this early implementation of the principle of the flywheel enabled them to produce a more regular thread with greater rapidity. Much later, perhaps under the Shang dynasty, simple hand-operated spinning wheels began to appear. They were followed by treadle-powered versions under the Han and water-powered versions by the time of the Song era. Also important in the development of spinning wheels was the increase in the number of spindles that could be powered by one wheel: a Yuan-dynasty belt-driven version with 32 spindles could produce 110 lbs (50kg) of yarn in a 24-hour period.

Cotton was not indigenous to China but had already made its way there from India by 200BCE or earlier. Although softer than ramie and, at its best, able to rival even silk in both appearance and durability, cotton was barely used in China for more than a thousand years. In part this was because the first species imported into China were ill-suited to most Chinese environments. Only with the gradual development of better plants, as well as tools and machines (such as the gin to get rid of the seeds and the bow to untangle and fluff up the fibers for spinning), were the Chinese able to produce cotton cloth economically enough to replace ramie and hemp as clothing for the masses. At that point (some time after 1000CE), the use of cotton spread dramatically—this was largely due to the fact that the simple equipment was affordable for peasant households.

A 14th-century piece of Chinese silk, finely embroidered with blue and gold thread.

TREASURES FROM THE EARTH

Partly because of its great size, China has benefited from a variety and abundance of natural resources, including deposits of all the metals used in premodern times: gold, silver, copper, tin, iron, lead, mercury, and zinc. The availability of clays, including kaolin ("china clay") for porcelain, allowed the Chinese to develop a ceramics industry unsurpassed anywhere for the scale of production and the aesthetic quality of the finished goods (see pp.198–201). Vast deposits of coal helped meet general fuel needs as well as those of a large-scale iron industry.

The extent of China's mining and related activities has seldom been properly appreciated. Even as early as the Han, or possibly a little later, besides the products mentioned above, the Chinese were mining and processing more than 50 other materials, of which the most important were jade, other precious and semiprecious stones, arsenic, sulfur, abrasives, alum, and potassium nitrate (which was used as a fertilizer and in gunpowder). Over the centuries, Chinese prospectors built up a vast store of knowledge that allowed them to find virtually all the significant deposits of useful minerals that could be economically exploited using traditional technology.

A magnificent bronze sheng ding— *a tripod vessel for offering food— found in the tomb of Chu Shuzhi Sun Peng (died in 548*BCE*), a chief minister of the Eastern Zhou state of Chu. The fine relief ridges on the tripod are decorated with tightly interlaced dragons.*

However, it was in the processing of the products of mining, especially metallurgy, that the Chinese showed themselves to be remarkably skilled and inventive. Bronzemaking provides a good example. By the Shang and early Zhou dynasties, the Chinese had learned to combine copper and tin in different proportions to form various versions of bronze, depending on the purpose for which it was to be used.

Most of China's metal deposits were in the form of ores that required heat treatment to separate the metal—long experience with the firing of pottery had taught the Chinese how to achieve and control very high temperatures in their furnaces. By the seventh or sixth century BCE they were able to extract iron from its ore, not only in the form of wrought iron (partly molten iron that had to be hammered by the smith to remove unwanted slag), but also cast iron, the fully molten metal which could be cast immediately into tools, weapons, and a range of other objects. It was at least a thousand years before techniques for producing cast iron appeared in the West.

The early availability of cast iron, as well as the discovery that it could be cast in durable iron molds, meant that a large number of mass-produced iron products were available from a very early period. This had a dramatic effect on Chinese economic development.

THE MINES OF TONGLÜSHAN

The earliest large copper mines in China date back to the latter part of the Shang period. The most fully excavated so far is the mine at Tonglüshan, just south of the Yangzi River in central China. Mining had begun here by at least 1000BCE. It continued, although perhaps with some breaks, for the better part of a millennium. By studying the mine's remains, it is possible to trace much of the early development of mining technology, such as various timbering methods to shore up the excavations; efforts to drain excess water and improve ventilation; and the use of firesetting (heating, then rapidly cooling, the rock), often the most effective and efficient way of breaking rock before dynamite became available in the late nineteenth century.

DRILLING FOR SALT BRINE IN SICHUAN

The presence of great amounts of salt brine in the western province of Sichuan not only provided an essential nutrient for millions of Chinese living far from the sea or the salt lakes of the north, but also encouraged uniquely early advances in deep drilling. Drilling of deep borehole wells, using iron drills, seems to have been invented in the eleventh century CE; by 1132, some 4,900 mostly deep-drilled wells had been registered by local officials. Brine was extracted by means of long bamboo tubes at the bottom of which was an iron container with flap valves—the valves opened when the tube was lowered, letting in the brine, and then closed as it was raised. The famous Xinhai well, built in 1835, employed the traditional drilling techniques to reach a depth of more than half a mile (1km)—about twice that of any contemporary borehole well outside China.

Wooden derricks at a Chinese salt mine in the late 19th or early 20th century.

TRANSPORT AND COMMUNICATION

This painted wooden model of an ox-cart with spoked wheels dates from the Han dynasty.

WHEELED TRANSPORT
The earliest evidence for wheeled vehicles in China dates from the Shang dynasty with the first appearance of the chariot with spoked wheels, an import from the northwest.

The wheelbarrow was first seen in China around the turn of the Common Era (it was not used in Europe until the twelfth or thirteenth century CE) and halved the number of laborers needed to transport loads beyond the capacity of one person.

By the fourth century BCE, Chinese wheelwrights were constructing well-crafted wheels with hubs, spokes (as many as 30 on chariot wheels), and sectioned rims (felloes). Also at about this time, "dishing," or the fixing of spokes at a slight angle to the plane of the circumference, had been invented, producing a wheel with better resistance to lateral shocks.

A vast communications and exchange infrastructure was needed to maintain the unity of China—one of the world's largest political and cultural entities.

The First Emperor, Qin Shihuangdi (ruled 221–210BCE), provided a model—among his greatest civil engineering achievements was the construction of an almost 4,350-mile (7,000km) road network radiating out from the capital Xianyang to the farthest reaches of his empire. Later emperors followed his example and by the end of the second century CE China had some 22,000 miles (35,400km) of specially constructed roads to serve an empire of about 1.5 million square miles (4 million km²).

However, in many parts of China, waterways played a more important role than roads, partly because the Chinese roads were often poorly maintained. Water transport, which made faster, cheaper communications possible, benefited greatly over the centuries from the government's canal-building activities. The "Magic Transport Canal"—a contour canal built on the orders of the First Emperor—linked the central Yangzi river region to Guangzhou by way of the West river. The first canal anywhere to connect two river systems, it has remained in continuous use for more than 2,200 years.

The first Grand Canal system (see p.22) was built in the early seventh century CE and was an economic lifeline between the grain-deficit area of north China and the surplus-producing southeast. With the help of gate locks, invented in the tenth century, it eventually linked the waters of five great river systems along a 1,250-mile (2,000km) route, forming the world's most extensive waterway network before modern times.

On China's inland waterways, hauling, poling, and fishtailing (a form of rowing over the stern) were all common methods of propulsion. Ship design varied considerably: barges along the Grand Canal bore little resemblance to ships intended for long ocean voyages (see box, opposite).

Where roads encountered waterways, bridges were often built (although ferries provided transport across some rivers). Most bridges were of the beam type, making use of one or more spans of wood or stone. Arch bridges were also very common. The world's first suspension bridges—constructed using iron chains rather than ropes—were also originally a Chinese invention, probably dating from the Han period.

MARITIME TECHNOLOGY

China was the world's greatest maritime power for 400 years, culminating in the early fifteenth century, when a Chinese fleet sailed unchallenged across the Indian Ocean and as far as the Red Sea and the east coast of Africa. This maritime supremacy was made possible by a range of developments in nautical technology, including stern-post rudders (invented under the Han), which could be raised or lowered depending on the depth of the water, and water-tight compartments to limit damage from leaks. The compass was adapted for use on ships by at least the eleventh century and sailors had the benefit of nautical charts and navigational diagrams showing precise compass bearings, as well as star positions to be maintained for various routes.

Probably the most distinctive characteristic of Chinese ship design was that no use was made of frames or ribs; instead, the planking was joined to solid, transverse bulk-heads, including one each at the stem and stern. Larger Chinese ships were also commonly outfitted with multiple masts, carefully staggered so that the sail of one mast would not becalm that of another. The sails themselves were usually made of bamboo matting strengthened by bamboo battens. Although not as strong as canvas sails, they were aerodynamically more efficient, less prone to tearing, and could be readily furled without complex rigging.

The Chinese also pioneered the use of human-powered paddle-wheel ships. The largest of these, first built in the twelfth century, had a dozen wheels on each side.

Chinese junks, with their flat prows, were for centuries the most seaworthy craft in Asian waters.

THE TECHNOLOGY OF WAR

The Attack of Mara (detail), a Buddhist prayer banner of the 10th century CE found at Dunhuang. It is the oldest depiction of firearms in the world. Among the demons assailing the Buddha (left) are two figures armed with early Chinese weaponry: one (top right) wields a hand-held canon; another, just below him, throws a grenade.

Despite a cultural tradition in which disdain for all things military was widespread, there is no lack of warfare, both internal and external, in Chinese history. It is therefore hardly surprising that the Chinese developed many sophisticated weapons long before they appeared in the West.

There can be little doubt that military power was central to the emergence of the Shang as a powerful state in ancient China (see pp.24–5). In addition to bows and bronze-headed arrows, a command of bronze metallurgy and a marked ability to organize production provided the Shang warriors with a variety of weapons including daggers, halberds, dagger-axes, and bronze-tipped spears.

From ca. 500BCE warfare in China underwent a revolution more far-reaching than even the introduction of gunpower weapons 1,500 years later. Responding to threats from mounted nomads from the north and west, the Chinese borrowed nomadic techniques and introduced cavalry into their armies. Yet even the invention of the stirrup many centuries later never led Chinese armies to rely predominantly on cavalry. They could usually depend on their organizational and logistical skills to deploy much larger numbers of troops than their enemies. Moreover, the rapidly increasing availability of iron from the Warring States period on made it possible to produce a great variety and quantity of arms, thus providing the weapons for mass armies on an unprecedented scale.

This elaborate bronze axe head dates from the 6th–5th centuries BCE.

The Chinese advantage in arms production also had a further dimension. By the Warring States era there appeared the two most important heavy weapons in use before the age of firearms: the crossbow and the catapult. Chinese craftsmen were able to make intricate trigger mechanisms as well as the aerodynamically effective bolt heads that increased the accuracy of crossbows. Moreover, by the third century BCE, Chinese armies were deploying mobile crossbows weighing 600 lbs (270kg) and shooting arrows that were more than seven feet (2.25m) long. Under the Tang, such crossbows were said to have a range of more than one 1,000 yards (900m). The culmination of crossbow design came in the eleventh or twelfth century CE with the invention of repeater crossbows capable of firing several bolts in rapid succession. The crossbow remained one of the Chinese army's key weapons until the nineteenth century.

Much combat within China took the form of siege warfare. Attackers made use of a whole panoply of weapons, including catapults, firebombs, smoke bombs, battering rams, and "cloud ladders" (folding siege ladders). Defenders attempted to minimize the effects of attacks with an equally wide-ranging array of similar weapons, as well as screens and curtains to intercept enemy projectiles, and firescreens with which to attack enemy soldiers who tried to scale the walls.

It was in the use of gunpowder (after its accidental discovery by alchemists in the later Tang) that the Chinese displayed particular ingenuity. However, after ca. 1400, the development of firearms and cannons came largely to a halt. This was probably partly due to a general absence in subsequent centuries of serious long-term military threats to China from outside—a situation that changed only with the arrival of Western imperial powers in the nineteenth century.

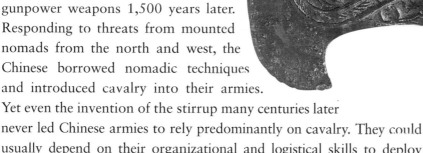

A CHRONOLOGY OF GUNPOWDER WEAPONS

ca. 850CE Some Chinese aware of the explosive power of a mixture of saltpeter (potassium nitrate), sulfur, and charcoal

919 First record of the use of gunpowder in a weapon

ca. 950 Gunpowder used in hand held flamethrowers

968 Incendiary arrows using low-nitrate gunpowder paste

11th century Semiexplosive bombs, grenades, and mines

Early 12th century Incendiary rockets and rocket-propelled bombs

Early 13th century Semiclosed containers of gunpowder mixed with projectiles that on ignition were propelled out along with the gunpowder gases

13th century Gunpowder as a rocket propellant; rocket arrows; high-nitrate explosives

Late 13th/early 14th centuries True guns and cannons with metal barrels; transmission of gunpowder formula and gunpowder weapons to Arabs and to Europe

14th century Winged and two-stage rockets

MECHANICS AND POWER

A Han-dynasty bronze model of a man operating a millstone using an early crank. The piece was excavated in Zhongxiang county, Hubei province.

While examples of technological ingenuity can be found in all periods of Chinese history, technical advances in machinery and its applications seem to have been especially prolific in the Warring States and Han period and again under the Song and Yuan. By contrast, China's inventive drive seems to have waned noticeably in the final centuries of the imperial period.

Several pieces of ingenious machinery made their first appearance around Han times. One of the most basic inventions of all was the crank. It became invaluable as the easiest means of interchanging rotary and reciprocal (back and forth) motion. Proto-cranks, consisting of a kind of peg or stick inserted at the edge of a wheel (such as a millstone) to serve as handles for turning, may well have be used much earlier. But the first evidence anywhere of the true crank with its pair of right angle bends are models found in Han tombs depicting cranks as the means for powering rotary-fan winnowing machines of a type still frequently seen on Chinese farms. Later, the crank would be applied to a great variety of machines, including mills, windlasses used for lifting something from a depth, such as water from a well or coal from a mine, and various complex textile machines, such as silk-reeling machines and spinning wheels.

The rotary-fan winnowing machine was one of two important devices developed under the Han for controlling a current of air. The second was the double-acting box bellows, consisting of a rectangular box within which a piston and valve arrangement made it possible for the piston to pump out air on both the forward and backward stroke, thus creating a continuous blast of air with a single piston. The most efficient air pump devised anywhere before the advent of modern machinery, this device was extensively employed to achieve the high temperatures needed in metallurgical furnaces.

While the Han period is notable for the many new machines that made their appearance at that time, the Song and Yuan periods, while not lacking in important inventions, are particularly significant for their greatly expanded use of better technologies. This era was especially marked by the sophisticated application of waterpower to manufacturing processes. Although the waterwheel had been used for irrigation purposes since before the Common Era (see box, p.180), it was as an industrial machine that it had most impact. It seems possible that the Chinese were even using water before animals to power machines.

Unsurprisingly, two of the major early industrial applications of waterwheels (for which there is evidence as early as the Han dynasty) were to rotate millstones and to power metallurgical bellows. In both cases, horizontal mountings proved highly efficient.

There was also a third major application of waterwheels under the Han—the activation of trip hammers, which were widely used for hulling grain and crushing iron ore. Indeed, this is the usage most commonly mentioned in the surviving literature. One or more hammers could be raised and allowed to fall by means of a series of catches or lugs on a revolving shaft leading from a waterwheel. Although a vertical waterwheel would clearly be the preferred choice here, there is no firm evidence until much later for the Chinese use of vertical wheels in this application; quite possibly, the early trip hammers were powered by horizontal waterwheels, together with right-angle gearing leading from a waterwheel.

After the Han period, there do not seem to have been any dramatic breakthroughs in the construction of waterwheels themselves, but larger

THE EARTHQUAKE DETECTOR OF ZHANG HENG

China is a land of frequent earthquakes. It is therefore hardly surprising that the Chinese, always keen observers of natural phenomena, were, from the earliest times, interested in detecting and recording earthquakes. The oldest Chinese record of an earthquake dates back to 780BCE. The first instrument designed specifically to detect earthquakes seems to have been invented in 132CE by an official named Zhang Heng, who had wide-ranging scientific interests.

The surviving account of Zhang's instrument tells us that it consisted of a bronze urn with eight dragons facing out from around the rim, each with a bronze ball in its jaw. Around the base and below each dragon was a toad with

A modern reconstruction of Zhang Heng's seismograph.

an open mouth facing upward. An earthquake caused the interior mechanism, with its pendulum-like central pillar, to trigger the jaw of the dragon facing in the direction from which the earthquake had come. This caused the dragon to release its ball into the mouth of the toad below it, thus leaving a record of the earthquake.

Instruments of this type appear to have been used in China from Zhang Heng's time until the seventh century CE, after which the technique for producing them seems to have been lost.

WATERWHEELS AND IRRIGATION

No invention before the steam engine did more to ease the toil of humans and animals than the waterwheel. The earliest waterwheels probably originated some time in the last centuries leading up to the Common Era as a means to raise water for irrigation (see p.169). There is some evidence that the *noria*, a vertical wheel equipped with buckets on its periphery, may have been used in Egypt as early as the second century BCE. The appearance of this version of the waterwheel may have been delayed in China because of the availability there around this time of the trough and pallets chain pump, which served very well for irrigation needs.

Waterwheels have appeared in many different forms. The names of the overshot vertical and the undershot vertical wheels distinguish whether the water power is directed at the top of the wheel or passes underneath. Horizontally mounted waterwheels, for which the Chinese showed a preference wherever possible, were also common.

But it was not as an aid to irrigation but rather as an industrial machine to transmit the energy of flowing water that the waterwheel was of great importance in the history of premodern technology, east and west (see main text).

A vertical wooden waterwheel still being used for irrigation purposes in Guangxi province.

wheels were increasingly used to power bigger and more complex installations. In the *Agricultural Treatise of Wang Zhen*, a famous illustrated work compiled in 1313, Wang discusses the use of waterwheels in textile manufacture and metallurgy. A water-powered blowing machine for use with metallurgical furnaces incorporates an elaborate mechanism for converting the rotary motion of the waterwheel to the reciprocal motion needed to propel the panel that forced air into the furnace.

Despite the sophistication of the linkages, however, one can easily imagine that the assembly illustrated by Wang, like most of the water-powered machines of traditional China, was heavy, clumsy, and inefficient. However, although they were typically limited to an output of five horsepower (3,700 watts) or less, waterwheels provided far more energy than other sources of power. This energy was eagerly harnessed from the Song period onward in large manufacturing operations. For example, a single waterwheel might drive a half dozen or more large millstones, or even a combination of millstones, trip hammers, and edge-runner mills (where the grinding was done by one or two disk-shaped stones rolling on their edges in a circular trough).

There is no simple answer to the question of why China's technological ingenuity flagged during the Ming and Qing periods. Some have suggested that, in many areas, most of the possibilities for economically feasible mechanization had already been exploited; only a great breakthrough in energy resources (such as the development of steam power) could have made a new wave of mechanization possible. It has also been argued that a burgeoning population was placing increasing pressure on available resources at this time, thereby pushing up the prices of the raw materials—wood and metals—needed for constructing machines, while at the same time making manual labor ever cheaper. Also worth noting is the existence in Ming and Qing China of an extremely efficient distribution system, able to draw on vast supplies of underutilized rural labor—this could have precluded the appearance of production bottlenecks at times of rising demand that might otherwise have stimulated innovation. It has also been suggested that a change in élite values discouraged interest in technology by some of those who might have been best able to contribute to technical progress.

China's relative technological stagnation occurred during the precise period when new technology was emerging in Europe. This left the country at a severe disadvantage when, in the nineteenth century, it had to defend itself against a Western imperialism based on overwhelming economic and military might.

Advances in the use of gearing and other kinds of linkages opened the way to one of the most ingenious "machines" of the Han dynasty, the south-pointing carriage. A kind of mechanical compass, this was a two-wheeled cart fitted with a statue of a pointing figure, as illustrated by this modern reconstruction. The statue and the wheels were interconnected through gearing so that the figure continued to point south (the primary cardinal direction for the Chinese) no matter which way the cart turned.

PAPER, PRINTING, AND PUBLISHING

In the history of technology, even inventions that came to have an enormous impact often emerged very gradually. Printing is a striking example of this. When it was first experimented with—perhaps as early as the seventh century CE—printing represented such a small change in the use of existing materials and techniques as to be almost unrecognizable as something truly new. Nevertheless, its further development, in China and elsewhere, led to such far-reaching changes in the societies in which it appeared that the invention is deservedly viewed as one of the great milestones in human history.

As their notation system developed, the Chinese experimented with a variety of writing surfaces, including pottery objects, turtle shells, and silk. It seems that the first efforts to produce paper date from the early Han—the process probably consisted of macerating old rags to reduce them to their fibers, mixing the fibers with water, and then using a mold to hold the fibers as the water was drained off. The water absorbed by the fibers led them to expand which, in turn, bound them together.

Once the basic technique of papermaking had appeared, the Chinese experimented with an ever-increasing variety of raw materials. The bark from the mulberry tree, rattan, bamboo, and rice and wheat stalks all provided fibers suitable for papermaking, and paper became the most widely used writing surface. Paper production led to the technique of taking rubbings or squeezes from texts engraved on stone or another hard surface to produce a white text on a black background. By the end of the second century CE, the seven works then considered to be the classics of the Confucian school of thought—consisting of some two hundred thousand characters—were engraved on a series of stones from which ink rubbings could be taken.

In order for the slow and difficult technique of rubbing to evolve into the rapid and efficient process of woodblock printing, text had to be reproduced in reverse so that it could be inked and used to create a positive copy. The close association between carved seals and writing facilitated the emergence of reverse-carving on woodblocks for printing.

Woodblock printing was in widespread use in China by the tenth century CE, and it continued to be the overwhelmingly dominant form of printing into the

An early example of Chinese watercolor printing, made using woodblocks. The aim of Chinese color printing was to achieve a style that resembled that of painting as closely as possible. This image is from a collection of leaves from two color-printed painting manuals entitled The Ten Bamboo Studio *and* The Mustard Seed Garden, *both of which date from the 17th century.*

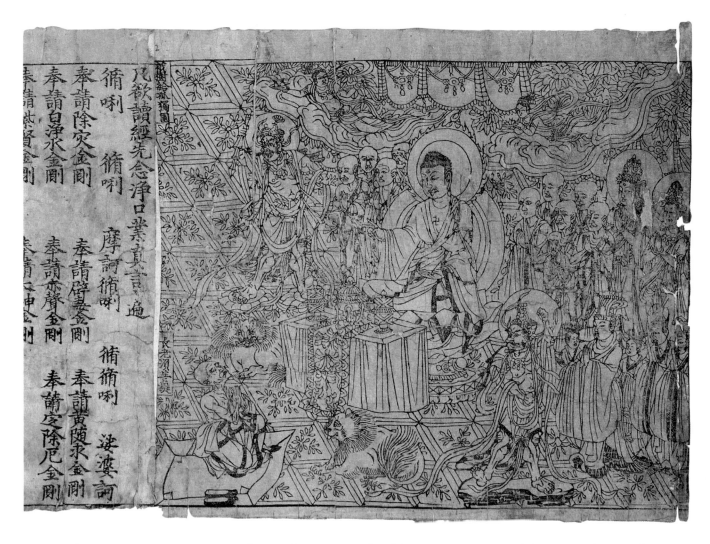

twentieth century. It was an extremely simple process—the thin, porous paper that the Chinese used for printing absorbed water-base ink with little pressure so that there was no need for a press. In addition, once the text was written and transferred to the blocks, the blocks could even be carved by illiterate craftsmen. This was an enormous advantage in a society in which the great complexity of the written language, together with limited opportunities for schooling, meant that literate artisans would always be at a premium. Jesuit missionaries in sixteenth-century Beijing commented that a skilled Chinese engraver could complete a page in the same amount of time as would be taken to typeset a page in Europe.

Woodblock printing also had the advantage of incurring low labor costs—a skilled artisan could print more than 1,500 pages in a single day. The price of books dropped by as much as 90 percent in China between the ninth and eleventh centuries and Chinese publishers could make at least a small profit in limited editions of a few hundred copies. Many private entrepreneurs were quite willing to print anything that promised to make even a modest profit.

Part of the Diamond Sutra, *the world's oldest printed book, dating from 868CE and discovered in 1907 at Dunhuang. It is in the form of a continuous 17-foot (5m) scroll. Printing in China appears to have begun as a Buddhist phenomenon. The mass production and distribution of Buddhist images and texts earned merit for the devout. A remarkably high proportion of early Chinese printed books are illustrated, since woodblocks with illustrations were just as easy to prepare as those with characters alone.*

THE ART OF DYNASTIC CHINA HAS MANY ANCIENT ORIGINS. IT DID NOT DEVELOP IN ISOLATION—CHINESE PAINTERS, POTTERS, SMITHS, AND SCULPTORS WERE INFLUENCED BY CULTURES AS DIVERSE AS PERSIA AND TIBET. THESE INFLUENCES CONTRIBUTED TO THE UNIQUENESSS OF CHINESE ART, WHICH CONTINUES TO BE A SOURCE OF INSPIRATION TO THE OUTSIDE WORLD.

THE FINE AND DECORATIVE ARTS

RITUAL JADE AND BRONZE

The stone called *yu* in Chinese and roughly translated into English as "nephrite jade" has been treasured by the inhabitants of what is now China for more than six millennia. Nowhere else in the world has a single type of stone been so widely venerated over such a long period of time. In the last hundred years or so, countless ancient jade objects have been unearthed in various parts of China. Their often dramatically different styles convincingly reveal that, far from being homogenous, prehistoric China was home to an extraordinary diversity of cultures.

There are more than five hundred Chinese characters based on the root denoting "jade," many of them with connotations relating to value, beauty, power, and riches. Confucius (551–479BCE) is believed to have summarized the five human virtues thought to be embodied by jade: he claimed that humanity, moral integrity, wisdom, justice, and perseverance were represented respectively by the warm glow, purity, pleasant ringing, hardness, and durability of jade. Over the centuries, these abstract human qualities came to be seen as intrinsic attributes of jade. The properties of the stone have impressed the Chinese to such an extent that the perfect sovereign—the Jade Emperor, ruler of Heaven—is envisioned as dwelling in an ideal paradise, a place bathed in jade's ethereal glow.

The earliest jade ornaments, including pendants and earrings dating from the fifth millennium BCE, were made by the Liangzhu culture in present-day Zhejiang province. Symbols of political and spiritual power typically appeared in the form of flat disks (*bi*) and segmented hollow tube-like objects (*cong*). Although evidence is still too scanty for scholars to reconstruct the significance of such artifacts, they must have been of considerable importance, since they were found in elaborate high-status burials. They were also very difficult to produce—jade is one of the hardest materials to work—and their form was not related to that of any everyday functional object. Sites in

Ancient jades were highly prized in the later empire. Here, two jade rings made in imitation of prehistoric bi-disks *form the basis of a Qing-dynasty pin, mounted with gold dragons.*

present-day Liaoning province once inhabited by people of the Hongshan culture (ca. 3500–ca. 2500BCE), although lacking in *cong* or *bi*, have yielded distinctive realistic-looking jades such as turtles, cicadas, birds, and, most characteristically, "C"-shaped "pig-headed dragons." The recently discovered remains at Sanxingdui (dated ca. 1200–ca. 1000BCE) included a unique type of ceremonial jade blade, among other remarkable artifacts (see illustration, right, and caption, below). During the Zhou dynasty, jade began to be used to cover the bodies of the deceased (see p.164) and to decorate the front of ceremonial robes. From the Han to the Tang dynasties, jade was worked into elaborate jewelry. In the later empire, from the Song to the Qing, more sculptural jade items were executed, sometimes modeled on ancient bronzes.

Bronze casting, as opposed to bronze hammering (the usual method of making bronze objects in the ancient world) emerged in China more than two millennia after the Chinese learned how to work jade. Over the next thousand years, the high raw-material and labor costs involved in creating bronze artifacts meant that such objects became symbols of wealth and power, and bronze vessels replaced jade for ritual purposes. Kings and nobles used bronze containers in sacred ceremonies to hold wine and food offerings to their ancestors and the spirits. Among the rival states of the Eastern Zhou period, bronzes were potent emblems of rulership. Bronze was also the preferred material for weapons.

Bronze vessels, such as *ding* (a round basin with three or four legs), usually derived their shapes from earlier pottery vessels. However, the use of metal cast in molds permitted greater precision and intricacy of both form and design. The ancient Chinese bronze casting method made use of piece-molding, whereby a mold was carefully assembled from many accurately modeled and carved clay sections. Such was the level of skill involved that after casting very little fettling (smoothing of rough edges where the molds had joined) was necessary (see also illustrations on pp.25–7).

In 1986 two pits dating from ca. 1200–ca. 1000BCE were found at Sanxingdui in Sichuan province. Among a mass of burned animal bones were various pottery, gold, jade, and bronze objects. These included a group of life-sized bronze heads with huge, staring eyes, such as the partly gilded one shown here, which is 19 inches (47.5cm) tall. The Sangxingdui culture is not mentioned in any surviving historical records. Evidently the pits represent a deliberate attempt to destroy some very valuable objects, but the motivation for such an act remains a mystery.

ART FOR THE AFTERLIFE

A detail of the murals that decorate the tomb of Princess Yong Tai in Chang'an (modern-day Xi'an). The paintings, which are dated 706CE, portray court ladies from Yong Tai's entourage.

Chinese tomb sculpture and paintings give us an insight into the rituals that accompanied the burials of people with power and wealth. The artifacts and images in tombs now provide a record of the artistic achievements of the Chinese and also shed light on our understanding of their notion of the afterlife. Each of these tombs was a dwelling for the deceased, built to resemble his or her daily life in every detail, through the arrangement of the chambers, the possessions buried with the body, and the pictures decorating the walls.

In the Shang and Western Zhou dynasties, ancestral temples housed elaborate ritual vessels made of jade and bronze (see pp.184–5). However, during the Eastern Zhou period, architectural decoration in palaces and tombs, rather than on ritual vessels, became the focus of artistic creativity, and representations of human figures assumed greater importance than those of mythological animals.

An early third-century BCE painting on silk, discovered in a tomb at Zidanku, Changsha (Hunan province) in 1973, provides evidence of one of the early signs of a new artistic genre. The painting bears a portrait representing the deceased as a dragon-riding swordsman. The image is presented in a fluid sketch: the folds of his clothes, the subtlety of his headdress, and the delicacy of his features are all effortlessly rendered— a stark contrast to the deeply-carved intricacy of bronze design. The artist adopted a drawing style eulogized by later connoisseurs as "the flowing silk threads of antiquity," and the heavy reliance on lines, rather than patches of color, has been a distinctive feature of Chinese painting ever since.

At the beginning of the first century BCE tombs constructed using bricks or stone began to replace timber-built ones. Decorated-to-order silk banners, which bore an individual likeness of the deceased, gave way to bricks bearing a large repertoire of decorative themes, which included depictions of everyday life, mythological creatures, and historical anecdotes. Some images were especially suitable for the tomb of a government official, such as depictions of past loyal ministers in action, while battle imagery was particularly apt for a military officer.

The large number of pictorial tomb bricks excavated indicates the existence in the mid- and late-Han era of a well-to-do population that was willing to spend considerable amounts of money on the decoration of their tombs.

THE TERRACOTTA ARMY

The burial of the First Emperor, Qin Shihuangdi (ruled 221–210BCE), epitomized the Chinese practice of duplicating the world of the living in an underground residence in which the deceased could live for eternity.

In 1974 a burial pit was discovered a little to the east of the emperor's mausoleum at Lintong near the city of Xi'an in Shaanxi province. The pit was excavated to reveal an army of more than 7,000 terracotta soldiers (of which around 2,000 have so far been unearthed). The soldier figures are remarkably lifelike and it appears that a limited number of standard elements (three types of plinth, two types of legs, eight torsos, and eight heads) were combined with a range of color schemes in order to make each figure as different as possible from the others. The individual modeling of facial features and hairstyles added to the effect. The creators of this formidable assembly apparently believed that the more realistic the terracotta soldiers were, the more effective they would be in serving and protecting the emperor in the afterlife.

In describing Qin Shihuangdi's tomb, the Han historian Sima Qian wrote that it contained mercury rivers and lakes, and that automated guards with crossbows were positioned in the passageways.

Both real items and replicas were found in the burial pit near the First Emperor's tomb: real horses were buried in their stables, but the massed ranks of the emperor's army, as seen in this view, were made from terracotta.

INSPIRATION AND ENLIGHTENMENT

A Qi-dynasty (479–501CE) ivory head portraying a bodhisattva.

The arrival of the Buddhist faith in China from India approximately two thousand years ago (see p.110) resulted in profound changes in Chinese culture and art. The first few gilded bronze icons representing the Buddha may have been brought into China from India for ritual use. Such images soon merged with indigenous Daoist motifs in China. The earliest surviving Chinese images of the Buddha (dating from before 265CE) are standing figures dressed in non-Chinese clothes with a double halo above the head.

A few bronze fourth-century CE Chinese Buddhist images have survived. Most of these bronzes are gilded figures that resemble the Indian Gandhara style, with a Chinese accessory—a leaf-shaped *mandorla* with a flaming edge. Most early Chinese sculptors played down the Buddha's human anatomical structure and produced statues with stiff, geometrically modeled garments.

In the fourth century, the Toba Tartar rulers of northern China (the Northern Wei dynasty) strongly encouraged the spread of Buddhism, and under imperial patronage cave-temples with colossal Buddhist imagery were constructed in Yungang and Longmen. In the process of cave building, a Sinicized style of Buddhist icon emerged, characterized by a slender waist, and a plump face with delicate facial features.

The Sui-dynasty style of Buddhist figures shows an awareness of the organic body under the folds of clothes. On the finest examples, graceful lines and subtle curves combine to imbue the image with a spirituality rarely seen since. In the Tang period Buddhist images were further humanized in that they all assumed a fully rounded torso with noticeably voluptuous contours. Tang Buddhist statues were often placed against a background of festive gatherings of deities, monks, donors, and other inhabitants of the Western Paradise. These bejeweled figures combined worldly grandeur and heavenly serenity, qualities that can be seen in copies found in places as far apart as Japan and Dunhuang near Central Asia (see sidebar, right)—a sure indication of the strength and influence of the Tang empire.

The Buddhist forms produced during the Tang were preserved in the languorous wooden icons popular in the Song dynasty. During the Mongol occupation of China, the Tantric school of Tibetan Buddhism was favored by the court. Throughout the next six hundred years of dynastic China, a distinctive Sino-Tibetan style of esoteric Buddhist art co-existed with a Chinese style that incorporated the ideal with the worldly.

CAVES OF THE SINGING SANDS

The cave-temples located to the east of the Hill of the Singing Sands at Dunhuang, a Chinese oasis town at the edge of the Gobi desert, house one of the most spectacular displays of Buddhist art in the world. The temples were created over a period of about 700 years, beginning in 366CE.

During the heyday of the Silk Road, Dunhuang was a major staging post used by traders and missionaries traveling between China and the West. Chinese and Korean Buddhist monks seeking images and scriptures and central Asian monks, merchants, and princes making the journey to China all left traces of their passage through the town. Every stage of the development of Buddhism in China is recorded in the murals and stucco sculptures that decorate the Dunhuang caves. Every cave wall and ceiling is covered with ornate painted motifs, Buddhist images, and narrative scenes. As an important Buddhist pilgrimage center, Dunhuang drew the rich and poor from near and far to sponsor the construction of shrines as a celebration of their devotion to the faith.

This Qing-dynasty painting of five bodhisattvas *is labeled "Shunzhi, tenth year" indicating that it dates from 1654, the tenth year of the reign of the emperor Shunzhi (ruled 1644–1661).*

THE ART OF WRITING

The Chinese considered calligraphy to be one of the higher art forms. When it first appeared in China, writing was thought to be imbued with magical power. The earliest forms found to date were written or carved on turtle shells, ox bones, and bronze vessels ca. 1200BCE for communicating with ancestral spirits during sacred divination ceremonies (see pp.132–3). In Chinese mythology, the creator of the writing system was Cang Jie, who invented ideograms by observing natural phenomena such as prints left by bird claws and animal paws, shadows cast by trees, and heavenly constellations. His achievement was so significant that nature, it is said, responded with miracles, such as showers of grain during the day and demons howling at night.

THE FIVE PRINCIPAL TYPES OF CHINESE SCRIPT

SEAL SCRIPT (*zhuan shu; xiao zhuan*). The First Emperor, Qin Shihuangdi (ruled 221–210BCE), had the seal script designed to unify the different scripts of his new empire. Seal script is stylized in form, with lines of even thickness and well-defined spacing to assist clarity. Although intended primarily for writing, it was also used for inscriptions and after the Han dynasty it was mainly used on seals, whence its name. It is often employed on works of art either to create a sense of antiquity or simply as a display of virtuosity.

CLERICAL SCRIPT (*li shu*). Literally "petty officials' writing," *li shu* was developed to meet the needs of the early empire's growing bureaucracy. It became widespread between the third century BCE and second century CE and was used for a wide variety of texts. More practical than seal script,

A calligraphic brush of ca. 1700 made of gilded copper and cloisonné *enamel. It is 13.5 inches (32cm) long including the brush tip.*

which demands lines of equal thickness, *li shu* is characterized by modulated horizontal sweeping lines displaying the "crescendo" progression of the brush tip.

STANDARD SCRIPT (*kai shu; zheng shu*). A modification of clerical script, *kai shu* was well established by the third century CE. Its short, terse characters make for greater legibility and ease of writing and it remains the most popular means of writing Chinese to this day. It is the script on which printed characters are based.

RUNNING SCRIPT (*xing shu*). A cursive form of standard script common in informal writing, such as letters, as well as on paintings (see pp.193). Developed in the second century CE, it combines speed with legibility. Arguably the most famous piece of Chinese calligraphy, *The Preface to the Orchid Pavilion Collection*, is in this style (see pp.192–3).

CURSIVE SCRIPT (*cao shu*). Representing a further step toward the freedom of the brush, *cao shu* originated as a shorthand version of either clerical or standard script. It is characterized by highly spontaneous, rapid, and light strokes of the brush tip, which permit infinite variations of form and shade. An extreme version, *kuang cao* ("wild cursive"), first appeared in the work of the monk Huaisu (active ca. 730–780CE).

OPPOSITE, LEFT, AND BELOW *Chinese calligraphy spawned a range of minor arts. These five inkcakes— solid blocks of pigment from which the required amount was ground and mixed with water to make ink—form part of a set made in 1689. They are decorated with the various types of script (see box, opposite):* OPPOSITE *seal script;* LEFT *(left to right) clerical script; standard script; running script with seal script;* BELOW *cursive script.*

Around the third and fourth centuries CE writing began to be viewed as an art form in itself: *shudao* ("way of writing") or *shufa* ("method, or standard, of writing"). From this time, the production of fine calligraphy featured prominently in the lives of the *literati*, the scholarly élite, for whom mastery of writing became a sign of personal cultivation. This period saw the birth of China's most famous calligraphic artist, the poet Wang Xizhi (303–361CE), who is known as the "Sacred Calligrapher."

Early forms of Chinese writing were pictographic imitations of natural objects; although the characters later evolved to become much more schematic, the bond between character and object is deeply rooted. The contents of calligraphic texts are often made more manifest by their physical form. Calligraphy is an embodiment of the writer's personality and mood as well as a demonstration of artistic creativity. As the theorist Su Guoting (648–703CE) pointed out in his *Shu Pu* (*Manual of Calligraphy*, 687CE), when Wang Xizhi wrote the *Lanting Ji Xu* (*The Preface to the Orchid Pavilion Collection*) in 353CE about a happy gathering of *literati* friends, his roaming thoughts and uplifted spirit took the form of "untrammeled brushstrokes" (see illustration, pp.192–3).

Chinese calligraphy is in many senses a ritualistic act in that the writer, who has undergone years of rigorous training, follows highly precise conventions such as the way to hold and manipulate the brush-pen, the sequence of strokes that must be followed in producing a character, and so on. Also, the content of a text and the physical setting in which a piece of calligraphy is to be presented help determine the type or style of script (*shu ti*; see box, opposite) that the calligrapher chooses.

According to the *Manual of Calligraphy*, a master calligrapher may evoke all kinds of natural forces, such as "the manner of wild geese cruising in the sky and beasts

running in fright" and "the posture of phoenixes dancing and snakes slithering away with a start." Brushstrokes can be as light "as a cicada's wings" or as voluminous "as rolling clouds." The calligrapher may move the brush "as a spring bubbles forth" or rein it back "as if the mountains are in repose." Crystallized in the form of calligraphy are the master's character, cultivation, and mood, as well as his skill and energy.

Calligraphy is one of the earliest forms of Chinese performance art: on viewing a calligraphic piece, a connoisseur savors the artist's effort and ingenuity, expressed in every thrust and pause and every contrast between blank and inked spaces and between light and dark patches. Furthermore, Chinese calligraphic works have an essential linear structure, which starts from the top right-hand corner of the page and moves downward character by character and leftward column by column to the lower left-hand corner. With the knowledge of the conventional sequences of strokes in each ideogram and of numerous different renderings of the same ideogram by generations of masters, a connoisseur achieves an intimacy with the work and its creator that no other forms of art can provide. The Northern Song calligrapher Mi Fu (1052–1107) described his infatuation with old masters' works: "Every time I spread out a scroll, I am oblivious even to the roar of thunder by

Part of Wang Xizhi's celebrated The Preface to the Orchid Pavilion Collection, *written in 353*CE *in a short burst of inspiration and regarded as one of the great masterpieces of Chinese calligraphy. It was* The Preface *that earned Wang the title of the "Sacred Calligrapher" (see p.191). Three centuries later, the Tang emperor Taizong (ruled 626–649*CE*) collected all extant work attributed to Wang and had exact copies engraved on stone pillars so that people could make ink rubbings of them. The* Preface *is written in "running script" (*xing shu*).*

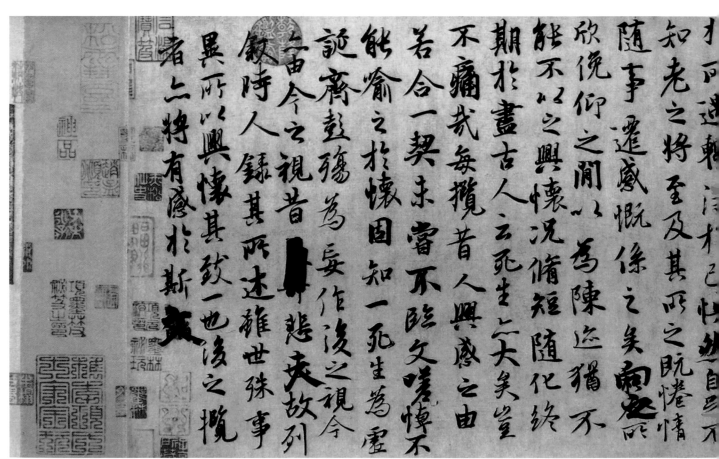

my side, and the taste of food is forgotten ... I suspect that after I die I will become a silverfish who enters into scrolls."

Since about the third century CE, collections of calligraphy have been arranged according to script types (see box, p.190), rather than by the literary genre of the content. The traditional way of classifying calligraphic works and the age-old practice of copying model calligraphy page by page have led to a separation of the content from its form—it is the fine ink strokes and composition of the characters that are objects of appreciation, not what is actually written. An extreme example can be found in the John B. Elliott Collection at Princeton University. A superb hanging scroll of script, which was the epitaph of a certain Madam Han, and therefore inauspicious, has been cut up into album leaves. The physical rearrangement of the text has preserved the art, but made its content less offensive to a Chinese reader.

The most popular form in which Chinese calligraphy is displayed is the pair of hanging scrolls (*dui lian*), often seen flanking doorways or family altars, or hung in the living room. On the first day of each Chinese New Year (which falls in late January or early February), almost every household is adorned with a pair of freshly-written scrolls conveying auspicious messages for the new cycle.

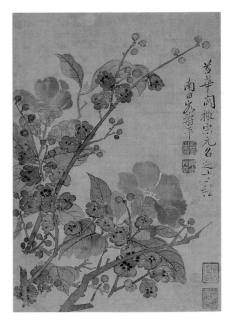

Plum Blossom and Camellias *by Shouping Yun (1633–1690). It bears an inscription in running script.*

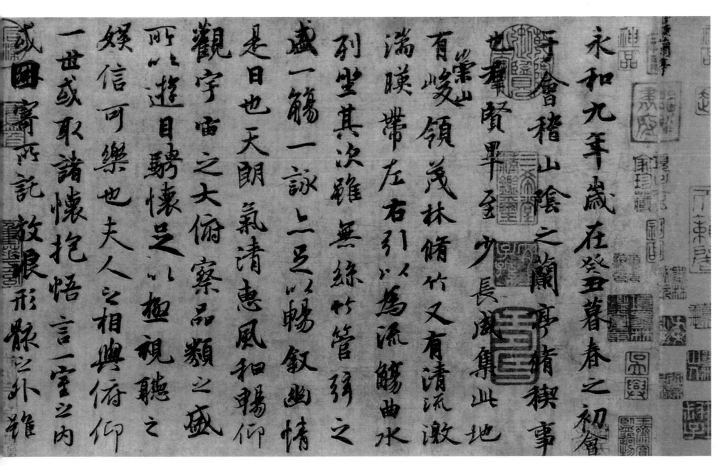

TRADITIONS OF COURT PAINTING

Apart from religious institutions, only the imperial court had the power and resources to patronize high art on a substantial scale in dynastic China. Kings and emperors gathered the best artists in the country around them, not only from a love of art, but also for propaganda purposes, since they constantly needed to justify their mandate to rule to competing political forces and the public.

In the waning years of the Tang dynasty and the chaotic 50-odd years of the Five Dynasties and Ten Kingdoms, the imperial artistic traditions were best preserved in the courts in Jinglin (present-day Nanjing) and Sichuan, where birds, flowers, mountains, and rivers gained the interest of painters, largely because there were few human glories to promote.

Both written and pictorial evidence for the efflorescence of paintings

VISIONS OF ORDER

The Song emperor Huizong (ruled 1101–1125 CE) was a great patron of the arts and himself a sophisticated painter. He advocated both "absolute" realism and an imagery of subtle and poetic suggestion (as demonstrated in his painting illustrated below).

In 1072, the court artist Guo Xi (after 1000–ca. 1090 CE) presented the emperor with *Zao-chun tu* (*Early Spring*), a pictorial spectacle of nature, order, and sublimity. Guo Xi synthesized the techniques of his northern and southern predecessors and ingeniously realized the objectives of landscape painting: to recreate the true image and mood of nature while glorifying the imperial system, for both are seen as forms of the superior cosmic order.

Another vision of order was provided by portraits of various worthies, to whom specific good deeds were attributed. These characters were intended to be role models for everyone in the imperial hierarchy. Examples from this category include *Zhelan tu* (*Breaking the Balustrade*) and *Quezuo tu* (*Declining the Seat*), which praised two loyal ministers of the Han dynasty. Enhanced by dramatic poses, such narrative paintings illustrate the force of Chinese political rhetoric.

Finch and Plum Blossom *by the emperor Huizong. The accompanying inscription is in his exquisite "thin-gold style" of calligraphy, later known simply as "imperial style."*

of birds and flowers during this period survives, such as the accounts given by the Song writers Shen Kuo (active 1086–1093CE) and Guo Ruoxu (active last half of the eleventh century CE), and the paintings attributed to Huang Quan (903–968CE) and Xu Xi (died before 975CE). This genre of court art was partly a product of the Confucian notion that society might be influenced by the contemplation of the order of nature in all its splendor. The emperors of the Western Shu (Sichuan) and the Southern Tang (Nanjing) courts chose to decorate their luxurious palaces with schemes of fauna and flora: images of peonies, narcissi, rabbits, cranes, and pheasants prevailed.

Shen Kuo's *Mengxi bitan* (*Casual Writing by the Stream of Dreams*) contains vivid descriptions of the styles employed by the two grand masters: "The extraordinary quality of Huang Quan's flower paintings lies in his way of laying on colors. First he drew an outline in very delicate lines (one can hardly discern them on the finished work). Then he applied light color washes upon the foundation to complete his painting. This was called the 'depicting-the-life' method." On the other hand, "Xu Xi drew an object summarily in ink and then applied very small amounts of cinnabar and white to the sketch. His work radiates a subtle but satisfying vitality." From then on, Chinese bird and flower painters consciously tended to follow one of these two major traditions.

During the first half of the tenth century, landscape painting underwent a profound transformation. With its further refinement sponsored by the Song court, it evolved into an unmistakably Chinese style. In the north, hard, crisply-drawn compact forms were favored, and the rocky surface of the mountains was emphasized to convey a sense of monumentality. In the south, however, paler ink and wet brushstrokes were preferred to depict the ethereal beauty of the mist-filled marshy waterlands.

The Ming court supported a large number of court artists, resulting in the rise of the Zhe school, which perfected the narrative and didactic elements of Chinese painting. As the Qing dynasty reached its zenith during the Qianlong reign, the style of court painting became increasingly meticulous and ornate—a combination of the emperor's personal taste and the contemporary Western influence brought to China by missionary painters such as the Italian artist Giuseppe Castiglione (1688–1768).

Two panels from an intricately detailed ten-panel screen made in the workshops of the emperor Qianlong (ruled 1736–1795). The elaborate decorations on this piece include imperial dragons (top left and bottom right) and a mountain, symbolizing stability (top left).

A NOBLE PASTIME:
LITERATI ART

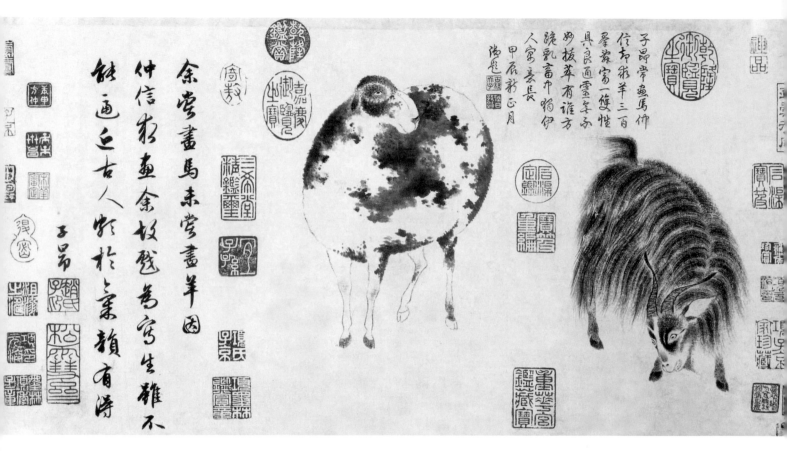

Sheep and Goat *by the Yuan dynasty*
literati *painter Zhao Mengfu
(1254–1322).*

In the late Northern Song dynasty (ca. 1050CE), the scholar-officials Su Shi, Mi Fu, and Li Gonglin initiated a new movement in art: so-called "*literati* painting," which diverged from the orthodox style practiced by professionals at the Imperial Academy of Painting. When the Mongols occupied China, most educated Chinese found themselves relegated to the bottom of the social scale. During that period, members of the *literati* (see pp.66–7) often formed mutual support groups, in which the wealthier members helped the less well-off. In this patronage system, paintings often served as a means of repaying a benefactor.

Owing to their Confucian education, Chinese scholar-gentlemen were all highly skilled with the brush pen, and a typical *literati* painting reflects the artist's expertise in the art of Chinese writing. For example, a fine calligraphic stroke might be transformed to portray a joint in a bamboo stem or a twig on a pine tree. According to Zhao Mengfu (see caption, left), the "guru" of Yuan *literati* painters, the solid black strokes used in writing the seal script (see p.190) embody the organic energy of trees, while the eight basic types of strokes employed in the regular script are adapted to depict the foliage and stems of bamboo. Dry, unevenly inked strokes shape the rocks and give them roughness and volume. A knowledgeable viewer can appreciate the brushstrokes in a *literati* painting both as components of an image and as the calligraphic movements of a master hand.

The scholar-gentlemen painters favored monochrome paintings of plant subjects such as bamboos, orchids, pine trees, and blossoming plum, each a symbol of admirable human qualities. This symbolism, derived from the Chinese classics, was used to convey congratulatory and auspicious messages and served, especially in the Yuan dynasty, to strengthen the common values among the *literati* at a time when Chinese identity was brutally subjugated.

A descendant of the Song imperial family who served at the Yuan court, Zhao Mengfu inaugurated the practice of expressing one's individual nature and feelings through the medium of ink on paper. The "Four Great Masters of the Late Yuan"—Huang Gongwang, Ni Zan (see box, below), Wu Zhen, and Wang Meng—further cultivated this genre to the extent that it became the hallmark of the whole *literati* school. The best *literati* paintings demonstrate how a personal style, developed within the new scholar-gentleman tradition, can effectively convey a sense of tranquillity and escape from worldly attachments. The plain, unimpressive scenery and the often schematic composition in a *literati* painting reject all that is overtly expressive. Both the brushwork and image communicate the idea of uncompromising integrity and aloofness.

Scholar Listening to a Waterfall *by Shizuo Li (1673–1747).*

NI ZAN

Ni Zan (1301–1374 CE), one of the "Four Great Masters of the Yuan," was born in Wuxi, near the Grand Canal and Lake Tai. He had an excellent classical education and spent a great deal of time studying paintings by past masters held in the art collections of his wealthy friends.

In the spring of 1352, in the declining years of the Yuan dynasty, Ni Zan was forced by the political and economic climate to leave his hometown. He moved around Lake Tai in a houseboat—the beginning of more than 20 years of wandering. Ni Zan felt he could only keep his high moral principles (and avoid being persecuted by Yuan officials) by living in complete reclusion, in accordance with his Daoist ideals.

Ni Zan is most famous for his compositional scheme, in which a wide watercourse typically separates two groups of features on different planes: trees in the foreground and mountains in the background. In compositions of this kind, Ni Zan attempted to reduce nature to a minimum. By being less representational, he could express his untrammeled spirit and display his aloofness from worldly concerns. The simplicity of his style is deceptive—he built up the trees and rocks with dry and transparent brushstrokes, and the seemingly sketchy brushwork is actually comprised of many light texture strokes. Ni Zan took *literati* landscape painting style to almost unsurpassed heights, epitomizing the *pingdan* ("unembellished elegance") aesthetics cherished by the scholar-gentleman class. Like most *literati* masters, Ni Zan was modest about his work, claiming it to be just "ink play"—a mere pastime.

THE CRAFT OF THE POTTER

Clay for making low-fired pottery (that is, fired below 1,000°C) can be found almost anywhere in the world, and China is no exception. However, the country is especially rich in deposits of *gaolin* (kaolin, or "china clay"), which is the main ingredient of high-fired hard porcelain (fired at about 1,350°C), for which China is famous. The body of low-fired earthenware is usually brown or gray in color, porous and brittle, while stoneware (fired at about 1,200°C) and porcelain are harder and non-porous. In turn, the body of porcelain is whiter, more translucent, and more glass-like than that of stoneware.

Earthenware has served from prehistoric times to the present day mainly as a material for cheap utensils, but also as an artistic medium. The aesthetic sensibilities of the earliest Chinese potters are reflected in the forms and decoration of the red, gray, and black Neolithic earthen-

TANG EARTHENWARE

The cosmopolitan and prosperous society of the Tang dynasty has left us a rich legacy in the form of the only substantial group of the secular clay sculpture in the whole dynastic history of China. Handsome pieces glazed in the *sancai* (literally "three colors," although in fact more were used) have been discovered, not only around the Tang capital of Chang'an (present-day Xi'an), but also as far as Xingjiang in the northwest and Liaoning in the northeast. The *sancai* palette, primarily consisting of brown, green, yellow, and white, and occasionally blue, appealed to the viewer with its almost baroque splendor, created through the free-flowing and intermingling of these glazes during firing. In addition to the bright glazing, the modeling style used to portray humans and animals (especially horses) was both naturalistic and vigorous, while a fantastic style was used to depict guardian spirits and heavenly kings.

Tang aristocrats were extremely dress-conscious and their tomb sculpture records every subtle change in fashion. The impressive figures of Tang court ladies belong to two distinct groups: slender and plump. It is believed that the latter type owes its appearance in the second quarter of the eighth century CE to the favor bestowed by the Emperor Xuanzong (ruled 712–756CE) on Lady Yang, a woman of Rubenesque beauty.

*This Tang figure representing a Buddhist guardian deity (*lokapala*) was glazed using the* sancai *("3-color") palette.*

ware (ca. 7000–ca. 2000BCE). It was on Neolithic red pottery that one of the earliest known Chinese paintings was produced during the fourth millennium BCE. The potters of one Neolithic culture, the Dawenkou (ca. 5000–3000BCE), even fabricated elegant eggshell-thin vessels such as goblets with pierced decorations in polished black earthenware. This ingenious manipulation of the intrinsically bulky material was not to be repeated for millennia—it next appeared in the late 1970s.

During the Shang dynasty, there arose another noteworthy example of earthenware: white ware duplicating bronzeware forms. Just as exquisitely fashioned and decorated as their bronze prototypes, these vessels were made in very small quantities for ritualistic use. After this period, low-fired pottery was rarely used again as a medium for high craftsmanship, although clay funerary objects (*ming qi*) representing everyday objects and activities (see pp.186–7) abounded between the Warring States period and the High Tang era (first half of the eighth century CE). The use of earthenware substitutes for vessels of more valuable materials greatly lowered the costs of funerals. The most famous example of *ming qi* is the army of terracotta warriors made to guard the mausoleum of the First Emperor of Qin (see p.187).

The growth of filial piety in the Han dynasty encouraged wealthy families to bury their dead in a competitively elaborate way and the new multi-chambered tombs could accommodate more *ming qi* items. The variety of grave goods further multiplied, covering practically every sphere of life, from stoves to latrines, and figures of entertainers to domesticated animals. Soft lead glazes were applied to funerary pottery, first in reddish or dark brown (iron oxide) and leaf green (copper oxide), then in yellow or amber, and later, in the Tang dynasty, in blue and turquoise (cobalt oxide). These glazes are both decorative and poisonous—a desirable quality for *ming qi*, as it could discourage tomb-robbers.

Low-fired pottery was also used for making molds for bronze-casting and for building houses, tombs, and drainage systems. The intricate shapes and patterns found on the molds in bronze foundries involve a very high level of craftsmanship, as do various forms of glazed roof tiles, some of which were assembled to create the gleaming palatial splendor of the Forbidden City in Beijing (see p.218).

A Han pottery model of a grain silo, made in the 2nd century BCE to be placed in a tomb. The five-story model is remarkable for its detailed decoration.

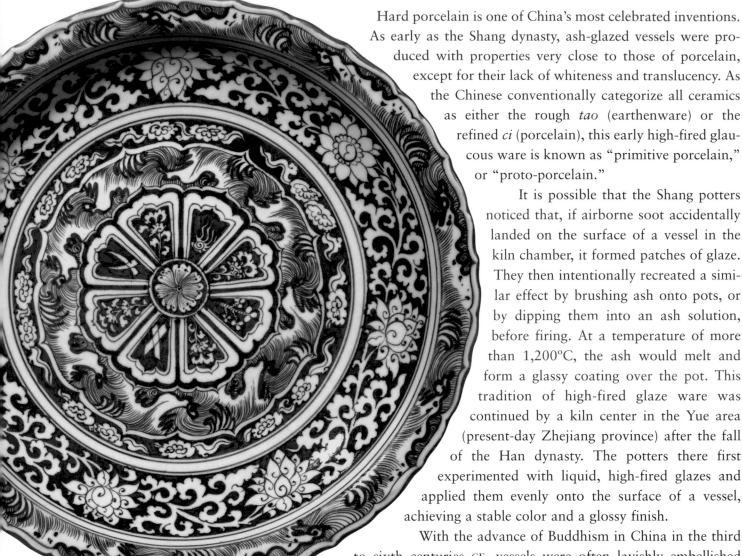

A Yuan dynasty dish. Blue-and-white Yuan ware bears a series of horizontally arranged decorative zones. The main design is usually painted with various kinds of textured strokes similar to those found in contemporary ink painting. It took more than a century for the Chinese élite to appreciate blue-and-white ware, which remained principally an export item until the reign of the Xuande emperor (1426–1435) during the Ming dynasty, when delicate and more refined forms were produced to cater for Chinese tastes.

Hard porcelain is one of China's most celebrated inventions. As early as the Shang dynasty, ash-glazed vessels were produced with properties very close to those of porcelain, except for their lack of whiteness and translucency. As the Chinese conventionally categorize all ceramics as either the rough *tao* (earthenware) or the refined *ci* (porcelain), this early high-fired glaucous ware is known as "primitive porcelain," or "proto-porcelain."

It is possible that the Shang potters noticed that, if airborne soot accidentally landed on the surface of a vessel in the kiln chamber, it formed patches of glaze. They then intentionally recreated a similar effect by brushing ash onto pots, or by dipping them into an ash solution, before firing. At a temperature of more than 1,200°C, the ash would melt and form a glassy coating over the pot. This tradition of high-fired glaze ware was continued by a kiln center in the Yue area (present-day Zhejiang province) after the fall of the Han dynasty. The potters there first experimented with liquid, high-fired glazes and applied them evenly onto the surface of a vessel, achieving a stable color and a glossy finish.

With the advance of Buddhism in China in the third to sixth centuries CE, vessels were often lavishly embellished with Buddhist motifs, such as premolded lotus blooms and jewels. The Tang dynasty saw abundant literary references to the aesthetic value of ceramics, in particular of Yue ware. Many poets extolled its beauty, comparing it to jade, green mist, spring water, or "a new lotus leaf scooping morning dew."

Ceramics produced in the Song dynasty conform to a new set of aesthetic ideals and display sensitively achieved simplicity. The Ru kilns near the capital of the Northern Song in Henan province operated for only 20 years (ca. 1086–ca. 1106CE), but the surviving Ru pieces have been avidly sought after ever since for their subtle shades of light grayish-blue, their faint cracking, and their simple yet elegant forms. After the Song court moved to Hangzhou in the south in 1127, new kilns were set up to continue producing the same type of ware. However, local materials were different, resulting in a ware later known as Guan (literally, "official"). Guan ware was greatly admired for its thick, jade-like, translucent glaze with a pronounced cracked-ice pattern.

The sudden emergence of mature blue-and-white porcelain at Jingdezhen in Jiangxi province in the early to mid-fourteenth century still puzzles scholars. In the Song dynasty, the Jingdezhen kilns started firing a *qing bai* ("bluish white") ware, which evolved in the following centuries into a pure white, translucent porcelain with a clear glaze. This provided an ideal surface for the brilliant cobalt blue imported from the Middle East, where only low-fired pottery existed. The war in northern China at that time forced the skilled potters of the Cizhou and Jizhou kilns to flee and settle in Jingdezhen. They carried with them sophisticated techniques of underglaze painting. When descriptions of Chinese hard porcelain arrived in the Middle East, collectors sent large orders to Jingdezhen. The Yuan government encouraged porcelain export, as it earned huge profits that were badly needed to fund the dynasty's colossal bureaucracy. Typical Yuan blue-and-white vessels include large pieces, such as dishes (see illustration, opposite), jars, and "prunus" vases (*mei ping*). In the Ming dynasty, the refined taste and sensibility of the Chenghua emperor (ruled 1465–1487) led to the creation of a collection intended for a more tactile appreciation in the hands of connoisseurs.

The potters of the Qing dynasty displayed great virtuosity; almost every material—including bamboo, ivory, lacquer, bronze, and pudding stone—was duplicated in ceramic form.

A pair of wall vases decorated in the fencai *("powder color," known in the West as "famille rose") palette, Qianlong reign (1736–1795). Qing-dynasty potters transferred the aesthetic ideal of the harmonious combination of poetry, calligraphy, and painting onto single pieces of porcelain, created under the direct supervision of the emperor.*

THE AESTHETICS OF DISPLAY

An inscribed ornamental jade carved with an image of two scholars at a mountain retreat.

OPPOSITE *An example of calligraphy in the style of Wen Zhengming, who is ranked eighth in Li Rihua's list of desirable works of art (see box, opposite).*

With the rapid development of the Chinese economy from the mid-Ming period, the Jiangnan area of the Yangzi delta enjoyed a similar status in China to that of Touraine in France at the beginning of the Renaissance. During the last quarter of the sixteenth and first half of the seventeenth century, Jiangnan's *literati* (see pp.66–7) created an extremely sophisticated cultural environment. They invented a genre of writing notes on how objects encountered by the leisured class should be appreciated, specifying precise rules of taste and style.

In spite of the fact that the declared aim of the Ming *literati* was to escape worldly attachment, many of them wrote books concerning material goods, the most famous of which is *Zhangwu zhi* (*Treatise on Worldly Possessions or Superfluous Things*). Its author, Wen Zhenheng (1585–1645), was born into a famous lineage with a respectable income from landholdings. According to Wen Zhenheng, a gentleman's residence should be imbued with the air of a man without worldly cares and emit the aura of a cultivated hermit. Living in a perfect aesthetic environment, it was believed, would nurture the inhabitant's soul and protect him or her from "corrosion" by the mundane.

"Good-taste guides" written by *literati* typically contained sections on buildings and rooms, trees and flowers, water and rocks, fish and birds, calligraphy and painting, and connoisseurship of various types of works of art and crafts. The books meticulously describe the qualities of numerous desirable objects and the ways in which they should be presented and appreciated—the display of carefully chosen pieces was intended to demonstrate the owner's good taste and reinforce his or her social and intellectual status.

The two terms used most frequently in discussions of *literati* taste are *ya* ("refined") and *su* ("vulgar"). One activity which illustrated the distinction between *ya* and *su* was the collection and appreciation of works of art. In this field, hierarchies of different categories of objects, and the preference for particular origins and styles within a category were exhaustively listed. One leading theorist, Li Rihua (1565–1635) produced a hierarchical list of works of art according to their level of cultural prestige (see box, opposite). The list reflected the *literati*'s cultural world, in which calligraphy and painting were ranked higher than bronzes and ceramics, and antiques were preferred over more recent products. It is interesting to note that—under the Ming dynasty—Chinese porcelain appears at the bottom of Li Rihua's list.

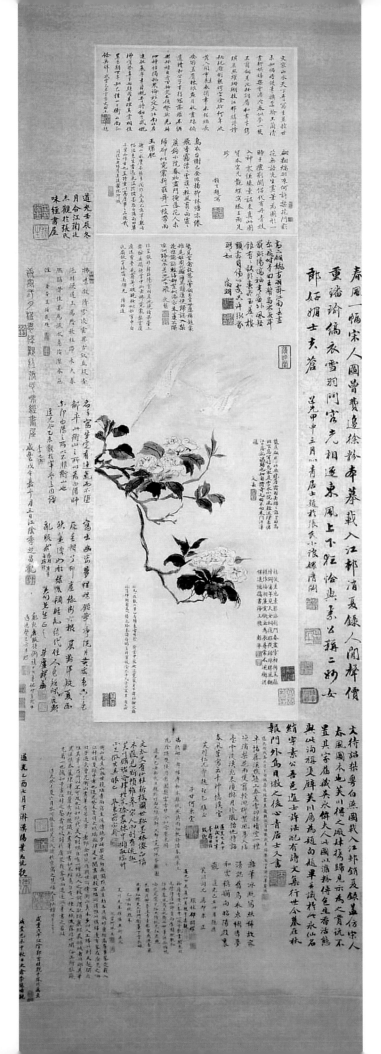

LI RIHUA'S LIST

In his *Zitaoxuan zazhui* (*Miscellanea from the Purple Peach Studio*), the Ming scholar Li Rihua ranked objects of beauty in order of their desirability to the discriminating *literatus*:

1. Calligraphy of the Jin and Tang dynasties.
2. Paintings of the Tang, Five Dynasties, and early Song.
3. Ancient calligraphic model-books of the Sui, Tang, and Song.
4. Calligraphy by Su Shi (1037–1101), Huang Tingjian (1045–1105), Cai Xiang (1012–1067), and Mi Fu (1052–1107).
5. Paintings of the Yuan dynasty.
6. Calligraphy by Xianyu Shu (ca. 1257–1302), Yu Ji (1272–1348), and Zhao Mengfu (1254–1322).
7. Paintings by Ma Yuan (active ca. 1190–1225) and Xia Gui (active ca. 1195–1230).
8. Masterpiece paintings by Shen Zhou (1427–1509) and Wen Zhengming (1470–1559).
9. Calligraphy in running or cursive style by Zhu Yunming (1461–1527).
10. Examples of calligraphy by various other famous *literati*.
11. Good examples of pre-Qin bronze vessels with a brilliant turquoise or vermilion patination.
12. Ancient jades, such as large *bi* disks.
13. Tang inkstones.
14. Ancient zithers and famous swords.
15. Finely printed books of the Five Dynasties and Song.
16. Fantastic rocks with a rugged texture and attenuated shapes.
17. An old, elegant pine tree accompanied by needle-like rushes in a fine pot.
18. Elegant blossoming plum trees and bamboos.
19. Imported perfumes of a subtle kind.
20. Foreign treasures of a rare and beautiful kind.
21. The highest grade tea, well prepared.
22. Foreign delicacies.
23. Lustrous white porcelains, green-glazed *mi se* ("secret color") ware, earthenware, and stoneware of all periods.

THE PERFORMING ARTS

THE CHINESE THEATER

MUSIC, DANCE, AND ACROBATIC SHOWS PLAYED A CENTRAL ROLE IN THE TRADITIONAL LIFE OF CHINA. THESE ART FORMS WERE USED TO COMMUNICATE WITH ANCESTRAL SPIRITS AND EXERCISE POLITICAL POWER IN RITUALS; TO EXPRESS FEELINGS, ESPECIALLY IN COURTSHIP; AND TO ADD COLOR TO SOCIAL OCCASIONS. IN LATE IMPERIAL CHINA ALL THE PERFORMANCE ARTS MERGED AND EVOLVED INTO A DISTINCTIVE FORM OF NATIONAL MUSIC-DRAMA WITH NUMEROUS REGIONAL VARIATIONS.

A Yuan-dynasty figure of a comic actor. Although this piece appears to represent a man, it was not uncommon for women to play both male and female roles.

Theater and drama are referred to in Chinese as *xi* and *ju*, terms that originally covered a range of activities including plays, games, and acrobatics. Traditional Chinese theater is characterized by highly stylized roles and stage movements, pantomine-like gestures and makeup, and by a unique combination of recitation, song, dance, acrobatics, and music.

As forerunner of Chinese theater, *canjunxi* (literally, "adjutant play") appeared in the court of Late Zhao during the Eastern Jin dynasty and evolved further in the Tang dynasty. In a *canjunxi* show, two performers—usually men—acted out comic dialogues, accompanied by string, wind, and percussion instruments. With the rise of a new merchant class during the Song dynasty, urban culture developed rapidly. In this environment *zaju* (literally, "variety play") and *nanxi* ("southern theater") emerged in north and south China respectively as the country's first fully-fledged theatrical traditions. A typical *zaju* show was performed by actors playing four or five roles in a set sequence: dancing, acrobatics, the central play, comic patter, and a musical conclusion. These short and often humourous plays were mostly romances or satires on officialdom. Popular role categories included those of the *fujin* (clown) and the *fumo* (jester).

There was a great flowering of drama under the Mongol emperors of the Yuan dynasty. When Khubilai Khan (ruled 1260–1294) reunited north and south China, *zaju* began to dominate the Chinese theater, marking its first golden age. The names of more than a 150 Yuan playwrights are recorded, and the most distinguished of them, Guan Hanging, is known to have written at least 60 plays. Yuan drama drew on the inexhaustible supply of stories provided by China's rich literary culture. During the Yuan era most *zaju* performances consisted of four acts, sometimes with a prologue or an interlude. The main character sang throughout the play. Although no musical scores from Yuan dramas have

THE BEIJING OPERA

In 1790, during the eightieth birthday celebrations for the emperor Qianlong (ruled 1736–1795), theatrical troupes from Anhui province made a great impact in the capital city with their innovatory performances. From these imperial birthday-shows evolved the much-loved form of national entertainment known as *jingxi* ("Beijing opera"). Its style is relatively simple and unpretentious, presenting familiar stories from history and literature. The repertory could be categorized as *wenxi* ("civil plays"), *wuxi* ("combat plays"), *daxi* ("epic plays"), and *xiaoxi* ("comic plays"). There were four principal roles: *sheng* (male), *dan* (female), *jing* (painted-face), and *chou* (clown). Each role was characterized by a set of distinctive speaking, singing, and acrobatic skills. By the early nineteenth century *jingxi* dominated the Beijing stage and eventually replaced *kunqu* (see main text) as the most popular form of theater in China.

survived, pictorial evidence from the period shows that they were commonly accompanied by flutes, drums, and clappers. Among characters portrayed in the Yuan *zaju* were scholars, courtesans, war heroes, rebels, judges, recluses, and supernatural beings.

Toward the end of the Yuan dynasty, southern drama was revived under the name *chuanqi* (literally, "spreading the incredible"). *Chuanqi* theater usually concentrated on romantic themes and was to dominate the Chinese stage for the next 200 years. The sixteenth century saw a surge in the popularity of *kunqu* (literally, "the tunes of Kunshan," a town near modern Shanghai)—an opera of sophisticated lyrics and scholarly librettos. *Kunqu*'s overall effect was atmospheric, elegant, and often melancholy. Many plays included 40–50 scenes, and took several days to perform. Around the end of seventeenth century, *kunqu* became popular among scholar-officials, who often took the actors with them on their postings—in this way *kunqu* spread to many parts of China.

MUSICAL TRADITIONS

The Chinese musical tradition has a long and rich history, attested to by a large amount of documentary and archeological evidence, including 21 seven-hole bone flutes discovered in an 8,000-year-old tomb. Music was an essential component of court rites and was believed to connect descendants with the spirits of their forefathers, and rulers with the power of Heaven.

The *Shi Jing* (*Classic of Poetry*), a collection of eleventh- to seventh-century BCE songs on themes as diverse as courtship and political satire, lists 29 types of percussion, wind, and stringed instruments. The Chinese employed a great variety of timbre in their musicmaking and they classified instruments according to the eight natural materials from which they were made. The most common instruments included bronze bells, stone chimes, bamboo or bone flutes, clay ocarinas, drums made of skin, mouth-organs fashioned out of a calabash, and zithers and lutes with silk strings and a wooden body.

The influx of central Asian and Indian musical influences during

Members of a traditional Chinese orchestra playing the two-stringed fiddle, or erhu.

A 2,400-YEAR-OLD ORCHESTRA

In 1978, the discovery of a complete ritual orchestra in the tomb of Lord Yi of Zeng (died ca. 433BCE) in Hubei provided rare evidence of the Chinese music of this period. Among the instruments found were large *se* zithers, small *qin* zithers, panpipes, flutes, and drums. Most sensationally, the tomb contained a set of 32 chimestones and a set of 65 bells suspended on stands. These instruments were used to produce what contemporary literature described as "suspended music"—a unique Chinese musical style. Both the bells and chimestones can still be used to play music composed on a five-pitched scale by striking them at a variety of specific points.

Bells or chimestones, such as those found in Lord Yi's tomb, served as standard-setters for an orchestra, emitting notes to which the other instruments could be tuned. They were also played to mark the beginning and the end of a performance.

Bronze bells originated in south China. They were imported into the Zhou capital and the surrounding area (in present-day Shaanxi province) halfway through the Western Zhou dynasty and appeared elsewhere in northern China at around the same time. Zhou court music came to rely heavily on the use of these impressive instruments.

Two bronze bells from the set found in the tomb of Lord Yi. The largest bell of the group weighs 175lbs (79.5kg).

the Han and Tang dynasties resulted in the introduction of new instruments and in changes in secular music. The Tang court organized music for entertainment into ten categories, mainly based on its ethnic origins. Among these, music from Qiuci (Kucha) in Turkestan and Xiliang (present-day western Gansu province) are of particular interest because many different musical traditions merged at these busy international trading centers. The Tang emperor Xuanzong (ruled 712–756CE) further arranged court music into two types: "sitting mode" and "standing mode." The former was chamber music played by three to twelve of the very best musicians, while the latter was performed in the open air by orchestras of 60–180 instrumentalists.

The *daqu* (long, formal pieces of music) of the Tang dynasty represent the zenith of Chinese instrumental ensemble music. It continued to be popular throughout the Song dynasty before it was finally overshadowed by theater music in late imperial China.

THE ART OF DANCE

This painted ceramic figure of a female dancer dates from the Eastern Han period and was found in a tomb near Xi'an in Shaanxi province. The dancer performs a long-sleeve dance—it is thought that such figures, many of which were later carved in jade, were intended to entertain the deceased after death. The figure is 20 inches (50cm) high.

In a preface to one of the Confucian classics, the *Shi Jing* (*Classic of Poetry*), a scholar of the first century CE summarized the contemporary Chinese view of dance: "Feelings arise within us and may be expressed in the form of words. If words alone do not suffice to express our feelings, we sigh. If sighing fails, we sing. If singing is still not enough, we express them by dancing with our hands and feet."

Like music, traditional Chinese dance originated in ritualistic activities such as courtship and ancestral worship. In ancient China, exorcistic dances were performed by professional sorcerers in order to guarantee a good harvest, to end a drought or flood, or to quell evil spirits. Subsequently, dance developed as part of political ceremonial and as an important form of entertainment. The folk and ritual songs collected in the *Shi Jing* describe female dancers of the Zhou dynasty entertaining guests at official banquets and private drinking parties with their splendid costumes, elegant movements, and dynamic formations. During the Zhou, dance was considered to be an essential part of the education of male aristocrats, who were expected to master and perform dance as a means of achieving harmony between body and mind. From the ages of thirteen to fifteen, boys from high-status families would learn "civil dances," before being trained in "military dances" until their early twenties.

The Tang dynasty saw a burgeoning of cultural exchange between China and other parts of Asia and many new dance styles were introduced. Exotic dances were regularly staged in palaces and great mansions, and also during seasonal festivals. The absorption of foreign choreographic ideas gave rise to a further new blossoming of local styles. The Tang emperor Xuanzong (ruled 712–756CE) is remembered as the founder of a court academy of dance and music called the Pear Garden (Liyuan), a name which has become a synonym for the dancing and acting professions in China. The emperor personally oversaw the training and rehearsal of hundreds of dancers and musicians in the academy.

Dance performances were not limited to court circles; in certain quarters of the capital hundreds of courtesans performed for public entertainment. As Tang paintings and figurines show, these dancers performed in low-necked robes with long pleated and flared skirts. The rippling of their long silk sleeves added to the swirling effect of the dance, which was much lauded by Tang poets.

With the rise of theater in later imperial China (see pp.204–5), dance developed further as an integral part of theatrical performance.

THE "WESTERN TWIRLING DANCE"

The *huxuan wu*, or "Western Twirling Dance," was popular in the Tang court and was a personal favorite of the dance-loving emperor Xuanzong (see main text). The *huxuan* dance is described in a book of the period, *Yuefu zalu* (*Random Notes on Music and Dances*), which states that it was performed by dancers from central Asia apparently balanced on small balls (*qiu*). This description has formed the basis of Edward H. Schafer's account in *The Golden Peaches of Samarkand* of girls who "skipped, tripped, and twirled on the tops of balls rolling about on the dance platform." However, all extant depictions of the dance (on murals, jade, and ceramics) show a twirling dancer on an oval rug. In Chinese, the character for "rug" (*tan*) is very similar to the one for "ball" (*qiu*) and so it may well be that a medieval copyist of *Yuefu zalu* mistook the character for *tan* as that for *qiu*.

Two prominent Tang poets, Bai Juyi (772–846CE) and Yuan Zhen (779–831CE), wrote vividly about the Western Twirling Dance. This extract is by Bai Juyi:

Western Twirling Girl! Western Twirling Girl!
Her heart beats to the tune of stringed instruments;
Her arms move in harmony with the drum's rhythm.
She lifts her sleeves as the music starts;
She dances like whirling snowflakes.
Tirelessly she revolves and endlessly she gyrates;
Nothing under the heavens matches her speed;
Carriage wheels are slower and even the whirlwind
    cannot catch her…

A depiction of the Western Twirling Dance in a detail from a Buddhist mural at Dunhuang caves, Gansu province.

ACROBATS AND CIRCUS

One of the most popular forms of entertainment in China, acrobatics originated from the desire to show off skill, dexterity, and courage using whatever tools, weapons, or utensils were available. The pre-Qin classics contain a wealth of documentary references to acrobats, and one tale even recounts the use of acrobatics during a battle between the armies of the states of Chu and Song—the Song soldiers were so transfixed by the sight of a Chu warrior juggling with nine balls that the Chu army was able to overwhelm them completely.

Acrobatics forms an intrinsic part of Chinese circus. Tomb bricks and pottery figurines dating from the Han dynasty portray circuses on a grand scale known as *baixi* ("100 performances") that represent an accumulation of native traditions and influences from various central Asian areas. During such spectacles, large numbers of people were entertained by chariot races, gladiatorial contests, staged wild-beast hunts, and acrobatic feats. A tomb brick discovered at Yinan in Shandong province in 1954 shows a performer balancing a large cross on his brow, on which

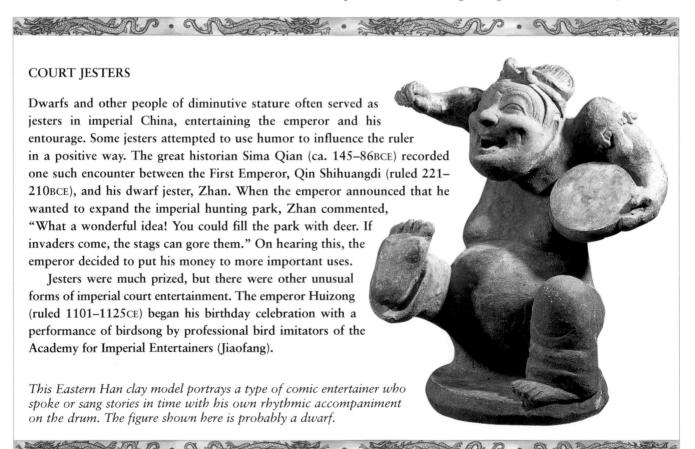

COURT JESTERS

Dwarfs and other people of diminutive stature often served as jesters in imperial China, entertaining the emperor and his entourage. Some jesters attempted to use humor to influence the ruler in a positive way. The great historian Sima Qian (ca. 145–86BCE) recorded one such encounter between the First Emperor, Qin Shihuangdi (ruled 221–210BCE), and his dwarf jester, Zhan. When the emperor announced that he wanted to expand the imperial hunting park, Zhan commented, "What a wonderful idea! You could fill the park with deer. If invaders come, the stags can gore them." On hearing this, the emperor decided to put his money to more important uses.

Jesters were much prized, but there were other unusual forms of imperial court entertainment. The emperor Huizong (ruled 1101–1125CE) began his birthday celebration with a performance of birdsong by professional bird imitators of the Academy for Imperial Entertainers (Jiaofang).

This Eastern Han clay model portrays a type of comic entertainer who spoke or sang stories in time with his own rhythmic accompaniment on the drum. The figure shown here is probably a dwarf.

three other figures are depicted performing gymnastic stunts. In another scene, a tightrope walker is executing a handstand in the middle of a rope strung above a line of sharp swords pointing upward. Two more figures are moving toward the middle of the rope from each end, swinging stone balls around them. A third scene shows a rider leaping onto a galloping horse. Also depicted is a man juggling with three swords.

Two authors of the Eastern Han dynasty, Zhang Heng (78–139 CE) and Li You (active ca. 89 CE), wrote about circus performances. Their accounts feature a strongman who lifted a cauldron "as though it were a feather"; gymnasts who jumped through hoops and wriggled through tubes; a giant-and-dwarf comedy duo; and magicians who altered the appearance of objects, appeared to slice bodies in half, swallowed knives, and breathed fire. Circus acts were not limited to acrobatics and conjuring tricks. Animal training also has a long tradition in China, where performing-animal shows included not only mammals but also fish and insects. Snake charmers were particularly popular.

The state occasionally attempted to restrict the development of circus in China. In 341 CE, the emperor Chengdi (ruled 326–342 CE) of the Eastern Jin dynasty banned feats such as walking on one's hands, jackknifing the body in order to squeeze through in a bamboo tube, and "horror magic" shows (such as "skinning a body") on the grounds that they disturbed social harmony. Anyone caught performing such stunts was punished by having their rice ration cut.

ABOVE *A Han pottery model of musicians, dancers, and acrobats performing before seven standing dignitaries.*

BELOW *This early 20th-century print depicts the exuberant acrobatics of a popular theatrical performance. The actor at bottom right uses precisely the same technique of walking on his hands with his legs about to curve over his head as the performers in the clay model above.*

● CHAPTER 15   *Nancy R. S. Steinhardt*

ARCHITECTURE AND PLANNING

THE TECHNOLOGY OF CHINESE ARCHITECTURE

FOR MILLENNIA, TRADITIONAL CHINESE ARCHITECTURE HAS BEEN GROUNDED IN A REVERENCE FOR THE "SON OF HEAVEN" AT THE CENTER OF A COSMOS OF ENCLOSED SPACES. BUILDINGS DESIGNED TO BE USED FOR WORSHIP OR TO BE INHABITED BY THOSE ENTERING THE AFTERLIFE FORM HIGHLY STRUCTURED ENVIRONMENTS, WHILE IN RESIDENTIAL AND GARDEN DESIGN THE ARCHITECT ENJOYS A GREATER DEGREE OF CREATIVE EXPRESSION.

Blue roof tiles decorated with dragons adorn the Temple of Heaven in Beijing (see also p.45).

The Chinese constructed buildings in a wide range of materials, including wood, brick, stone, mud-earth, ceramic tile, and even metal. Since earliest times, however, Chinese construction above-ground has been dominated by wood. The timber frame is China's major technological contribution to architecture worldwide—Chinese builders achieved unparalleled flexibility, adaptability, and versatility using wood.

In Zhejiang province in southeastern China, archaeologists have excavated interlocking pieces of wood that are over 6,500 years old. More than three thousand years ago, during China's Bronze Age, building complexes featuring several gates, principal structures interconnected by causeways, multiple courtyards, and enclosing arcades were constructed solely in wood.

The timber-frame building was to remain the norm for the most eminent Chinese structures throughout the imperial period. From the Song dynasty onward, the traditional Chinese building stood on a raised earthen or stone foundation platform and had a heavy tiled roof, the weight of which was borne by an elaborate construction of decorative bracket sets and columns made of wood. Walls and internal partitions were built using wattle and daub. The most important buildings faced south, sometimes with no openings on the other three sides.

The main hall of Foguang monastery on the sacred Buddhist mountain Wutai in Shanxi province is a typical example of Chinese timber-frame architecture. Built in 857CE, the hall rises more than 26 feet (8m) at its highest point and has 36 wooden columns, which support the rafters and roof structure. Fundamental to Chinese building technology is a modular system defined by its wooden members. A Chinese builder would have perceived the Foguang hall as

being eight columns wide by five columns deep, or, alternatively, as a nine-rafter frame building of eight rafter-spans. The rafter-span number refers to the number of spaces between each pair of rafters. It is probably the ability of wood to expand and contract according to climatic conditions, combined with the bulge around the middle of the columns and their slight incline, that made it possible for wooden halls such as the one at Foguang monastery to survive weathering and earthquakes for more than a millennium.

Between the columns and wooden structure that supported the roof is the feature most often associated with Chinese building technology—wooden bracket sets. These join the columns to the roof frame and lend additional support to the characteristically broad overhanging roof eaves. The timber-module system makes it possible for columns and corresponding beams and purlins to be easily added when more space is needed. Chinese timber-frame technology not only made it possible to accommodate an increase in family size or prosperity—reflected in the construction of more side rooms in private residences—but meant that essentially the same design was easily adaptable for the hall of a palace, a Buddhist hall (whereby the place of the throne would be taken up by an altar), or the hall of any other group or sect.

A view of the Forbidden City, Beijing, showing the decorated brackets on top of the columns that lend extra support for the heavy, ceramic-tile roof with its characteristic upturned overhanging eaves. The number and complexity of such bracket sets reflect the importance and designated use of a Chinese building.

THE GREAT WALL

The Great Wall is at once China's greatest monument and one of its most powerful symbols. Known in Chinese as the "Long Wall," it has captivated the imagination of both Chinese and non-Chinese alike for centuries. It is said to be the only human monument visible from the moon.

In the first millennium BCE, during the Springs and Autumns period (ca. 770–475BCE), feudal states constructed defensive walls—some of them stretching several hundred miles—along their borders. During the following Warring States period (ca. 476–221BCE) higher, longer, and more heavily fortified defensive walls were built.

The remains of a Han-dynasty signal tower on the Great Wall near Kupa in western China.

The figure most often associated with the Great Wall is the First Emperor, Qin Shihuangdi, who unified the Chinese states into an empire in 221BCE. In his most ambitious construction project, the First Emperor decided to join together various extant city and state walls to form one long wall, complete with forts and watchtowers, separating Chinese civilization from its "barbarian" northern neighbors. The Chinese nickname, "the 10,000-*li*-long wall," is not so much a literal statement (1 *li* = about 500m) as an expression of the wall's seemingly endless east–west span.

The rulers of the succeeding Han dynasty, equally anxious to protect China from external influence and attack, continued the construction and reinforcement of the wall, particularly across north China. They also added watchtower-beacons, so that troops stationed along the wall could use smoke signals to communicate urgent messages. It has been estimated that by the end of the Han in 220CE more than 6,000 miles (10,000km) of fortified wall had been built.

The dynasties that followed the Han undertook repairs to the wall, and some remarkable monuments were erected, such as the white marble gateway known as the Juyongguan ("Cloud Terrace Pass") about 35 miles (60km) north of the Forbidden City, originally built in the 1340s by the Mongol (Yuan) dynasty and restored under the following dynasty, the Ming. The Ming emperors renewed the commitment to a fortified northern frontier, and the Great Wall seen today is mainly a Ming construction (see box, opposite).

Under the Qing, the last imperial dynasty, both construction and repair work on the Great Wall were halted. The Qing emperors were Manchu, peoples from the north, beyond the wall, whom the Ming and earlier dynasties had sought to prevent from crossing into China. Allowing the wall to fall into ruin symbolized the incorporation into the empire of the Manchus and other non-Chinese peoples to the north.

The building of the wall represented an almost unbelievable accomplishment in engineering and logistics. A wealth of legends and stories recalls the construction of the Great Wall and the suffering of those who toiled on it (see p.51). Incessant national organization on a huge scale was needed to transport the vast quantities of materials and tools required to the construction sites. On the pre-Ming wall in the east and during Ming wall construction north of western China, local building materials were exploited wherever possible. For example, a mixture of pebbles, tamarisk, and twigs was used to build the sections of the wall that crossed the Gobi desert, and in the northeast oak and pine wood were employed to encase rammed earth.

THE MING WALL

Fearing Mongol invasion, the founder of the Ming dynasty, Hongwu (ruled 1368–1398CE), ordered his general Xu Da to repair all the strategic passes along the Great Wall. Subsequent Ming emperors built new stretches of the wall several miles to the south of the original one. Construction continued almost without interruption until ca. 1500. In the second half of the sixteenth century (when a northern tribe called the Oirats posed a serious threat), another 300 miles (500km) of Great Wall were erected.

Although it was farther south, the Ming wall across north China roughly followed the lines of the Qin and Han walls. The eastern section was built in ashlar or a combination of ashlar and brick, more solid materials than the layers of rammed earth used in former times. The average height of the Ming Great Wall is about 26 feet (8m); the average width at the base is about 23 feet (7m), tapering to about 20 feet (6m) at the top.

Many parts of the Ming wall are still standing today, such as this section at Simitai, north of Beijing.

WALLED CITIES AND TOWNS

THE WARDS OF CHANG'AN

In the seventh century CE, the imperial capital of Chang'an (modern Xi'an) was the largest and most populous city in the world, with more than a million inhabitants within its 23-mile (37km) outer wall in an area measuring 32 square miles (84km²). The enclosed palace city, home to the imperial family, stood in the center, with the government offices directly to the south. The rest of the city was divided into 108 wards, each enclosed by a wall. Every ward was subdivided into four by two main streets, one running north–south and the other east–west, each ending at a guarded ward gate. These four subdivisions were in turn subdivided into four, so that every ward contained sixteen bounded spaces, which made it relatively easy for the government to monitor the inhabitants' movements.

Two other wards—one on the east side of Chang'an and the other on the west—were designated as market areas.

Until the mid-twentieth century, whenever the Chinese built a city, they also built a wall. The Chinese character most often used to express the English word "city" is *cheng*, the same character that is usually chosen to translate the word "wall." Walled settlements, some of which were surrounded by moats, existed all over China from as early as the fourth or third millennium BCE. Neolithic walls were constructed by ramming layers of pounded earth. The shapes of the enclosures were usually four-sided, although oval-shaped walls have also been found.

The four-sided enclosure remained the main characteristic of the Chinese town or city through the seventeenth century CE, although rammed earth strengthened with pieces of rubble or wood was gradually replaced by brick as the main building material. It is thought that enclosure walls were initially constructed for defense purposes or to delineate boundaries. As weaponry and warfare became increasingly sophisticated, however, walls became less effective as defensive barriers. In spite of this, the Chinese continued to enclose their towns and cities, indicating that the purpose of such walls had always been partly symbolic.

The concept of the four-sided enclosure is so fundamental to the Chinese view of space that not only was every premodern Chinese settlement enclosed by walls but also the spaces within the settlement, from the most expansive monastery or government building to the humblest residence. Thus an imperial monastery in the Chinese capital city might be surrounded by a wall faced with plaster or brick and decorated with ceramic tiles; a smaller temple complex might be enclosed by an arcade supported by wooden pillars and open on the interior courtyard side;

and a city merchant's residence might be fronted by a plaster wall, while side walls were shared with his neighbors.

Within or adjacent to the main city walls of most Chinese state capitals was a smaller walled enclosure in which the ruler's palace and government offices were located. In the last decade of the third century BCE, under the Han dynasty, the Chinese capital was built at Chang'an. The city was expanded during the first century BCE—by the beginning of the Common Era, five enclosed palace complexes occupied at least half of the area within the capital's outer walls. By the Period of Disunion (fourth to sixth centuries CE), every state capital in China had a walled enclosure known as the "palace city" or "inner city" for the ruler and his government, as well as the standard outer wall. From the sixth century CE, the plans for Chinese urban construction were often modeled on Chang'an when it was the capital city of Sui and Tang China (581–907CE; see sidebar, opposite). From Japan to Inner Mongolia, the remnants of enclosure walls, wards, and gates can still be seen in cities and towns influenced by Chinese urban patterns.

This handtinted photograph of a city gate in Beijing was taken in 1906 and clearly shows the capital's old city walls. They were demolished in the 1960s during the Cultural Revolution.

A HOUSE FOR THE "SON OF HEAVEN"

Every Chinese palace symbolized the authority of the emperor—all its buildings, which sometimes numbered more than a hundred, were positioned and arranged to reflect the ruler's supreme power. Standard features at all periods within what the Chinese aptly call the "palace-city" (*gong*) were the emperor's throne room and private apartments.

It is believed that the large, centralized structures that dominated Neolithic and Bronze Age Chinese settlements were the prototypes for later palace architecture. During the Eastern Zhou period, each ruler's city had its own palace area. After the unification of China in 221BCE, emperors tended to govern from more than one capital and, to meet increasingly complex bureaucratic needs, the imperial spaces in the capitals gradually became standardized.

Both the Sui and the Tang built palace-cities in their two main capitals, Chang'an and Luoyang. In 634CE, the Tang emperor Taizong (ruled 626–649CE), began work on a palace complex at Chang'an, the

The first court of the Forbidden City. Beijing's famous imperial palace complex was the primary residence of fourteen emperors of the Ming and Qing dynasties.

Daminggong, which was typical of imperial residences of 600–800CE. Approached by a wide street from the south, the focus of the 1.2 square-mile (3.1km²) complex was a "U"-shaped group of buildings. A dynasty such as the Tang also had "detached," or "traveling," palaces, where the imperial family could stay when they were away from the capital.

Little remains of the main palaces of Song China, but records suggest that they were at least as grand as the Daminggong and followed the same principles. Much more is known about Khubilai Khan's *gong* in Dadu (Beijing), which was designed according to classical Chinese architectural principles as part of a program to legitimize Mongol rule in China. He also built the famous detached palace of Shangdu, described by Marco Polo and the inspiration for the poet Coleridge's *Xanadu*.

However, the best-preserved example of palace construction is the Forbidden City in Beijing, home to rulers of China's last two dynasties. Like the ideal Chinese state, the palace is perfectly planned. The first court (see illustration, below) is traversed by an elegantly conduited stream that runs south of the main palace, as required by Chinese geomancy (*feng shui*). Beyond the court are ceremonial halls, the apartments of the emperor and empress, and an array of government buildings (see also illustrations, pp.42–3, 46, and 213).

A bronze statue of a guardian lion in the Forbidden City. An imperial symbol, the creature grasps a pearl representing wisdom.

PLACES OF WORSHIP

Like the Chinese palace, the Chinese temple or monastery, or *miao* or *si*, consists of a complex of buildings—indeed from the outside, a temple complex and a palace complex can appear almost indistinguishable. Most temples in China are associated with one of the country's three great traditions: Buddhism, Daoism, and Confucianism.

Only a handful of temples of any denomination survive in China from before the tenth century CE. Nevertheless, we know from records, excavated evidence, and paintings that, within a few centuries after the introduction of Buddhism from India during the Han period, huge monasteries consisting of dozens of courtyards and hundreds of bays of buildings existed in every major city and throughout the Chinese countryside. Palace architecture (see pp.218–19) greatly influenced the design of these monasteries. The emperor's throne room was transformed into the main worship hall, in which the chief Buddhist image was the largest and most central. The cave temple, a uniquely Buddhist place of worship, was also introduced to China from India by way of central Asia.

The Pavilion of the Buddha's Fragrant Incense temple is located within the imperial Summer Palace complex of the Qing emperors on the shores of Lake Kunming, northwest of Beijing.

PUNING TEMPLE

Occasionally, temple architecture would break out of the strict confines of the Chinese building tradition. This was especially true during periods of rule by non-Chinese dynasties, when foreign religions and sects received extensive imperial patronage. The temple complexes of Tibetan Buddhism in China—such as Puning Temple in Chengde (Jehol), Hebei province—are examples of the successful marriage of Chinese planning and Tibetan architectural style.

The 39,500-square yard (33,000m²) site of Puning Temple was built in 1755 by the Qing emperor Qianlong (ruled 1736–1795) to celebrate his victory over a Mongolian tribe known as the Zungars. The building complex follows the strict axial plan of Chinese religious space, but Tibetan traditions are reflected in the tall, boxy, gilded structures with bulb-shaped roof decoration, and the deities depicted inside them.

Puning Temple at Chengde, Hebei province. Under the Yuan (Mongol) and Qing (Manchu) dynasties, the Tibetan form of Buddhism had an important influence on Chinese society and culture (see pp.115 and 222).

Cave temples dating from the fourth and fifth centuries CE onward survive in all parts of China.

The early (pre-twelfth century CE) wooden buildings preserved at Longxing *si* (monastery) in Zhengding, Hebei province, are typical of Buddhist temple complexes constructed in the ninth through fourteenth centuries. Oriented southward, the monastery is constructed along a north–south axis that begins at the front gate, accessible from the town, and includes a cruciform hall dedicated to the Buddha, a hall (now destroyed) dedicated to a patriarch, and smaller side halls. An additional multistory, 79-foot (24m) high pavilion was dedicated to the *bodhisattva* Guanyin. To the east lay the monks' living and eating quarters—the monastery was, of course, as much a place for the accommodation and education of monks as for worship by outsiders. This was also true of Daoist temple complexes. Yonglegong, one of the grandest, was built in the thirteenth century for the Complete Perfection (Quanzhen) Daoist sect (see p.93). This complex is also oriented southward, and includes halls to two Daoist patriarchs associated with the sect and buildings in which the monks lived and studied.

THE PAGODA

Together with the monastery and the cave temple, the pagoda is one of three important forms of Indian Buddhist architecture that was transmitted via central Asia to China. The Indian prototype for the pagoda is the *stupa*, initially an earthen mound with an egg-shaped dome used for housing relics. Over time, the *stupa* came to be built of stone, its dome topped by a multilayered finial mast, perhaps in imitation of an Indian ceremonial parasol.

By the time the *stupa* appeared in China, probably just before the end of the Han dynasty, it had become taller and more slender, although it was still circular in plan. The Chinese urban gate tower was combined with the *stupa* to produce the pagoda—a tall structure consisting of several stories (each story defined by a roof with overhanging eaves) and crowned by a roof. These early pagodas probably dominated every Buddhist monastery in China—it has been estimated that some of the most magnificent pre-Tang pagodas soared more than 425 feet (130m)—but most of them were made of wood and have not survived. The sole surviving examples of pre-500CE pagodas were hewn from solid rock inside Buddhist cave temples. Supported by a central pillar of rock, each story

THE WHITE PAGODA

A pagoda style sometimes called *dagoba*, particularly associated with Tibetan Buddhism, first appeared in China during the period of Mongolian rule (the Yuan dynasty). Perhaps the most famous example is the White Pagoda, a white brick *dagoba* that forms part of the Miaoying monastery in Beijing. It was built in 1279 under the influence of Anige, the Nepalese advisor of the emperor Khubilai Khan, founder of the Yuan dynasty. Elevated on a high platform, the White Pagoda consists of a large, bulb-like structure rising from a square base, above which are thirteen rings of decreasing size, representing the thirteen levels through which an adept must pass in order to attain Buddhahood. The spire is capped by a metal parasol and spire.

Almost four hundred years later, in 1651, the new Manchu rulers of China (the Qing dynasty), who were also followers of Tibetan Buddhism, erected a similar white pagoda in what is today Beihai Park in Beijing, to commemorate the advent of the new conquering dynasty.

The White Pagoda in Beijing. In plan it takes the form of a mandala, *a Buddhist cosmic diagram consisting of a circle within a square.*

has a decorative ceiling with rafters, eaves, and bracket supports carved into the stone in imitation of their wooden counterparts.

Pagoda architecture flourished during the Tang dynasty. Most pagodas of this period were four-sided and built of stone, brick, or wood. Smaller structures known as funerary pagodas were erected at monasteries throughout China to commemorate influential monks; these might have a circular, hexagonal, octagonal, or square ground plan. From the tenth to at least the twelfth centuries every Chinese Buddhist monastery had at least one pagoda. Among the hundred or more pagodas to survive from the tenth to the twelfth centuries in China and along its borders, the octagon is the most common ground-plan. However, from the Southern Song period pagodas began to disappear from monasteries. This was due to the marked growth in Chan (Zen) Buddhism (see p.113), which did not include worship in or around a pagoda as part of its rituals.

The 10th-century stone pagoda at the Kaiyun temple complex, Fujian province.

BUILDING FOR THE AFTERLIFE

The respectful burial of corporeal remains is one of the fundamental features of Chinese civilization. Few images have aroused as much interest about early China as those of excavated royal tombs, such as the Shang dynasty tombs at Anyang and that of the First Emperor, Qin Shihuangdi (ruled 221–210BCE), near Xi'an in Shaanxi, with its nearby pits containing thousands of life-size terracotta warriors (see pp.54 and 187).

Before the arrival of Buddhism at the beginning of the first millennium CE, the concept of rebirth on Earth did not exist in Chinese thought. Rather, Chinese writings inform us that careful preparations were made—often long before death was imminent—for the preservation of the corpse (see p.164) and its comfort in the afterlife.

The stone doorway leading to the inner chamber of the tomb of Li Shou, a prince of the Tang dynasty who was buried in 631CE.

Although the hallmark of Chinese architecture above ground was the timber frame, underground funerary constructions—which replicated the spaces of residential architecture—were built mainly of earth, brick, or stone. The materials used for Chinese tombs were more permanent than those used for palaces or great monasteries. Funerary architecture was often innovative—the earliest vaulting in China was accomplished underground in the last centuries BCE.

Some Chinese dynasties built royal necropolises, while others preferred to create an individual burial site for each emperor. The body of the deceased was buried beneath a mound, a custom dating from before the end of the first millennium BCE.

Like palace architecture, the above-ground portion of an emperor's tomb was enclosed by walls and was usually oriented according to the cardinal directions. Individuals close to the emperor—sons, daughters, other relatives, or honored officials—were often buried nearby in auxiliary tombs.

Access to the grave began at the end of the spirit path (see box, opposite).

SPIRIT PATHS

The approach to an imperial tomb above ground was dramatic. By the early centuries of the Common Era it was marked by a formal gateway set in surrounding walls, freestanding gate towers, and stone stelae commemorating the deeds of the deceased. Later, the *shen dao* ("spirit path"), as the way to the tomb was called, might be lined with life-size statues of officials, animals, exotic creatures, foreigners, or imperial bodyguards. It is thought that such figures may have served to guard the tomb or they may represent a sort of permanent funeral procession in stone. Each individually positioned imperial tomb had its own spirit path. In the case of grouped tombs, as in the imperial necropolises of the Ming and Qing dynasties, one path served the entire group.

Stone elephants, representing the southern imperial domains, line the spirit path to the tombs of the early Ming emperors at Nanjing.

A ramp led to the wooden or stone doors of the burial chamber, beyond which a richly decorated passageway descended into the tomb itself. Imperial tombs were known as "underground palaces" and were elaborate architectural complexes that were intended to reproduce in every possible way the buildings that had been home to the deceased in life.

Wealthy citizens were interred in tombs that were smaller than those built for emperors, but also filled with all the accoutrements of their lives on earth. In 1971, one of the largest non-imperial tombs from the Han dynasty, 65 feet (20m) in length, was excavated in Helinge'er, about twelve miles (20km) north of the Chinese border in Inner Mongolia. The tomb belonged to a Chinese military official stationed there in the second century CE and contains three main chambers, each with its own vaulted ceiling, and a total of three side chambers.

Inside the subterranean tomb, wallpainting and sometimes relief sculpture narrate the life of the deceased. He or she may be depicted at a banquet or being entertained. Those who had served the deceased in life are almost invariably also portrayed in the tomb murals. The most common subjects for tomb-ceiling decoration are celestial bodies, mainly the sun, moon, and lunar lodges (Chinese equivalents of constellations), and occasionally planets or signs of the zodiac.

DESIGNS FOR LIVING

This pottery model of a Han-dynasty walled manor house was found in a tomb of the 2nd century BCE in Huaiyang county, Henan province. It has a single entrance and is built around two courtyards. The living area, around the rear (north) court-yard (top), is entered by a two-story gateway. Opposite this is a multi-storied manorial hall. The enclosed area on the left of the model is a vegetable garden.

In imperial China, every person who could afford to build a house did so, and residential architecture is probably the oldest continuous building tradition in China. Vernacular architecture can be said to bring us closer to what is fundamentally Chinese about archi-tecture than any other form of construction and, although houses representing that tradition have all but vanished from China's cities, nevertheless they exist and continue to be built in the countryside.

Examples of traditional Chinese houses can still be seen in Putian county in Fujian province, southeast China. Although the southern style of a family dwelling in Fujian is often indicated by the dramatic slope of the roof eaves, and materials for specific parts of the house may vary, the plan of such a home is similar to that of rural houses in most other parts of the country. Each house is built around a front courtyard that is entered through a gate (a skywell often replaces the courtyard when less space is available). The front central room, which may be open to the courtyard or hidden behind doors, is a formal room, which provides a place to eat and entertain guests. Further rooms are added symmetrically to the central one.

The sturdy but simple *chuandou* framework (a wooden skeleton of columns and beams joined together), roof purlins (to support the rafters) positioned directly on beams, and non-weight-bearing walls that character-ize Chinese wooden construction can easily be adapted to accommodate family changes. If a growing family does not possess enough land to build outward, bays can be added around the interior of the front court-yard. Two-story dwellings with bedrooms upstairs have also played a role in the Chinese residential tradition, perhaps since the early imperial era.

Chinese courtyard-style houses could be adapted to village or urban settings. The residential system of much of pre-twentieth-century Beijing, for example, allowed for each house to have its own courtyard, but houses were arranged side by side, all facing the same street.

In traditional China, families took every aspect of the building process very seriously. Today, as throughout the imperial period, the family first chooses a location for the house according to the rules of *feng shui*—a system that attempts to guarantee that a site is as auspicious as possible, and takes best advantage of wind, rain, and other natural factors. Timing is also important—the days and hours at which the various stages of construction occur are considered lucky or unlucky.

PROVINCIAL HOUSES

Many village houses in the Chinese provinces are built in an architectural style that is characteristic of the region or of the local ethnic minority. Some of the earliest extant Chinese residences are in Anhui province and date in some instances from the Ming dynasty. Most Anhui houses have two stories and are rarely more than three bays wide. They are fully enclosed by whitewashed walls built around a sky-well rather than a courtyard.

The large communal houses built by the Hakka (Keija) people—who live in Fujian province and Hong Kong and are now referred to by the Chinese as an ethnic minority—usually have three or four stories and are rectangular or circular in plan. Hakka houses accommodate a large number of families in a single building constructed around an open central courtyard.

Other ethnic groups within China have their own distinctive residential styles—for example, the Dong, Zhuang, and Miao of south China construct houses raised entirely or partly on stilts. The largely nomadic Mongols erect yurts—round tents consisting of a framework of poles covered with felt or skins.

The waterside family houses in this village in Anhui province date from the Ming era.

GARDENS OF DELIGHT

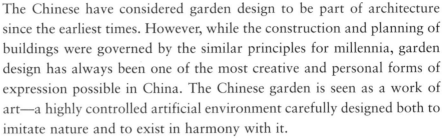

THE SUMMER PALACE

The Qing dynasty transformed the area northwest of Beijing into a vast series of pleasure gardens or parks, often called the "three hills and five parks." One of these, sometimes known simply as the Summer Palace, was rebuilt by the Qianlong emperor from 1751–1764 and named Yiheyuan ("Garden of Nurtured Harmony"). Its vast stretches of water, which account for three-quarters of the garden's 715 acres (290ha) were originally channeled from north of the capital in the thirteenth century. The garden's 796-yard (728m) Long Gallery contains an individual painting on each of its beams and has four double-roofed, octagonal pavilions. Yiheyuan was notorious for the extravagances of the dowager empress Cixi (see p.59). Among these is a lakeside pavilion in the form of a ship—built with funds intended for the imperial navy.

Chinese gardens often feature pavilions and bridges—such as this one in the gardens of the Summer Palace—as sites for contemplation.

The Chinese have considered garden design to be part of architecture since the earliest times. However, while the construction and planning of buildings were governed by the similar principles for millennia, garden design has always been one of the most creative and personal forms of expression possible in China. The Chinese garden is seen as a work of art—a highly controlled artificial environment carefully designed both to imitate nature and to exist in harmony with it.

A traditional Chinese *yuan* (a term that can be translated as either "garden" or "park") resembles a three-dimensional landscape painting, often strewn with unusually-shaped rocks and planted with flowers and blossoming trees. Many traditional Chinese gardens included symbolic artificial landscape features, such as hills in the shape of the Chinese character for mountain (a tall central peak and two flanking lower ones) and islands constructed in lakes to represent the isles of the immortals (see p.95). It is believed that a small detail, such as the shape of an aperture, or the view from around a curve can alter the panorama enough to inspire a different mood in the observer, or create a new association.

One of the earliest imperial gardens about which records exist is Shanglinyuan, which was built by the First Emperor, Qin Shihuangdi outside his capital Xianyang, later known as Chang'an (modern Xi'an). Said to have been 93 miles (150km) in circumference, Shanglinyuan included an imperial game reserve as well as a 740-acre (300ha) artificial lake that was used both for training the imperial navy and as a reservoir. It has even been suggested that Shanglinyuan was designed to be a re-creation of the empire in miniature. More a park than a garden, some experts believe it set the standards for garden construction for the rest of the imperial era.

The names of private gardens and garden-builders are recorded from as early as the Han dynasty. Prince Liangxiao is said to have built his own garden, named Rabbit Garden, in the Western Han period. In the beautiful city of Suzhou in Jiangsu province, the Wangshiyuan (Garden of the Master of the Fish Nets) was founded by the official Shi Zhengzhi during the Song dynasty. Its name is a reference to an official of the state of Chu named Qu Yuan (ca. 340–ca. 278BCE), who was inspired by the words of a fisherman. Poetic references to the past, metaphors for good government, and words to stimulate a reflective mood can be found

in the names of most natural phenomena and structures in a Chinese garden. In the Garden of the Master of the Fishing Nets, for example, one finds the Pavilion for Viewing Pines and Enjoying Paintings, the Late Spring Abode, the Stick to Peace Mansion, and the Lute Chamber.

Many of China's most famous gardens were constructed in Beijing during the Qing dynasty (see sidebar, left). Like earlier dynasties, the Qing also had summer palaces and detached palaces (residences away from the capital) that were primarily parkland. The most famous was the resort called Bishushanzhuang (Hill Station to Escape the Heat), built in 1703 by the emperor Kangxi (ruled 1661–1722). It was one of nineteen such resorts that stretched between Beijing and the Manchu hunting grounds and military training area known as the Mulan, some 250 miles (400km) northeast of the capital.

A 19th-century painting depicting part of the series of imperial pleasure gardens developed by the Qing emperors northwest of Beijing.

THE LEGACY OF 4,000 YEARS

The poem *Prayer* (right) was written by one of the most remarkable cultural figures of post-imperial China's twentieth century. Wen Yiduo, born November 24, 1899, burst onto the literary scene in China in his early twenties, just after the language reforms associated with the New Culture Movement of 1915–23 eliminated the traditional stranglehold of the classical language on literary expression. Wen was the first person to adapt the rhythm of the spoken language to the meter of Chinese verse, and his poetry, as exemplified by *Prayer*, bridged the gulf separating tradition and modernity in both its form and its content. A man of many talents, Wen achieved similar prominence through his painting (see p.232). Then, when the responsibilities of a growing family required a steadier income than that provided by either poetry or art, he became a professor of literature. Demonstrating his creative genius yet again, he developed into the most imaginative classicist of his age, in many ways still ahead of the times.

As the Chinese expression has it, Wen lived in interesting times. But he was able to turn crisis into opportunity. When the Japanese invasion of China in 1937 forced the relocation of China's universities from the eastern seaboard to the distant western provinces, Wen rejected the bus transport offered to the professors, preferring instead to walk with the students. The two-month, 1,000-mile march from Wuhan to Kunming was transformed into a moving classroom, as professor and students alike observed and annotated the rural areas through which they passed. Perhaps most important, they collected folksongs all along the route, establishing an invaluable written corpus that ethnographers and literary critics alike still mine. Finally, with the end of what Chinese call the "War Against Japan" in 1945, Wen Yiduo shaved off his scholar's beard and turned his powers of expression to matters of state. In this too he quickly attracted attention, but unfortunately it was from the government of the day. On July 15, 1946, he was assassinated.

The martyr's death of Wen Yiduo immediately won him the place in the pantheon of Chinese cultural icons that the multidimensional accomplishments of his life would eventually have brought, his canonization unique only for its speed. It is not so much that time moves

PRAYER

Please tell me, who are the Chinese?
Show me how to cherish memory.
Please tell me of this people's greatness.
Softly tell me; don't shout it out.

Please tell me, who are the Chinese?
In whose hearts are the hearts of Yao and
  Shun;
Whose blood is the blood of Jing Ke and
  Nie Zheng;
Who are the children of Shennong and
  Huangdi?

You tell me that wisdom came so strangely,
You say it was a present brought by the
  river horse,
You even tell me that this song's rhythm
Was first handed down by the nine-hued
  phoenix.

Who will tell me of the Gobi's silence,
And the five peaks' majesty? And tell me
  too
That Mount Tai's stonedrops still drip
  patiently,
And that the Yangzi and Yellow rivers still
  flow calmly?

Tell me again, which drop of pure tear
Is the grief Confucius cried for the dead
  unicorn?
Which fool will tell me truly
Of the laughing of Zhuang Zhou, Chunyu
  Kun, and Dongfang Shuo?

Please tell me, who are the Chinese?
Show me how to cherish memory.
Please tell me of this people's greatness.
Softly tell me; don't shout it out.

Wen Yiduo, 1927

A scene that has probably changed little in centuries: cormorant fishers near Guilin, Guangxi region.

slowly in China, but rather that the collective memory is very long. Like the figures to whom Wen Yiduo refers in his poem, most members of the Chinese cultural pantheon earned their places long ago: Yao and Shun were already part of it some 2,000 years before the Common Era (see pp.80–81). Jing Ke and Zhuang Zhou lived in the third century BCE, another tumultuous century, and one to which the name "China" can be traced (from Qin, the first imperial dynasty). When Chinese seek to define themselves, they almost invariably turn to the past.

The tension between past and present is pervasive in China. Wen Yiduo's poem "Prayer" was written at a time of great self-doubt on the part of Chinese intellectuals. The empire of the Qing dynasty—which, though foreign (Manchu), was so culturally assimilated that many if not most Chinese accepted it as a native dynasty—had collapsed just fifteen years before. In the meantime, Chinese territory was divided among various warlords, a civil war having just concluded the year before. What is more, Western powers and Japan controlled virtually every major port along the eastern seaboard. This caused Chinese intellectuals to feel a keen sense of national shame, and many of them questioned whether there was not some fundamental flaw in the traditional Chinese worldview itself that had brought China to such a state of weakness vis-à-vis the West. Some, such as Zhang Binglin (1868–1936) and Hu Shi (1891–1962), even suggested that perhaps China's problem was that it lacked a transcendental savior figure such as Jesus; they proposed developing a similar cult around the figure of Confucius. The traditional status of Confucius proved as impervious to this assault as it did to that of the First Emperor, Qin Shihuangdi (ruled 221–210BCE), or as it would to that of Mao Zedong.

Other intellectuals, loosely associated by a shared iconoclasm ("doubting antiquity" in Chinese), joined together to publish between 1926 and 1937 a series of volumes entitled *Debates on Ancient History* (*Gu shi bian*). The editor of the series was Gu Jiegang (1893–1980), the leading historian of the day, who attempted to discern the "stratigraphy" of the Chinese textual tradition. In the case of mythology, for instance, he began with the basic premise that the earliest forms of myth should be the simplest. As time passed, the myth would become ever more elaborated. Moreover, he argued, the dates attributed to mythical figures reveal a similar progression—the earlier the date, the later it was given. According to this argument, Yao and Shun, who were traditionally dated to the late third millennium BCE, were in fact products of the third century BCE—another time of great intellectual debate in China. Extending this argument to all genres of literature and to its logical extreme, Gu and his adherents ended up rejecting as spurious virtually all of China's earliest literary heritage—including, most prominently, most of the Confucian classics.

Facing the Mirror *(1927), a watercolor painted by Wen Yiduo to serve as the cover of his friend Fan Guangdan's novel* Feng Xiaoqing. *Wen was renowned for blending old themes with new media or, as here, blending new themes with old media. The mirror itself is an old motif; since ancient times in China it has been a metaphor for history.*

In retrospect, it seems clear that the conclusions of the contributors to *Debates on Ancient History* were representative of their own era—in China the 1920s and 1930s was a time of political weakness and cultural uncertainty. But, as noted in the Introduction to the present volume, fundamental to the Chinese worldview is the notion that what is below will eventually rise (again). As if a demonstration of this, China as a nation could not be kept down for long. After the defeat of Japan in 1945, and four more years of civil war, the People's Republic of China was established.

Although this regime has meant different things to different people, both inside and outside of China, it cannot be denied that during its 50 years of rule the Chinese people have developed a renewed sense of

Mao Zedong. Apparently identifying with the First Emperor, Mao tried to "rebury" the Confucians during the Cultural Revolution, one of his rallying cries being "Criticize Confucius and Lin Biao!" Lin, Mao's defense minister, was killed—possibly assassinated—in 1971.

pride in themselves. Sometimes this pride has been in contemporary achievements; sometimes it is a manifestation of an ingrained xenophobia (such as that evident in the recent book *The China that Can Say No*, an anti-Western polemic). More often it has derived from a new recognition of the unique place in world history to which the traditional culture of China is entitled.

Much of this recognition has come from the magnificent archaeological discoveries that have been made in China since the establishment of the People's Republic. Although the government itself has had an ambivalent attitude toward traditional culture, Mao Zedong's call to "let the past serve the present" served to protect archaeology probably more than any other field of the humanities and social sciences. Even during the Cultural Revolution, when products of traditional culture that had long been preserved above ground were being desecrated and destroyed, archaeologists were authorized to continue to explore under the ground. Indeed, it was during the Cultural Revolution that they made some of their most impressive discoveries, most famously the astonishing terracotta army buried near the tomb of the First Emperor, Qin Shihuangdi, which was discovered just outside the city of Xi'an in

Stalls and tourists, mainly Chinese, at the tomb of the First Emperor. For the hundreds of millions of Chinese born in the 1950s and 1960s, historical figures such as Qin Shihuangdi loomed early in their memories. Traditionally condemned for having "burned the books and buried the Confucians" (see p.84), the First Emperor was proclaimed a great cultural hero by Mao Zedong during the "Great Proletarian Cultural Revolution" of the late 1960s and early 1970s.

1974. Probably even more important for understanding early Chinese culture—and cited throughout the present volume—are the three tombs at Mawangdui, excavated between 1971 and 1973 in the middle of Changsha, the capital of Hunan province. Tomb 1 was that of Lady Dai, probably the wife of Li Cang, prime minister of the Han state of Changsha 193–186BCE, buried in Tomb 2. Dai's corpse was almost as astounding as the terracotta warriors, since it was perfectly preserved, even the skin still being pliable. But it was Tomb 3, containing the body of their son, who died in 168BCE, which gave Mawangdui its great significance for Chinese history. In it were more than 20 texts written on silk, including the oldest copies of the *Yi Jing* (*Classic of Changes*) and the *Dao De Jing*, two of the most important works in all of China's long textual tradition.

Discoveries of manuscript versions of traditional texts such as these, and the other discoveries that have continued apace from throughout China over the last quarter century, have led Chinese historians to do an about-face with respect to the iconoclastic views of the 1920s and 1930s. Now the reigning orthodoxy among Chinese historians is termed "believing antiquity." As the name suggests, it holds that China's traditional history, including especially the dates attributed to famous figures and texts, is by and large reliable. This new orthodoxy is every bit as polemical as the earlier "doubting antiquity" movement was, and will almost surely eventually be supplanted by some new conclusion.

As ancient history has come to be seen as more reliable over the last half century, so too have other aspects of traditional culture. Some, such as traditional Chinese medicine and martial arts, have gained additional prestige by becoming international cultural phenomena. As explained in the chapter "Healing and Medicine," traditional Chinese medicine (now often abbreviated simply "TCM" in the West) has had a long pedigree. Since the establishment of the People's Republic, several research institutes devoted to the discovery and development of a modern, scientific basis for traditional Chinese medicine have been founded. Today most hospitals in China offer both traditional and Western treatments side by side.

Despite the scientific terms in which traditional Chinese medicine is now often discussed, it still partakes of the same holistic worldview as it did during the Han dynasty—the same worldview that finds expression, for instance, in Daoism, the native Chinese religion. Daoism too has experienced a tremendous resurgence in recent years. Although freedom of religion is protected under the constitution of the People's

A Confucian shrine dedicated to a god called the Official of Heaven. Confucianism has survived onslaughts from successive Chinese regimes, including the Communist one. The virulence of Mao's anti-Confucius campaign demonstrated beyond doubt that the Confucians—and especially Confucius himself—were still very much alive, as they still are today. It is not surprising that the so-called "Little Dragons" of east Asia (Hong Kong, Singapore, Taiwan, and South Korea) should have attributed their economic success of the 1980s and early 1990s to their Confucian heritage.

A still from Farewell My Concubine *by Chen Kaige, a film about a Beijing opera star caught up in China's turbulent 20th century. Many modern Chinese writers, artists, and moviemakers continue to draw their inspiration from China's recent and ancient history.*

OPPOSITE *A parade before the Gate of Heavenly Peace (Tiananmen) celebrating the 50th anniversary of the People's Republic in 1999. Although the style and form of official communist symbols have changed little in half a century, the regime itself has undergone radical transformations—today many of its policies are unequivocally capitalist.*

Republic, in fact the government has viewed religion as a form of superstition and for the first four decades of the regime it sought—generally successfully—to suppress it. But an unusual combination of pride in Chinese traditions, as discussed above, and an "open-door" economic policy, which has brought a sudden influx of money from Chinese communities in Hong Kong, Taiwan, Singapore, and elsewhere, has served to reinvigorate Daoism, and indeed Buddhism and the other religions in China.

In place since the 1980s, the open-door economic policy has also resulted in massive urban renewal. Most of the China's city walls have long since been torn down to accommodate traffic, and now even the traditional *hutong* alleys of central Beijing are being razed to make room for office buildings—for the most part in an undistinguished modern international style—that will tower over the adjacent Forbidden City. This is as tangible a symbol of the tension between past and present, tradition and modernity, as one could want to see.

With the new construction, China's cities are fast becoming ever more congested and polluted. Many of the inhabitants have come to believe that they have paid a tremendous price in terms of both their physical health and spiritual well-being for this economic progress. It is perhaps not surprising that many of them should now be looking to traditional Chinese medicine and religion for some relief. It is perhaps also not surprising that the government should view this interest as criticism of its economic policies. At the present time, the government—like all its predecessors—prizes stability above all else.

And so, the tension between tradition and modernity that is so evident in Wen Yiduo's *Prayer* continues to characterize China still today:

> Please tell me, who are the Chinese?
> Show me how to cherish memory.
> Please tell me of this people's greatness.
> Softly tell me; don't shout it out.

We are perhaps no better placed than he was to hazard an answer. But, just as he directed his inquiry to the cultural heroes of the past, so too it seems should we. If we are to understand "who are the Chinese," if we are to understand something "of this people's greatness," it is appropriate that we seek first to understand who *were* the Chinese. *China* cherishes memory, and tells of it not in a loud way, but rather subtly—in a hundred different facets.

LANGUAGE AND PRONUNCIATION

Chinese is the mother tongue of around 94 percent of the citizens of the People's Republic of China (PRC), as well as of many overseas communities. However, in the course of around 3,000 years, the ancient Chinese language—spoken in roughly the area of the North China Plain—has evolved into ten main dialects (and countless subdialects) that today are distinct enough from each other to be considered as separate languages. Four of these dialects are referred to collectively as Mandarin, or Northern Chinese, and are spoken mainly in the north, northeast, and southwest of the Chinese provinces as well as in adjacent areas of the Autonomous Regions (see map on p.21).

The dialects of Mandarin differ less from each other than they do from the Chinese dialects of the east, south, and southeast, such as Wu (spoken in east China including Shanghai) and Cantonese (spoken in Guangdong province, Hongkong, and many overseas communities). All the dialects are characterized by their use of tones, whereby the intonation of a syllable affects its meaning. In Beijing dialect there are four tones (level, rising, falling then rising, and high falling), but others have more. The differences between dialects is illustrated by the following examples (these romanizations take no account of tones):

ENGLISH	MANDARIN	CANTONESE
one	yi	yat
two	er	yi
three	san	sam
mother	mu-qin	mou-ts'an
father	fu-qin	fu-ts'an
hand	shou	sau
foot	jiao	kiok
good	hao	hou
bad	huai	wai
Happy New Year!	gongxi fa cai![1]	kung hei fat choy!

[1] Literally: "Respectfully Wishing You Prosperity!"

The term Mandarin also refers, as in these examples, to the modern standard Chinese language. This has its roots in a variety of Beijing dialect spoken by senior imperial civil servants as an administrative language throughout the empire. In the early 20th century this "speech of officials"—hence the term "Mandarin"—formed the basis of moves to create a national standard language which all citizens could learn, whatever their first tongue. Attempts to spread this language in the early republic foundered owing to political disunity, foreign invasion, and war, but after 1949 the PRC renewed efforts to implement it as a means of promoting national unity. This effort has met with considerable success, and modern standard vernacular Mandarin, or Putonghua ("Common Speech"), is in general use today in government, education, and official media. It is the means by which a Uighur will communicate with a Shanghainese, and also the language usually learnt by foreigners.

For educated Chinese, at least, the wide divergences in the spoken language have always been of relatively little importance because the written script can be read in any dialect. This is because by and large all dialects consist of the same stock of meaningful syllables, some of which are words in their own right, while others are used in compounds. The pronunciation of these syllables can differ widely from dialect to dialect, but they are always written with the same distinctive character. Chinese has the world's oldest system of writing still in use—it is well over 3,000 years old—and one that has remained remarkably unchanged since the development of *kai shu*, or "standard script," by the 3rd century CE (see p.190). Many of the 6,000 or so traditional characters that a literate person has on average to learn for everyday use are very elaborate, and in its literacy drive of the 1950s the PRC therefore encouraged the teaching of about 2,000 simplified characters. Some of these simplifications were new, but many had existed for centuries as alternative forms.

The PRC also introduced a new way of writing standard Chinese phonetically in a Latin script. Called "Chinese Spelling" (Hanyu Pinyin, or "pinyin" for short in the West), for most purposes this romanization system has now superseded all others both inside and outside China, except in some overseas communities (Taiwan adopted it in 1999).

Pinyin is less complicated than the 19th-century Wade-Giles (WG) romanization, formerly the most widely used system. Thus Ch'ing, *ch'i-kung*, and *t'ai ch'i ch'üan* (WG) are rendered in pinyin as Qing, qigong, and *taijiquan*. In general the letters of pinyin have broadly similar values to those of English. The following are the most important points to note, with WG equivalents for reference:

PINYIN	ENGLISH EQUIVALENT	WG
c	ts in tsar	tz'
z	dz in adze	tz
j	j in jib	ch
zh	j in job	ch
q	ch in chin	ch'
x	between s and sh	hs
ui	as "way"	ui, wei

TABLE OF DYNASTIES

PRE-IMPERIAL PERIOD

SHANG DYNASTY	ca. 1500–1045 BCE
ZHOU DYNASTY	ca. 1045–256 BCE
Western Zhou	ca. 1045–771 BCE
Eastern Zhou:	ca. 770–256 BCE
Springs & Autumns Period	722–481 BCE
Warring States Period	480–222 BCE

IMPERIAL PERIOD

QIN DYNASTY	221–207 BCE
HAN DYNASTY	206 BCE–220 CE
Western Han	206 BCE–23 CE
All dates from here are CE	
Reign of Wang Mang ("Xin dynasty")	9–23
Eastern Han	25–220
THE THREE KINGDOMS	220–264
Wei kingdom	220–264
Wu kingdom	222–280
Shu Han kingdom	221–263

THE PERIOD OF DISUNION	
Western Jin dynasty	265–316
Eastern Jin dynasty	317–419
Liu Song dynasty	420–479
Qi dynasty	479–501
Liang dynasty	502–556
Chen dynasty	557–618
SUI DYNASTY	581–618
TANG DYNASTY	618–907
THE FIVE DYNASTIES	907–960
Later Liang	907–923
Later Tang	923–935
Later Jin	936–947
Later Han	947–951
Later Zhou	951–960
SONG DYNASTY	960–1279
Northern Song	960–1126
Southern Song	1127–1279
YUAN DYNASTY	1279–1368
MING DYNASTY	1368–1644
QING DYNASTY	1644–1912

BIBLIOGRAPHY

General Bibliography

Blunden, Caroline and Elvin, Mark. *Cultural Atlas of China.* Oxford: Phaidon Press, 1983; New York: Facts on File, 1983.

Chan, Wing-tsit. *A Sourcebook in Chinese Philosophy.* Princeton: Princeton University Press, 1963.

de Bary, William T., Wing-tsit Chan, and Burton Watson, comps. *Sources of Chinese Tradition,* Volume 1. New York: Columbia University Press, 1960.

Elvin, Mark. *The Pattern of the Chinese Past.* Stanford: Stanford University Press, 1973.

Overmyer, Daniel L.; Alvin P. Cohen; N.J. Girardot; and Wing-tsit Chan. "Chinese Religions" in the *Encyclopedia of Religion* (ed. Mircea Eliade), vol 3, pp. 257–323. New York: Macmillan, 1987.

Overmyer, Daniel L. *Religions of China: The World as a Living System.* San Francisco: Harper and Row, 1986.

Thompson, Laurence G. *Chinese Religion: An Introduction,* fifth edition. Belmont, Calif.: Wadsworth, 1998.

Chapter 1. All Under Heaven
Richard von Glahn

Buchanan, Keith M. *The Transformation of the Chinese Earth: Aspects of the Evaluation of the Chinese Earth from Earliest Times to Mao Tse-tung.* London: Bell, 1970.

Harrell, Stevan, ed. *Cultural Encounters on China's Ethnic Frontiers.* Seattle: University of Washington Press, 1994.

Leeming, Frank. *The Changing Geography of China.* Oxford and Cambridge, Mass.: Blackwell, 1993.

Mackerras, Colin. *China's Minority Cultures: Identities and Integration Since 1912.* New York: St. Martin's Press, 1995.

Marks, Robert B. *Tigers, Rice, Silk, and Silt: Environment and Economy in Late Imperial South China.* Cambridge and New York: Cambridge University Press, 1997.

Smil, Vaclav. *The Bad Earth: Environmental Degradation in China.* Armonk, N.Y.: M.E. Sharpe, 1984; London: Zed Press, 1984.

Stein, Aurel. *On Ancient Central-Asian Tracks.* Chicago: University of Chicago Press, 1964.

Strassberg, Richard E., ed. *Inscribed Landscapes: Travel Writing from Imperial China.* Berkeley and Los Angeles: University of California Press, 1994.

Thomson, John. *Thomson's China: Travels and Adventures of a Nineteenth-Century Photographer.* Oxford and New York: Oxford University Press, 1993.

Tuan Yi-fu. *China.* Chicago: Aldine, 1969.

Xu Guohua and L.J. Peel, eds. *The Agriculture of China.* Oxford and New York: Oxford University Press, 1991.

Chapter 2. Continuity and Change
Mark Edward Lewis

Chang Kwang-chih. *Shang Civilization.* New Haven: Yale University Press, 1986.

Ch'ü T'ung-tsu. *Han Social Structure.* Seattle: University of Washington Press, 1972.

Gernet, Jacques. *A History of Chinese Civilization.* Cambridge: Cambridge University Press, 1989.

Ebrey, Patricia. *Cambridge Illustrated History of China.* Cambridge: Cambridge University Press, 1989.

Gernet, Jacques. *Daily Life in China on the Eve of the Mongol Invasion, 1250–1276.* Stanford: Stanford University Press, 1962.

Holcombe, Charles. *In the Shadow of the Han.* Honolulu: University of Hawaii Press, 1994.

Hsu Cho-yun. *Ancient China in Transition.* Stanford: Stanford University Press, 1965.

Hsu Cho-yun and Katheryn Linduff, *Western Chou Civilization.* New Haven: Yale University Press, 1988.

Huang, Ray. *1597: A Year of No Significance; the Ming Dynasty in Decline.* New Haven: Yale University Press, 1981.

Langlois, John D., ed. *China Under Mongol Rule.* Princeton: Princeton University Press, 1981.

Lewis, Mark Edward. *Sanctioned Violence in Early China.* Albany: State University of California Press, 1990.

Lewis, Mark Edward. *Writing and Authority in Early China.* Albany: State University of California Press, 1999.

Naquin, Susan, and Evelyn Rawski. *Chinese Society in the Eighteenth Century.* New Haven: Yale University Press, 1987.

Paludan, Ann. *Chronicle of the Chinese Emperors.* London: Thames and Hudson, 1998.

Pulleyblank, Edwin G. *The Background of the Rebellion of An Lu-shan.* Oxford: Oxford University Press, 1955.

Spence, Jonathan. *The Search for Modern China.* New York: Norton, 1990.

Twitchett, D. and J. F. Fairbank. *The Cambridge History of China.* 10 vols. Cambridge: Cambridge University Press, 1979– .

Chapter 3. The Role of the State
John Chinnery

Anderson, Mary M. *Hidden Power: The Palace Eunuchs of Imperial China.* Prometheus, 1990.

Geguin, Gilles and Dominique Morel. *The Forbidden City, Heart of Imperial China*. London: Thames and Hudson, 1997.

Lo, Winston W. *An Introduction to the Civil Service of Sung China*. Honolulu: University of Hawaii Press, 1987.

McMullen, David. *State and Scholars in T'ang China*. Cambridge: Cambridge University Press, 1988.

Schram, S. R., ed. *Foundations and Limits of State Power in China*. London: School of Oriental and African Studies; Hong Kong: Chinese University Press, 1987.

Spence, Jonathon D. *Emperor of China: Self-Portrait of Kang-hsi*. New York: Knopf, 1974.

Chapter 4. Family and Society
John Chinnery

Chu T'ung-tsu. *Local Government in China Under the Ch'ing*. Cambridge, Mass.: Harvard University Press, 1962.

Fei, Hsiao-Tung. *Peasant Life in China*. London: Kegan Paul, Trench, Trubner (first printing), 1939.

Fitzgerald, C. P. *The Empress Wu*. London: Cresset Press, 1968.

McKnight, Brian E. *Law and Order in Sung China*. Cambridge: Cambridge University Press, 1992.

Skinner, William G., ed. *The City in Late Imperial China*. Stanford: Stanford University Press, 1977.

Wolf, Margery, and Roxana Witke, eds. *Women in Chinese Society*. Stanford: Stanford University Press, 1975.

Yang, C. K. *Religion in Chinese Society*. Berkeley: University of California Press, 1967.

Chapter 5. The Creation of Wealth
Richard von Glahn

Bray, Francesca. *Technology and Gender: Fabrics of Power in Late Imperial China*. Berkeley and Los Angeles: University of California Press, 1997.

Brook, Timothy. *The Confusions of Pleasure: Commerce and Culture in Ming China*. Berkeley and Los Angeles: University of California Press, 1998.

Chao, Kang. *Man and Land in Chinese History*. Stanford: Stanford University Press, 1986.

Eastman, Lloyd E. *Family, Field, and Ancestors: Constancy and Change in China's Social and Economic History, 1550–1949*. New York and Oxford: Oxford University Press, 1988.

Huang, Philip C.C. *The Peasant Economy and Social Change in North China*. Stanford: Stanford University Press, 1985.

Li Bozhong. *Agricultural Development in Jiangnan, 1620–1850*. Houndmills, England: Macmillan, 1997.

Li, Lillian M. *China's Silk Trade: Traditional Industry in the Modern World, 1842–1937*. Cambridge, Mass.: Harvard University Press, 1981.

Perdue, Peter C. *Exhausting the Earth: State and Peasant in Hunan, 1500–1850*. Cambridge, Mass.: Harvard University Council on East Asian Studies, 1987.

Pomeranz, Kenneth. *Great Divergence: China, Europe, and the Making of the Modern World Economy*. Princeton: Princeton University Press, 2000.

Richardson, Philip. *Economic Change in China, c. 1800–1950*. Cambridge: Cambridge University Press, 1999.

von Glahn, Richard. *Fountain of Fortune: Money and Monetary Policy in China, 1000–1700*. Berkeley and Los Angeles: University of California Press, 1996.

Chapter 6. Confucianism: Order and Virtue
Jennifer Oldstone-Moore

Birrell, Anne. *Chinese Mythology: An Introduction*. Baltimore: John Hopkins University Press, 1993.

Confucius; Lau, D.C., trans. *The Analects*. Harmondsworth, England, and New York: Penguin Books, 1979.

Fingarette, Herbert. *Confucianism: The Secular as Sacred*. New York: Harper and Row, 1972.

Mencius; Lau, D.C., trans. *The Mencius*. New York: Penguin Books, 1970.

Tu Wei-ming . *Confucianism Thought: Selfhood as Creative Transformation*. New York: State University of New York, 1985.

Chapter 7. Following the Dao
Jennifer Oldstone-Moore

Chuang-tzu; Graham, A.C., trans. *The Chuang-tzu*. London: Unwin Paperbacks, 1986.

Lao-tzu; Lau, D.C., trans. *The Tao Te Ching*. Trans. D.C. Lau. Harmondsworth, England: Penguin Books, 1963.

Translated by Wilhelm, Richard and from German to English by Cary F. Baynes. *The I Ching*. 3rd edition. Princeton: Princeton University Press, 1967.

Saso, Michael. *Taoism and the Rite of Cosmic Renewal*. Pullman, WA: Washington State University Press, 1990.

Schipper, Kristofer. *The Taoist Body*. Berkeley: University of California Press, 1993.

Stepanchuk, Carol, and Charles Wong. *Mooncakes and Hungry Ghosts*. San Francisco: China Books, 1991.

Welch, Holmes. *Taoism: The Parting of the Way*. Boston: Beacon Press, 1966.

Chapter 8. The Way of the Buddha
Jennifer Oldstone-Moore

Chen, Kenneth. *Buddhism in China: A Historical Survey*. Princeton: Princeton University Press, 1964.

Johnson, Willard L., Sandra A. Wawryko, and Geoffrey De Graff. *The Buddhist Religion: A Historical Introduction*. 4th Edition. Belmont, Calif.: Wadsworth Publishing, 1996.

Yampolsky, Philip B. trans. *The Platform Sutra of the Sixth Patriarch*. New York: Columbia University Press, 1978.

**Chapter 9. The Harmony of
Heaven and Earth** *and*
**Chapter 10. The Realm of Ghosts
and Spirits**
Edward L. Shaughnessy

Allan, Sarah. *The Shape of the Turtle:
Myth, Art, and Cosmos in Early China.*
Albany: State University of New York
Press, 1991.

Bilsky, Lester. *The State Religion of
Ancient China.* 2 vols. Taipei, Taiwan:
Chinese Association for Folklore, 1975.

Bodde, Derk. *China's First Unifier.*
Leiden: Brill, 1938; rpt., Hong Kong:
Hong Kong University Press, 1967.

Chang Kwang-chih. *Early Chinese
Civilization: Anthropological
Perspectives.* Cambridge, Mass.: Harvard
University Press, 1976.

Creel, Herrlee Glessner. *The Birth of
China: A Study of the Formative Period
of Chinese Civilization.* New York:
Reynal & Hitchcock, 1937; 6th printing,
New York: Ungar, 1967.

Falkenhausen, Lothar von. *Suspended
Music: Chime-Bells in the Culture of
Bronze Age China.* Berkeley: University
of California Press, 1993.

Fung Yulan; Bodde, Derk, trans. *A
History of Chinese Philosophy,* vol. 1:
The Period of the Philosophers; vol. 2,
The Period of Classical Learning.
Princeton, N.J.: Princeton University
Press, 1953.

Graham, A. C. *Disputers of the Tao:
Philosophical Argument in Ancient
China.* La Salle, Ill.: Open Court, 1989.

Graham, A. C. *Yin-Yang and the Nature
of Correlative Thinking.* Singapore:
Institute of East Asian Philosophies,
1986.

Granet, Marcel. *La pensée chinoise.*
1934; rpt. Paris: Albin Michel, 1968.

Granet, Marcel; Freedman, Maurice,
trans. *The Religion of the Chinese
People.* Oxford: Basil Blackwell, 1975.

Harley, J. B., and David Woodward, eds.
The History of Cartography, vol. 2, book
2: *Cartography in Traditional East and
Southeast Asian Societies.* Chicago:
University of Chicago Press, 1994.

Harper, Donald. *Resurrection in Warring
States Popular Religion* in *Taoist
Resources* 5.2, 1994.

Hung Wu. *Monumentality in Early
Chinese Art and Architecture.* Stanford:
Stanford University Press, 1995.

Kalinowski, Marc. *Cosmologie et
divination dans la Chine ancienne.* Paris:
École française d'Extrême-Orient, 1991.

Kalinowski, Marc. "Les instruments
astro-calendériques des Han et la
méthode de Liu ren" in *Bulletin de
l'École française d'Extrême-Orient* 72:
pp.309–419, 1983.

Keightley, David N. "Archaeology and
Mentality: The Making of China" in
Representations 18: pp. 91–128, 1987.

Keightley, David N. *Sources of Shang
History: The Oracle-Bone Inscriptions of
Bronze Age China.* Berkeley: University
of California Press, 1978. (2nd printing,
with minor revisions, 1985.)

Legge, James. *The Chinese Classics.* 5
vols. London, 1865–72, Oxford 1893–4;
rpt. Hong Kong: Hong Kong University
Press, 1960.

Legge, James. trans. *Li Chi, Book of
Rites.* 2 vols. New York: University
Books, 1967.

Li, Xueqin; Chang, K.C., trans. *Eastern
Zhou and Qin Civilizations.* New Haven,
Conn.: Yale University Press, 1985.

Loewe, Michael. *Divination, Mythology
and Monarchy in Han China.* Cambridge
University Press, 1994.

Loewe, Michael. *Ways to Paradise: The
Chinese Quest for Immortality.* London:
Allen & Unwin, 1979; rpt. Taipei:
Southern Materials Center, 1994.

Loewe, Michael, and Edward L.
Shaughnessy, eds. *The Cambridge
History of Ancient China: From the
Origins of Civilization to 221 B.C.* New
York: Cambridge University Press, 1999.

Major, John. *Heaven and Earth in Early
Han Thought: Chapters Three, Four, and
Five of the* Huainanzi. Albany: State
University of New York Press, 1993.

Maspero, Henri. "Le Ming T'ang et la
crise religieuse chinoise avant les Han" in
Mélanges chinois et bouddhiques 9: pp.
1–171, 1951.

Mathieu, Rémi. *Etudes sur la mythologie
et l'ethnologie de la Chine ancienne;
Traduction annotée du* Shanhai jing. 2
vols. Paris: Collège de France, 1983.

Munro, Donald J. *The Concept of Man
in Early China.* Stanford: Stanford
University Press, 1969.

Ngo, Van Xuyet. *Divination, magie, et
politique dans la Chine ancienne.* Paris:
Presses Universitaires de France, 1976.

Poo, Mu-chou. *In Search of Personal
Welfare: A View of Ancient Chinese
Religion.* Albany: State University of
New York Press, 1998.

Rawson, Jessica. *Western Zhou Ritual
Bronzes from the Arthur M. Sackler
Collections.* Cambridge, Mass.: Harvard
University Press, 1990.

Rickett, Allyn. *Guanzi: Political,
Economic, and Philosophical Essays from
Early China,* vol. 1. Princeton: Princeton
University Press, 1985.

Riegel, Jeffrey, trans. "Do Not Serve the
Dead as You Serve the Living: The *Lüshi
chunqiu* Treatises on Moderation in
Burial" in *Early China* 20, 1995.

Rutt, Richard. Zhouyi: *The Book of
Changes.* Durham, England: Curzon
Press, 1996.

Schafer, Edward H. *Pacing the Void:
T'ang Approaches to the Stars.* Berkeley:
University of California Press, 1977.

Schwartz, Benjamin I. *The World of
Thought in Ancient China.* Cambridge,
Mass.: Harvard University Press, 1985.

Seidel, Anna. "Buying One's Way to
Heaven: The Celestial Treasury in
Chinese Religions" in *History of
Religions* 17, pp.419–31, 1978.

Shaughnessy, Edward L. *Before
Confucius: Studies in the Creation of
the Chinese Classics.* Albany: State
University of New York Press, 1997.

Shaughnessy, Edward L. *The Composition
of the Zhouyi.* Ph.D. dissertation,
Stanford University, 1983. University
Microfilms International, no. 8320774.

Soothill, William E. *The Hall of Light: A Study of Early Kingship*. London: Lutterworth, 1951.

Thorp, Robert L. "The Sui Xian Tomb: Re-thinking the Fifth Century" in *Artibus Asiae* 43, 5: pp.67–92, 1981.

Thote, Alain. "The Double Coffin of Leigudun Tomb no. 1: Iconographic Sources and Related Problems" in *New Perspectives on Chu Culture During the Eastern Zhou Period*, ed. Thomas Lawton. Washington, D.C.: Authur M. Sackler Gallery, pp. 23–46, 1991.

Tsien, T.H. *Written on Bamboo and Silk: The Beginnings of Chinese Books and Inscriptions*. Chicago: University of Chicago Press, 1962.

Watson, Burton, trans. *The Complete Works of Chuang Tzu*. New York: Columbia University Press, 1968.

Watson, Burton, trans. *Han Fei Tzu: Basic Writings*. New York: Columbia University Press, 1964.

Watson, Burton, trans. *Hsun Tzu: Basic Writings*. New York: Columbia University Press, 1963.

Watson, Burton, trans. *Mo Tzu: Basic Writings*. New York: Columbia University Press, 1963.

Watson, Burton, trans. *Records of the Grand Historian*. 3 vols. New York: Columbia University Press, 1961, 1993.

Whitfield, Roderick, ed. "The Problem of Meaning in Early Chinese Ritual Bronzes. Colloquies on Art and Archaeology" in *Asia* 15. Percival David Foundation of Chinese Art. London: School of Oriental and African Studies, 1993.

Yates, Robin. *Five Lost Classics: Tao, Huanglao, and Yin-Yang in Han China*. New York: Ballantine Books, 1997.

Chapter 11. Healing and Medicine
Vivienne Lo

Allan, Sarah. *The Way of Water and Sprouts of Virtue*. Albany: State University of New York Press, 1997.

Brashier, K.E. "Han Thanatology and the Division of 'Souls'" in *Early China* 21, pp.125–158, 1996.

Cullen, Christopher. "Patients and Healers in Late Imperial China: Evidence from the *Jinpingmei*" in *History of Science*, vol. 31, 1993.

Feher, Michel, ed. *Fragments for a History of the Human Body*. New York: Zone, 1989.

Harper, Donald. "Early Chinese Medical Literature: The Mawangdui Medical Manuscripts" in *Sir Henry Wellcome Asian Series*, vol. 2. London and New York: Kegan Paul International, 1998.

He Zhiguo and Vivienne Lo. "The Channels: A Preliminary Examination of a Lacquered Figurine from the Western Han Period" in *Early China* 21, pp.81–124, 1996.

Kohn, Livia, ed. *Taoist Meditation and Longevity Techniques*. Ann Arbor Center for Chinese Studies, Mich.: University of Michigan Press, 1989.

McKnight, Brian E. *The Washing Away of Wrongs—Song Ji*. Ann Arbor Center for Chinese Studies, Mich.: University of Michigan Press, 1989.

Sivin, Nathan. *Traditional Medicine in Contemporary China*. Ann Arbor Center for Chinese Studies, Mich.: University of Michigan Press, 1989.

Unschuld, Paul. *Medicine in China: A History of Pharmaceutics* Berkeley: University of California Press, 1986.

Wile, Douglas. *The Art of the Bedchamber: The Chinese Sexual Yoga Classics Including Women's Solo Meditation Techniques*. Albany: State University of New York Press, 1992.

Yamada, Keiji. *The Origins of Acupuncture, Moxibustion, and Decoction*. Kyoto: International Research Centre for Japanese Studies, 1998.

Chapter 12. Technology and Science
Peter J. Golas

Bodde, Derk. *Chinese Thought, Society, and Science: the Intellectual and Social Background of Science and Technology in Pre-modern China*. Honolulu: University of Hawaii Press, 1991.

Bray, Francesca. *Technology and Gender; Fabrics of Power in Late Imperial China*. Berkeley: Univ. of California Press, 1997.

Hommel, Rudolf P. *China at Work*. New York: John Day, 1937. Repr. Cambridge, Mass.: M.I.T. Press, 1969.

Institute of the History of Natural Science, Chinese Academy of Sciences. *Ancient China's Technology and Science*. Beijing: Foreign Languages Press, 1983.

Needham, Joseph et al. *Science and Civilisation in China*. 7 vols. Cambridge: Cambridge University Press, 1956– .

Ronan, Colin A., ed. *The Shorter Science and Civilisation in China* (vols. 1–5). Cambridge: Cambridge University Press, 1976–1995.

Sung Ying-hsing, E-tu Zen Sun, and Shiou-Chuan Sun, trs. *T'ien-kung k'ai-wu: Chinese Technology in the Seventeenth Century*. University Park, Penn.: Pennsylvania State University Press, 1966.

Temple, Robert. *The Genius of China*. New York: Simon and Schuster, 1986, and London: Prion Books, 1998.

Williams, Trevor I. *The History of Invention: From Stone Axes to Silicon Chips*. New York: Facts on File, 1987.

Wagner, Donald B. *The Traditional Chinese Iron Industry and its Modern Fate*. Richmond, Va.: Curzon Press, 1997.

Vogel, Hans Ulrich. "The Great Well of China" in *Scientific American* 268 no. 6, pp.116–121, 1993.

Chapter 13. The Fine and Decorative Arts
Ni Yibin

Barnhart, Richard M., James Cahill, and Wu Hung. *Three Thousand Years of Chinese Painting*. New Haven: Yale University Press, 1997.

Bickford, Maggie. *Ink plum: the making of a Chinese scholar-painting genre*. Cambridge: Cambridge University Press, 1996.

Chu-tsing Li and James C. Y. Watt, eds. *The Chinese scholar's studio: artistic life in the late Ming period: an exhibition from the Shanghai Museum*. New York: Thames and Hudson, in association with the Asia Society Galleries, 1987.

Clunas, Craig. *Art in China*. Oxford: Oxford University Press, 1997.

Fong, Wen C., and James C.Y. Watt. *Possessing the Past: Treasures from the National Palace Museum, Taipei*. New York: The Metropolitan Museum; Taipei: National Palace Museum, 1996.

Harrist, Jr. Robert E., and Wen C. Fong. *The Embodied Image: Chinese Calligraphy from the John B. Elliott Collection*. Princeton: The Art Museum, Princeton University Press, 1999.

Krahl, Regina. *Chinese Ceramics from the Meiyintang Collection*. London: Azimuth Editions, 1994.

Ledderose, Lothar. *Ten Thousand Things: module and mass production in Chinese art*. Princeton: Princeton University Press, 2000.

Lee, Sherman. *China: 5,000 Years: Innovation and Transformation in the Arts*. New York: Guggenheim Museum, 1998.

Michaelson, Carol. *Gilded Dragons: Buried Treasures from China's Golden Ages*. London: British Museum Press, 1999.

Mowry, Robert D. *Worlds within worlds: the Richard Rosenblum collection of Chinese scholars' rocks*. Cambridge, Mass.: Harvard University Art Museums, 1996.

Rawson, Jessica. *Chinese bronzes: art and ritual*. London: Published for the Trustees of the British Museum in association with the Sainsbury Centre for Visual Arts, University of East Anglia, 1987.

Rawson, Jessica. *Chinese Jade: from the Neolithic to the Qing*. London: British Museum Press, 1995.

Rawson, Jessica, ed. *Mysteries of Ancient China: New Discoveries from the Early Dynasties*. London: British Museum Press, 1996.

Weidner, Marsha, ed. *Latter days of the law: images of Chinese Buddhism, 850–1850*. Lawrence, K.S.: Spencer Museum of Art, University of Kansas; Honolulu, Hawaii: University of Hawaii Press, 1994.

Chapter 14. The Performing Arts
Ni Yibin

Chung-wen Shih. *The Golden Age of Chinese Drama, Yuan Tsa-Chu*. Princeton, N.J.: Princeton University Press, 1976.

DeWoskin, Kenneth J. *A song for one or two: music and the concept of art in early China*. Ann Arbor Center for Chinese Studies, Mich.: University of Michigan Press, 1982.

Lai, T. C., and Robert Mok. *Jade flute: the story of Chinese music*. Hong Kong: Hong Kong Book Centre, 1981.

Mackerras, Colin, ed. *Chinese Theatre from its Origins to the Present Day*. Honolulu: University of Hawaii Press, 1983.

Mackerras, Colin. *Peking Opera*. New York: Oxford University Press, 1997.

Yang Mu. *Chinese musical instruments: an introduction*. Canberra: Coralie Rockwell Foundation, Australian National University, 1993.

Chapter 15. Architecture and Planning
Nancy R.S. Steinhardt

Boyd, Andrew. *Chinese Architecture and Town Planning*. London: Tiranti Press, 1962.

Chinese Academy of Architecture. *Ancient Chinese Architecture*. Beijing and Hong Kong: China Building Industry and Joint Publishing Company, 1982.

Keswick, Maggie. *The Chinese Garden*. New York: Rizzoli, 1978.

Knapp, Ronald. *China's Traditional Rural Architecture*. Honolulu: University of Hawaii Press, 1986.

Luo, Zewen, et al. *The Great Wall*. New York: McGraw; Hill, 1981.

Paludan, Ann. *The Chinese Spirit Road*. New Haven: Yale University Press, 1991.

Pirazzoli-T'Serstevens, Michele. *Living Architecture: Chinese*. New York: Grosset and Dunlop, 1971.

Sickman, Laurence and Alexander Soper. *The Art and Architecture of China*. Harmondsworth: Penguin Books, 1968.

Ssu-ch'eng Liang. *A Pictorial History of Chinese Architecture*. Cambridge, M.A.: M.I.T. Press, 1984.

Steinhardt, Nancy R. S. *Chinese Imperial City Planning*. Honolulu: University of Hawaii Press, 1990.

Steinhardt, Nancy R. S. *Chinese Traditional Architecture*. New York: China Institute, 1984.

INDEX

T

U

V

W

PICTURE CREDITS

Abbreviations:
t top; c center; b bottom; l left; r right

AKG	Archiv für Kunst und Geschichte, London
BAL	Bridgeman Art Library, London/New York
BL	British Library
BM	British Museum, London
Christie's	Christie's Images, London
DBP	Duncan Baird Publishers
Images	Images Colour Library, London
Mainstream	Mainstream Photography/Ray Main
RHPL	Robert Harding Picture Library
SOAS	School of Oriental and Africa Studies, University of London
Stone	gettyone Stone
V&A	Victoria & Albert Museum, London
WFA	Werner Forman Archive, London

Jacket Charles Walker Collection/Images; **page 1** Art Archive; **2** Stone/Robert Everts; **3** Mainstream/Institute of Archaeology & Cultural Relics Bureau, Henan Prov., China; **6** Christie's; **7** Corbis/Wolfgang Kaehler; **8** Corbis/Georgia Lowell; **9** Art Archive/Freer Gallery of Art, Washington D.C.; **10** Stone/Keren Su; **11** Art Archive/Freer Gallery of Art; **13** BPK/Staatsbibliothek zu Berlin, Berlin; **14** RHPL/Gina Corrigan; **16l** BM (OA1941.7-12.04); **16r** Stone/Keren Su; **18** Stone/Yann Layma; **19** AKG; **20** CWB; **22** Art Archive/Bibliothèque Nationale de France, Paris; **23** Stone/Herb Schmitz; **24** Mainstream/Institute of Archaeology, Beijing; **25** Mainstream/Institute of Archaeology & Cultural Relics, Sichuan Prov., China; **26** Corbis/Asian Art & Archaeology Inc.; **29** AKG/National Museum of Beijing; **30** RHPL; **31** Axiom/Guy Marks; **32** Art Archive/National Palace Museum, Taiwan; **34** Art Archive/National Palace Museum, Taiwan; **35** Stone/Glen Alison; **37** BAL/V&A; **38** Christie's; **40** BAL/V&A; **41** Art Archive/SOAS; **42–3** Stone/Mike McQueen; **44** DBP; **45** Stone/Jean-Marc Truchet; **46** CWB; **47** BAL; **48** Art Archive; **49** BL (Add.16358); **50** Corbis/Eugene Fuller Memorial Collection, Seattle; **51** Stone/D.E. Cox; **52** Art Archive/BM; **53** AKG; **54** AKG; **55** BAL/BL; **56** RHPL; **57** Art Archive/National Palace Museum, Taiwan; **58** Art Archive; **59** AKG; **60** *Taohuawau Woodblock New Year Prints*, Jiangsu Ancient Book Publishing House, Suzhou; **61** Art Archive/V&A; **62** Stone/Yann Layma; **64** Art Archive; **65** AKG; **66** BAL/V&A; **67** Christie's; **68** Art Archive; **69** *Taohuawau Woodblock New Year Prints*, Jiangsu Ancient Book Publishing House, Suzhou; **70** Art Archive/Freer Gallery of Art; **71** Axiom/Gordon Clements; **72** Popperfoto; **73** Art Archive/V&A; **74** BM ; **75** RHPL; **76** Axiom/Guy Marks; **77** Magnum/Fred Mayer; **78** CWB; **79** DBP; **80** BM (OA Add. 226.1942-11-13.023) ; **81** BAL/National Museum of India; **83** BAL/BL; **84** BAL/Bibliothèque Nationale de France, Paris; **85** CWB; **86** Council for World Churches/SOAS; **87** BAL/Oriental Museum, University of Durham, England; **88** Corbis/Pierre Colombell; **89** WFA; **90** Christie's; **91** BAL; **92** BAL/National Palace Museum, Taiwan; **93** AKG/Bibliothèque Nationale de France, Paris; **94** Art Archive/BL; **95** Christie's; **96** Art Archive; **97** BM; **98** Christie's; **99** Corbis/Peter Harholdt; **100** Magnum/Fred Mayer; **101** BAL/Oriental Museum, University of Durham; **103** Magnum/Fred Mayer; **104** Art Archive; **105** Corbis/Bettman Archive; **106–7** Stone/Keren Su; **108** Stone/Paul Grebliunas; **109** Axiom/Gordon Clements;

110 Christie's; **111** Art Archive/BM; **112** Kyoto National Museum, Japan; **113** BM; **114** BM (Or8210/S.6983); **115** Christie's; **116** Corbis/Royal Ontario Museum; **117** CWB; **118** Christie's; **119** Stone/Simone Huber; **120** Corbis/Asian Art & Archaeology Inc.; **121** China Pictorial Press; **123** Panos/Jeremy Horner; **124** BL (Stein 3326); **125** Axiom/Gordon Clements; **126t** Art Archive, National Palace Museum, Taiwan; **126b** Hunan Publishing House, Changsha; **127** Charles Walker Collection/Images; **128** Hunan Publishing House, Changsha; **129** Corbis/Dean Conger; **130** Charles Walker Collection/Images; **131** Charles Walker Collection/Images; **132** Corbis/Royal Ontario Museum; **133t** Charles Walker Collection/Images; **133b** Corbis/Nik Wheeler; **134** Michael Holford, London; **135** Charles Walker Collection/Images; **136** Charles Walker Collection/Images; **137t** BM (1963.12-14-03); **137b** Hunan Publishing House, Changsha; **138** BAL/BM; **139** Hunan Publishing House, Changsha; **140** Christie's; **141** Hunan Publishing House, Changsha; **143t** Charles Walker Collection/Images; **143** Mainstream/Hubei Provincial Museum, Wuhan; **144** Art Archive/BL; **145** Christie's; **146** Corbis/Nik Wheeler; **147** Science and Society Picture Library; **148** Science and Society Picture Library; **149** Corbis/Owen Franklin; **150** Science and Society Picture Library; **151** The Wellcome Trust; **153** Stone/Keren Su; **154** Science and Society Picture Library; **155** The Wellcome Trust; **156** The Wellcome Trust; **157** Art Archive; **158** The Joseph Needham Research Institute, Cambridge; **159** RHPL; **160** RHPL/Gavin Heller; **161** Corbis; **162** Corbis/Roger Tidman; **163** Ancient Art and Architecture; **164** Mainstream/Hebei Provincial Museum; **165** Christie's; **166** BAL/SOAS; **167** BAL/Oriental Museum, University of Durham; **168** Art Archive/Musée Guimet; **169** Art Archive/Freer Gallery of Art; **170** Christie's; **171** WFA/Kunstgewerbe Museum, Berlin; **172** Mainstream/Henan Provincial Museum, Zhengzhou; **173** Cecil Beaton Collection/Imperial War Museum; **174** Christie's; **175** RHPL/Nigel Cameron; **176** Michael Holford/Musée Guimet; **177** Mainstream; **178** Mainstream/Jingzhou Museum, Hubei Province; **179** Science and Society Picture Library; **180** Stone/Michael Townsend; **181** Science and Society Picture Library; **182** Sam Fogg Rare Books, London; **183** Art Archive/BL; **184** BAL/Freud Museum, London; **185** Mainstream/Institute of Archaeology & Cultural Relics Bureau, Sichuan Province; **186** RHPL; **187** Superstock, London; **188** Corbis/Asian Art & Archaeology Inc.; **189** Christie's; **190t** Christie's; **190b** Christie's; **191** all Christie's; **192** National Palace Museum, Beijing; **193** Superstock/Christie's; **194** Corbis/Bettman Archive; **195** Christie's; **196** BAL/Freer Gallery of Art; **197** BAL; **198** Michael Holford; **199** Mainstream/Henan Provincial Museum, Zhengzhou; **200** Christie's; **201** Christie's; **202** Christie's; **203** Superstock/Lowe Art Museum, University of Miami; **204** AKG/National Museum, Beijing; **205** Stone/Sylvain Grandadam; **206** Mainstream/Historical Museum, Beijing; **207** Corbis/Pierre Colombell; **208** RHPL; **209** Mainstream/M2 Leigudun Sui county, Hubei Province, China; **210** Mainstream/Cultural Relics Bureau, Xindu county, Sichuan Province; **211t** Corbis/Asian Art & Archaeology Inc.; **211b** *Taohuawau Woodblock New Year Prints*, Jiangsu Ancient Book Publishing House, Suzhou; **212** CWB; **213** Axiom/Gordon Clements; **214** RHPL/Gina Corrigan; **215** Axiom/Gordon Clements; **216** BAL/BL; **217** AKG; **218–9** Axiom/Guy Marks; **220** CWB; **221** AKG; **222** Axiom/Gordon Clements; **223** RHPL/Rolf Richardson; **224** AKG; **225** Superstock; **226** Mainstream/Henan Provincial Museum, Zhengzhou; **227** Corbis/Keren Su; **228** CWB; **229** Art Archive/Bibliothèque Nationale de France, Paris; **230** Stone/James Nelson; **232** *Facing the Mirror*, painting by Wen Yiduo from *Poet, Scholar, Patriotic Warrior: Wen Yiduo*, first published 1927. Beijing: Zhongguo sheying chubanshe [China Movie Publishing House], 1996; **233** BAL/Private Collection; **234** Corbis/The Purcell Team; **235** Corbis/Derek M. Allan/Travel Ink; **236** Ronald Grant Archive; **237** Frank Spooner Pictures.